Praise for Law and Theology

"This volume offers an authoritative and accessible tour of natural law and positive law from the garden of Eden to the latest machinations of the United States Supreme Court. David W. Opderbeck brings both theological discernment and legal acumen to bear on the weightier matters of the law, on the quotidian questions of legal practice, and on the current cultural battles over sexual liberty and religious liberty. Judicious, candid, briskly paced, and cogently argued, this book deserves a wide readership." – *John Witte Jr., Emory University*

"I know of no other book like this. Opderbeck develops a constructive theology of law that draws upon his deep knowledge of theology and the theory and practice of law. He offers substantive reflection on God's being and attributes, superbly navigating the various controversies such reflection brings, for the purpose of constructing a theology of law that makes a significant contribution to moral and political theology. The breadth of knowledge is impressive. The masterful attempt to reconcile Christianity's nonviolent ethics with law is a joy to observe. But this is only the first part of this splendid work. The second applies his theology of law in the US context, showing its relevance to the pharmaceutical industry, the lingering effects of slavery and racism, and much more. Opderbeck has set the standard by which all other attempts to address law theologically will be judged." – *Stephen Long, Cary M. Maguire University Professor of Ethics, Southern Methodist University*

"David W. Opderbeck has given us a fascinating theology of law. His work is rooted in a sophisticated narrative approach to ancient scriptural texts and extends to the most pressing church-state issues of our time: controversies surrounding LGBTQ and abortion rights. Important for specialists, this book is also a fine choice for seminars on law and religion at both the graduate and undergraduate level." – *Cathleen Kaveny, Darald and Juliet Libby Professor of Law and Theology, Boston College*

"Simultaneously lawyer, theologian, and law professor, David W. Opderbeck is a wise and expert guide into the fascinating nexus of theology and law. From Genesis to Revelation, Clement to Cone, natural law to positive law, *Brown v. Board of Education* to the Masterpiece Cakeshop case, usury to pharmaceutical product regulation, theory to praxis, Opderbeck covers immense ground and convincingly demonstrates along the way that a proper understanding of God's mission can (and ought to) guide everything from how one lives and votes to how one litigates—even if one should—and why. The end is a vision of Christian life amid theology, law, and mission that is marked by patience and hope." – *Brent A. Strawn, Duke University, and Senior Fellow, Center for the Study of Law and Religion, Emory University*

"In this extraordinary tour de force, David W. Opderbeck tackles some of the most difficult questions at the heart of the interdisciplinary dialogue between theology and law. His nuanced and thoughtful discussion of classical theological sources and history illuminates the metaphysical foundations of debates about the most contested legal issues of our time. His extended argument for recognizing a more modest and limited role for positive law is a welcome salve for a body politic suffering from heated legal and cultural polarization." – *Amy Uelmen, Georgetown University Law Center*

"As a young professor, I remember hearing a Hebrew Bible professor discuss the laws of Israel as a constitution, concluding that thus the laws were not unlike contemporary laws. Since then, I have always tried to keep that larger constitutional perspective in reading what the Bible says about law as covenant obligation for Israel. However, few books have crossed my desk that seriously took up the discussion of how the Bible's law emerges into or relates to contemporary law–natural, positive–and how Christians relate to laws of the land. David W. Opderbeck offers to Bible professors as well as to pastors and serious readers a full-orbed discussion of law in the Christian tradition. This book will generate much light and many discussions." – *Canon Dr. Scot McKnight, Northern Seminary*

"David W. Opderbeck shows positivism's limits and pragmatism's shortcomings, not through a circle-the-wagons effort to thwart the premises of modern law, but by reclaiming premodern sources of Christian wisdom in an effort to delve more deeply into those premises. He pulls forward insights from Scripture and the Christian intellectual tradition, crafting a helpful lens through which to view some of our most deeply contested legal issues. Whether or not one agrees with all of his conclusions, the accessibility and relevance of his analysis underscores the importance of theology to legal discourse." – *Robert K. Vischer, Dean and Mengler Chair in Law, University of St. Thomas School of Law*

"David W. Opderbeck has written a learned guide for navigating the culture wars. He uses Scripture, the Christian intellectual tradition, and legal history to challenge the church to be faithful witnesses amid troubled times." – *John Fea, Messiah College*

Law and Theology

Law and Theology

Classic Questions and Contemporary Perspectives

DAVID W. OPDERBECK

FORTRESS PRESS
MINNEAPOLIS

LAW AND THEOLOGY
Classic Questions and Contemporary Perspectives

Print ISBN: 978-1-5064-3432-2
eBook ISBN: 978-1-5064-3433-9

Unless otherwise noted, Scripture quotations are from New Revised Standard Version Bible, copyright © 1989 by the Division of Education of the National Council of Churches of Christ in the United States of America.

Cover image: VTT Studio/Shutterstock
Cover design: Brad Norr Design

Contents

Introduction   1

Part I. Theology

1. Law and the Narrative of Scripture   17
2. Law and History   67
3. A Constructive Theology of Law after Modernity   103

Part II. Praxis

4. Praxis of Law in Ordinary Time   145
5. The First Big Question: Slavery and Race   159
6. The Second and Third Big Questions: Abortion and LGBTQ Rights   187

Conclusion: Law, Fear, and Eschatology   223

Acknowledgments   231

Names and Subjects Index   233

Scripture Index   245

Introduction

This book provides an introduction to a Christian theology and praxis of positive law. By a theology of positive law, I mean theological reflection on the nature and purposes of positive law. By a praxis of positive law, I mean ways of life and spiritual and missiological practices of the church relating to positive law.

If you ask a non-lawyer, "What is law?" the answer likely will focus on "laws on the books," passed by Congress or a state legislature. Statutes and ordinances issued by legislative bodies certainly are a source of law, but lawyers would give a broader answer. As leading law and religion scholar John Witte notes, "Law is much more than the rules of the state and how we apply and analyze them. Law is also the social activity by which certain norms are formulated by legitimate authorities and actualized by persons subject to those authorities."[1]

For example, regulations and certain kinds of guidance documents issued by administrative agencies and official executive orders issued by the president or a state governor are also law. In different kinds of political systems, law might also include the dictates of a king or tribal leader. In legal systems derived from England, including the American system, we also include the "common law" within the category of positive law. The common law is a body of legal rules based on judicial precedents rather than on statutes. This kind of law, made by humans, is called *positive law*.

Lawyers also recognize forms of law that are not found in law codes or case law issued by a political sovereign. Particularly in the field of international law, there are customs and practices that are recognized as normative and binding even though they are not a form of positive law. Such customs and practices include, for example, the idea that the high

1. John Witte, *God's Joust, God's Justice: Law and Religion in the Western Tradition* (Grand Rapids: Eerdmans, 2006), 454.

seas are not subject to political control by any one nation. This is called *customary law*, which may become part of positive law in treaties or court decitions.

Black's Law Dictionary defines positive law as a "system of law promulgated and implemented within a particular political community by political superiors."[2] Notice that positive law is created by human authorities, within human governments exercising power over organized human jural societies. Christian theology also asserts that God issues "law" in the form of commands. Divine commands also can be considered a form of positive law, since they issue from the will of an authority. Some Christian thinkers, however, have distinguished divine commands from positive law made by human beings.

In traditional Christian thought about law, and in other classical Western sources, positive law is contrasted with "natural" law. Natural law is composed of rights and related responsibilities that are inherent in the natural order. For traditional Christian thought, natural law was considered part of creation that could be known, at least to some extent, through the ordinary exercise of human reason.

In Western thought, the question of how to define "law" historically has been closely linked to the question of the *legitimacy* of positive law. Law compels and constrains through force. Part of the force of the positive law can be through example, as if the law were a kind of inspirational literature. The positive law's real force, however, arises through the exercise of physical power. If you don't obey the positive law, you can be fined, arrested, jailed, or even executed. Why is it legitimate—that is, right, or just—for some ruling power to compel you to obey a rule through force? In traditional Western and Christian thought, the answer to this question was that the positive law was promulgated by a properly constituted authority and was at least broadly consistent with the natural law. If a particular rule within the positive law was promulgated improperly—say, by a pretender to the throne—or was substantively evil or unjust, it was not truly "law" and could be disobeyed or resisted.

The understanding of law and legal legitimacy sketched above is premodern. Today, belief in any sort of natural law is a minority view in Western academic legal theory. Some of the reasons for this shift are related to the broad cultural and intellectual changes leading up to, and including, the Enlightenment. In Western Christendom, late medieval scholastic thinkers arguably began to weaken the link between natural law and God's inherent goodness. In the various movements of the European Reformations, human ability to perceive the natural law in our

---

2. "Positive Law," *Black's Law Dictionary* (New York: Thomson-West, 2014).

sinful, fallen state came into question. During the Enlightenment, just as the natural sciences began to discard explanations for natural phenomena beyond the "laws of nature," legal theorists began to argue that positive law does not relate to any phenomenon that is not accessible to human reason. The European "Wars of Religion" in the sixteenth and seventeenth centuries left many people skeptical of claims to political authority rooted in sectarian religious ideas.

Modern skepticism about law also is rooted in everyday experience. A theorist might say the natural law justifies disobedience of or resistance to an unjust law, but such disobedience or resistance, of course, could still result in punishment, including death. There have always been those who have suggested that talk of natural law and legitimacy are only smokescreens for the exercise of raw power. Look back into the history of today's "legitimate" rulers, after all, and you will find a war, revolution, murder, betrayal, coup, or some other violent seizure of power.

Careful observers have also long noticed that, in addition to more traditional sources of positive law, many other sorts of social and even technological rules and conventions govern our conduct. I sometimes ask my law students whether they would want to come to school in a clown costume. Apart from a Halloween party, the answer usually is "no." The reason is that the social norm of how law students should dress favors ordinary, modest street clothes, not silly costumes. When lawyers appear in court, the "dress code" is a business suit, with a jacket and tie for men and a very conservative look for women. There is no formal rule about this in most courtrooms, but as a matter of social convention the court will not take an "underdressed" lawyer seriously. We can also include here cultural, family, and religious norms. Some of these kinds of norms, particularly in some religious communities, might become part of formal law codes that apply within the community. Even technological limits, such as the parameters set by computer code, can constrain conduct and form a kind of "law."[3]

The move away from the supernatural after the Enlightenment, the history of religious wars, and observations about the violence of the law and about how social norms constrain behavior are part of why many modern legal theorists doubt whether "law" is even a meaningful concept it itself. Many contemporary legal scholars effectively subsume "law" within social sciences such as economics, sociology, political science, and psychology. Others think "law" is mostly a proxy for identity

3. See Lawrence Lessig, *Code and Other Laws of Cyberspace, Version 2.0* (New York: Basic Books, 2006).

based in race, gender, or socioeconomic status. For these thinkers, "law" does not invoke any broader moral or metaphysical principles.

Other modern legal theorists do think "law" remains a meaningful concept and that it must connect with deeper moral principles, but they assume those principles must be located in a source that does not invoke the supernatural, such as God. Yet others—a small but influential minority—try to reinvigorate the concept of "natural law" without any direct reference to God on principles of reason they think should be acceptable to everyone.

I will argue in this book that a meaningful Christian theology of law requires a recovery and reevaluation of premodern sources for our modern context. The first and most basic premodern source is Scripture, which has much to say about "law" and its relation to God's saving mission in the world. The second premodern source is the Christian intellectual tradition, which also has been deeply concerned with the concept of law.

But why does any of this matter? Many modern legal theorists are either explicitly or implicitly philosophical pragmatists. Pragmatism suggests that knowledge is instrumental, that is, that what is true is what works, and what "works" is determined by values that are culturally conditioned.[4] The nineteenth-century American jurist Oliver Wendell Holmes Jr. applied pragmatism to legal theory in work that remains influential today.[5] One of the benefits of pragmatism is that it allows people to bracket big, divisive, seemingly insoluble questions from more "practical" concerns that require immediate solutions.

Let's say, for example, that large numbers of people are purchasing medicines that are ineffective and dangerous. I might believe this is a problem the law should address because I believe every human person is created in God's image and therefore is endowed with inherent dignity and natural rights. Another person who does not believe in God might approach the problem from a consequentialist perspective and might agree on this basis that regulation is appropriate because the social costs of injury and death from these medicines outweighs any potential social benefits from the market in sales of such medicines. Yet another person might think it's impossible to know whether God does or doesn't exist but might agree that regulation is appropriate based on an intuitive feeling that something is wrong. We could mix and match these categories and reasons and come up with a nearly infinite list of other categories and reasons, but as long as enough people believe regulation is appropri-

4. See Robert Audi, ed., "Pragmatism," *The Cambridge Dictionary of Philosophy*, 3rd ed. (Cambridge: Cambridge University Press, 2015).

5. Oliver Wendell Holmes Jr., "The Path of the Law," *Harvard Law Review* 10 (1897): 457.

ate, we don't need to debate the validity of those categories and reasons. We can table the bigger metaphysical question of whether humans are created in God's image and move on to the practical question of what, specifically, the pharmaceutical regulations should require.

Pragmatism's minimal account of what's required for action is appealing in our bitterly divided world. Certainly, it's better to work together on crafting an effective and fair rule about pharmaceutical regulation than to spend all our time arguing about God and never getting down to the business of law making.

The problem, in my view, is that a concept of "law" requires metaphysical justification if we're really interested in a stable, peaceable society. Remember, the force of the law is *force*. The pharmaceutical company subject to regulation and its investors might argue that the *caveat emptor*—"let the buyer beware"—principle should govern medicine sales rather than any legal regulation. Why should the company be forced to comply with a regulation it doesn't like, ultimately under threat of financial penalties and possible jail time for its officers, all backed by the government's police powers? What prevents the company from raising a private army to resist enforcement? No doubt a substantial part of the equation is that no private company could possibly raise an army that could compete with US federal or state government forces. No doubt another part of the equation is that such an extreme conflict would not advance the company's self-interests in the long run, since the company's financial success depends on a regular, functioning economy. Another important consideration, we hope, is that the company's trustees, officers, managers, and employees hold in common some broad values about the rule of law versus the rule of guns. The thought of violence under these circumstances is inconceivable as an ethical matter even aside from practical concerns about whether the battle is winnable.

The pharmaceutical company example is far-fetched because the disparity in firepower is so overwhelming. What if the firepower hung in the balance? I like to give my constitutional law students a hypothetical scenario like this:

The president issues an Executive Order on immigration that is challenged under the religion clauses of the first amendment. A 5-4 majority of the Supreme Court holds that the Executive Order is unconstitutional and unenforceable. The president argues that he has the same authority as the Supreme Court to interpret the Constitution, declares that he will ignore the Supreme Court's decision, and orders the National Guard to mobilize to enforce the Executive Order at the border. Congress by a large majority passes a resolution condemning the president's action, but the president remains steadfast. How should the National Guard leadership respond?

There is not a single "correct" answer to this question as a matter of American constitutional law. The Supreme Court decided in 1803 in *Marbury v. Madison* that the court has the final authority to interpret the Constitution, at least in relation to legislation passed by Congress, a principle lawyers call "judicial review."[6] The court has also asserted its authority to interpret the Constitution in relation to regulations passed by executive branch agencies, although under a standard that is highly deferential to agency interpretations.[7] The question of a *direct* conflict between Supreme Court opinion and the president's interpretation of the Constitution has never been decided by the court. Even if the court had decided such a case in the past, this would still represent the *court's* interpretation. The president might reject that interpretive move as well. The National Guard—the military—would then have to decide whether to throw its support behind the president or behind the Supreme Court and Congress. It would be far from the first time in world history when an army's support for one rival claimant to power or another determined the fate of a nation.

Why don't we get to the point of this kind of showdown? Is this also just more pragmatism? Is it merely the recognition by political and military leaders that the costs of war are not in anyone's long-term personal interests? We do have national experience with a final breakdown of legal authority leading to the breakup of our government and to war: the Revolutionary War and the Civil War. The memory of the Civil War chastens any inclination to internecine violence. This streak of pragmatism undoubtedly contributes to the restraint of presidents and military leaders alike.

I think, however, that the restraint also has to do with commitment to a higher set of principles. Since the Civil War, our leaders have at least tacitly agreed that higher principles of freedom, democracy, and commitment to the rule of law surpass other disagreements well before actual shots are fired. The central cultural and legal issue that drove the Civil War—slavery—and slavery's aftermath into the civil rights era, further supported a general commitment to abide by constitutional principles *as interpreted by the Supreme Court.* A philosophical commitment to the common good, which necessarily entails a set of metaphysical beliefs

---

6. 5 U.S. (1 Cranch) 137 (1803).

7. See *Chevron U.S.A., Inc. v. Natural Resources Defense Council, Inc,* 467 U.S. 837 (1984).

about what "common" and "good" might mean, holds together the rule of law, which in turn holds together civil society's laws.

But what if the law is unjust? The Civil War erupted because of what all reasonable people today understand was a grave injustice: black slavery. The 1789 Constitution allowed this injustice to fester by tacitly upholding black slavery's legitimacy. After the Civil War, when slavery was outlawed by the Thirteenth Amendment and equal protection of the law was extended to all citizens regardless of race by the Fourteenth Amendment, the grave injustice of racial inequality persisted because the law was interpreted to permit segregation and other forms of legal discrimination.

The civil rights movement of the 1950s and 1960s was led by people such as Martin Luther King Jr. who combined advocacy for legal change in the courts and legislatures with civil disobedience to laws they believed were unjust. The civil rights movement was deeply contested by conservative whites at the time and remains deeply contested today. As with the question of black slavery, any reasonable person today should recognize that the broad principles of the civil rights movement were right and just and that racial segregation and legalized discrimination are grave evils, even if we might reasonably disagree on some of the particulars of how past discrimination should be remedied. Until recently, much of the current ongoing "mainstream" opposition to the civil rights movement occurred in subtle and coded forms. In recent years, racism has once again surfaced more directly, even in statements by high public officials. But if the law encodes an evil like racism, when and how can or should an affected individual or group resist? And who decides when the issue really is a clear systemic evil rather than a more complicated, morally ambiguous policy difference?

All of these questions raise deeper philosophical issues about the relationship of the *individual* to the *community*. This basic question goes to the heart of any political philosophy and therefore to any theory of law. Classical Western legal theory historically embedded a notion of *consent* into concepts of positive law. The notion of consent was particularly important in Roman law, which informed the early Christian tradition of legal thought, although the fact of consent usually was more of a historical fiction than a reality. Consent is closely related to the question of *conscience*—the moral duties of an individual who believes the law is unjust, and the consequences of violating a law perceived to be unjust. It is also closely related to the question of *rights*—the claims (if any) an individual has against certain actions of the state.

From a modern American perspective—particularly in branches of the

Christian church influenced by American populism—we tend to view the relationship between the individual and the community as a zero-sum game, which the individual must win. "Big government" is a disease to be avoided, and the most damaging political label to pin on a political foe is "socialist." The fullness of the biblical witness and the Christian intellectual tradition about law and society, however, is far richer than this populist trope. Both themes are prominent in Scripture and the tradition—on the one hand, the individual created in God's image and responsible directly to God, sometimes in prophetic opposition to the political rule of the present age, and on the other, the community formed by God's grace under God's law, through which individual preferences are disciplined and cultivated for the broader common good.

This reference to a community living under God's law raises the problem of church and state. Again, from a modern American perspective, the relationship between church and state is often viewed in radical terms. Church and state are viewed as competing domains. For many conservative evangelicals and Catholics, the problem is state interference with church, while for many liberal secularists, the problem is church interference with state. The biblical witness reflects varying theological perspectives, forged in very different historical contexts, which cannot always be reconciled. These include, for example, the vision of a unified political community of Israel under the Levitical and Deuteronomic law reflected in the "priestly" sources in the Old Testament; the condemnation of external legal observance in favor of true inner piety reflected in much of the Old Testament's prophetic literature; differing pictures of Jesus in the Gospels, at turns undermining and reaffirming the Jewish law; and Paul's complex and confounding understanding of the Torah's role in Jewish history.

The relationship between church and state was a defining problem in Christian antiquity and remained a defining problem in later European and American history. As we'll see, the competition between church and state—and, during the Reformation, between competing visions of both church and state—was sometimes dramatic and violent. Further, as we'll see, radically separatist movements have at times arisen, which have deeply influenced contemporary populist evangelical Christianity as well as an important stream of sophisticated political theology often called *ecclesial ethics*.

Finally, the possibility of a community living under God's law, and the related question of church and state, surfaces deeper questions about history and eschatology. How does our present lived experience relate to God's final judgment and redemption of humanity? Is the human future realized at all in our present social and political communities, or are the possibilities of "heaven" and "hell" entirely otherworldly realities? Does history have a direction and purpose, and if so, can human beings know anything about that direction and purpose? Is history on the brink of a disastrous cataclysm, as dispensational and other chiliastic eschatologies claim, or is history gradually progressing toward perfection, as in some postmillennial eschatologies, or does history reflect a kind of unresolved tension, as in many amillennial perspectives? As St. Augustine asked, how does the "City of Man" relate to the "City of God?" A person's eschatological perspective will profoundly influence his or her view of the purposes and limits of the positive law.

I take up these themes in this book as follows. Part 1, "Theology," covers the biblical witness, the Christian theological tradition, and thoughts on a constructive Christian theology of positive law. Part 2, "Praxis," discusses Christian practices relating to the positive law, particularly in light of historical and current culture wars in the United States.

Chapter 1 surveys the biblical witness relating to "law." The question of "law" is so pervasive in the Bible that it is impossible to cover comprehensively in a single chapter. My purpose in this chapter is to offer a survey that highlights the role of law in the narrative arc of Scripture from creation to consummation. This, of course, raises many fraught and intractable issues relating to methodology and interpretation. Nevertheless, I think it is possible to discern, and fruitful to tease out, a narrative thread through the Scriptures concerning the *missio Dei*—God's mission of redeeming a fallen creation. Law is central to this narrative in ways that many narrative theologies have not emphasized. At the same time, I have tried to remain sensitive to critical and historical biblical scholarship. The original writers and editors of the diverse texts that eventually came to comprise the canonical Christian Scriptures more often than not probably would not have perceived the narrative shape that a person influenced by contemporary narrative theology might see today. We can and must learn from the "world behind the text," but the approach I take in this book is that the inspiration of the text as Scripture inheres finally in its witness to the life, death, and resurrection of Christ, which is also God's address to the "world in front of the text"—our world today.

Chapter 2 surveys the witness of the Christian intellectual tradition relating to the nature and purpose of law. Again, the primary and secondary literature here is so vast that it cannot be comprehensively covered in one chapter, so this survey is necessarily selective. Nevertheless, my approach to the Christian intellectual tradition in this book is consistent with my approach to the Bible, not least because the great early

Christian theologians I reference in this book also read the Bible, in what they understood as its various senses of meaning, ultimately as a pointer to Christ. Further, the development of the Christian tradition is itself part of the narrative of the *missio Dei*, because God works within history. Indeed, as this Introduction suggests, any theology of law must be closely tied to a theology of history.

Like my methodological choice of reading Scripture narratively, my choice to look for meaning in a theology of history regarding Christian thought and law may prove particularly controversial. This will be true even among Christian thinkers who share some of my theological inclinations. There is a tendency among many who focus on narrative and missional theology to view the period beginning in the fourth century with the Emperor Constantine—the "Constantinian shift"—as a disaster. Prior to the Constantinian shift, Christianity was an illegal religion in the Roman world, and Christians were sometimes harshly persecuted by government officials. After the Constantinian shift, Christianity became a legal religion and eventually became the empire's official religion.

The historical significance of these events for the life of the church is deeply contested—including whether it was really a "shift" or more of a "bump." At the very least, it is clear that positive law was central to the Constantinian shift. It is not the case, however, that Christian thinkers prior to the Constantinian shift held dramatically different views about positive law than those after the shift. In my discussion of tradition, I try to show the great *continuity* in Christian thought about law both prior to and after Constantine. Core Christian beliefs about the relationships between creation, natural law, positive law, and justice, I will argue, were widely held by the great Christian theologians before and after Constantine, as well as through the Reformation. The *discontinuity*, or at least complication, after Constantine concerned the boundaries of the relationship between crown and church and the expectation for what positive law could accomplish in this present age. As to that issue, today's ecclesial theologians who are critical of the Constantinian shift are right to note that many Christians who are most concerned about positive law today, at least in the context of the American culture wars, often seem to take radically unbalanced and missionally unproductive positions on hotly disputed issues. At the same time, in my judgment, the ecclesial theologians have not paid sufficient attention to the role of positive law in mediating peace. In this respect I view this book as an effort to bridge some of the differences between "Augustinian" and "ecclesial" Christian ethics.[8]

Chapter 2 also examines the problem of "church and state," calling into question any simplistic narrative about the Constantinian shift. The church's mission is incarnational and embodied, and therefore must interface directly with systems of temporal governance. Even the "Benedict Option" of isolated monastic communities requires access to land, which necessarily involves property law.[9] At the same time, ecclesial ethicists who decry the Constantinian shift rightly note that the history of Christendom involved sustained efforts by the church, both in Rome and in Constantinople, to control the temporal government, and that these efforts often implicated the church in terrible violence.

Chapter 3 begins to sketch a contemporary constructive theology of law drawn from the materials in chapters 1 and 2. I am particularly concerned in chapter 3 to illustrate positive law's limits. This is not based in a "small government," *laissez-faire* political philosophy but rather on our recent cultural experience of extreme polarization and rhetorical hostility. The driving force behind much of this polarization, I believe, is the misplaced feeling within some segments of American Christianity that changing the positive law regarding certain hot-button issues—abortion and homosexuality, in particular—is more important than nearly any other value, include basic virtues of humility, patience, and truthfulness. I try to show in chapter 3 that any discussion of positive law involves trade-offs between what is ideal and what is possible. Moreover, even in the realm of what is possible, usually there are numerous alternatives that could be supported or criticized from different ethical perspectives. The nitty-gritty of the law is almost never a matter of simple absolutes.

At the same time, I argue in chapter 3 that because creation participates in God's being, there is a natural law toward which all legitimate positive law must tend. Because the natural law bends the universe toward justice—a justice disclosed in the death and resurrection of Christ on behalf of a humanity oppressed by sin and death—I conclude chapter 3 with a discussion of the relationship between law and liberation. The focus of this section is on how positive law can help create the conditions for freedom, equality, and human flourishing. I pursue this discussion with a focus on Christian perspectives about law, black slavery, and racism in America. The discussion of law and "liberation" surfaces the central problem of how the positive law relates to violence.

8. See D. Stephen Long, *Augustinian and Ecclesial Ethics: On Loving Enemies* (Lanham, MD: Lexington, 2018).
9. For one popular approach to the Benedict option, see Rod Dreher, *The Benedict Option: A Strategy for Christians in a Post-Christian Nation* (New York: Sentinel, 2018).

Chapter 4 opens part 2 of the book, "Praxis," with a discussion of some examples that seem far removed from the culture wars: usury and bankruptcy law, and pharmaceutical product regulation. These examples show how complex any discussion about biblical faith, ethics, and positive law can become, even when emotions do not run hot.

Chapter 5 continues the "Praxis" section with a discussion of slavery and race. Unfortunately, this is a troubling discussion. What was considered "orthodox" theology before the Civil War supported both black slavery and legal principles of federalism that argued against the federal government's intervention in the "slave code" laws of the southern states. The abolitionists, most of whom also were Christians, were considered unbiblical and radical by Christians who supported slavery. Long after the Civil War, racist attitudes persisted, justified by Christian theology and encoded in legalized segregation, the "black codes," and through other institutions of law and society. The civil rights movement starting in the 1950s began to roll back many of these legalized vestiges of slavery, spurred by other Christians, such as Martin Luther King Jr., rooted in minority communities and offering a theological perspective that foreshadowed later liberation theologies.

Today, even in conservative theological circles, the tide has dramatically shifted, and no one outside what is considered a lunatic fringe of white supremacists would argue that slavery or racism are justified by Christian theology. At least, the tide has dramatically shifted on the surface. In the deeper waters of political theology, conservatives today often make the same arguments rooted in states' rights, small government, judicial activism, executive overreach, and personal responsibility that were made in the southern states prior to the Civil War. And, even more directly, Christian conservatives recently have reverted to overtly racist language and tropes against nonwhite migrants while claiming respect for the "rule of law" against the "illegal" status of these immigrants—with eerie echoes of pre–Civil War fears about race wars spurred by rebellious slaves and about loss of respect for the rule of law as stated in the southern slave codes.

Chapter 6 address the two most divisive legal issues of our times: abortion and LGBTQ rights. I argue in this chapter that Christian conservatives express legitimate concerns about some strands of constitutional jurisprudence relating to these issues, but that some conservatives have elevated change in the positive law to a degree of priority that borders on idolatry, at grave cost to the church's real mission in the world.

In the conclusion, returning to the theme of a theology of history, I argue that one key driver of this distortion is a kind of multiple personality eschatology that blends a dispensationalist expectation of imminent doom with an incongruous belief that the apocalypse can be delayed through political action. This toxic combination, I suggest, ironically has seriously eroded the rule of law.

PART I

Theology

Part 1 surveys the biblical witness and the historic Christian tradition for insights about the nature and purposes of law. It concludes with thoughts on a constructive contemporary theology of law. I argue that there is a natural law connected with creation's participation in God's being. Because God is altogether loving, good, beautiful, true, and just, the love, goodness, beauty, truth, and justice toward which creation tends are not merely arbitrary accidents but rather possess metaphysical substance. At the same time, creation is not necessary, so that even the natural law as realized in this present creation exhibits a degree of contingency. Further, God relates to humanity in history, so that divine commands to humanity also exhibit a significant degree of contingency, even in the garden before human sin. Beyond the ordinary contingency of creation and divine command, because of sin, human society often tends away from the true ends of creation. Prior to the eschaton, human positive law is therefore necessary to restrain evil, mirror God's righteousness, guide human conduct, and promote human liberation. However, because of sin, no human society can fully realize the natural law, so that human positive law is radically contingent on history and plays a limited role in God's economy of salvation.

1.

Law and the Narrative of Scripture

INTRODUCTION

The Bible is "full of legal material."[1] This includes, for example, the specifically legal texts in the Torah, reflections on law and justice in the prophetic and wisdom literature, the summations of the law in Jesus's teaching, particularly in the Sermon on the Mount, the moral exhortations (*parenesis*) in Paul's epistles, and further wisdom and prophetic reflections on law and justice in New Testament wisdom texts, such as James and Hebrews, and in apocalyptic texts, including Revelation. Various parts of these biblical texts have been central to religious and social life in the Christian West, the Islamic world, and the Jewish diaspora, and through that influence have directly impacted ideas about law and justice in Western and Arab civilizations since antiquity. As biblical scholar Brent Strawn has noted, "It does not seem to be going too far to say that all of the Bible is—or has been or could be—law, even if only (!) of a religious sort."[2]

The diversity of literary genres in which this biblical legal material is embedded, the vast differences in ancient cultural and historical contexts through which the biblical literature was produced, and the distance between those ancient contexts and later moments in history—including our present moment, of course—presents enormous challenges for how (or whether) we should use the Bible as a source for reflection about law today.[3] Consider just this one command from the Torah:

1. Brent Strawn, ed., *The Oxford Encyclopedia of the Bible and Law* (Oxford: Oxford University Press, 2015), pref.
2. Strawn, ed., *Oxford Encyclodepia of the Bible and Law*, pref.
3. For a general discussion of these sorts of exegetical challenges, see, e.g., Michael J. Gorman,

17

If someone has a stubborn and rebellious son who does not obey his father and mother and will not listen to them when they discipline him, his father and mother shall take hold of him and bring him to the elders at the gate of his town. They shall say to the elders, "This son of ours is stubborn and rebellious. He will not obey us. He is a glutton and a drunkard." Then all the men of his town are to stone him to death. (Deut 21:18–21 NIV)

Very few contemporary Christian, Jewish, or Muslim interpreters would suggest that this law, or anything like it, should be enacted today. Nor did the ancient Jewish rabbis interpret such laws inflexibly. Indeed, the Talmudic jurists understood this law about the rebellious son to *limit* the otherwise unilateral power of a father who is head of a family by requiring a kind of trial before the elders, and further restricted the circumstances under which the punishment of stoning could be applied, such that the text served a more symbolic than practical purpose.[4] Many modern biblical scholars believe the Deuteronomic Code, from which this text is drawn, was the product of reforms of King Josiah (c. 639–609 BCE) or reflects forms of Assyrian and other ancient Near Eastern laws brought into the context of Israel's covenant relationship with God.[5]

With this historical background, many modern scholars understand the Deuteronomic Code primarily as theological and hortatory—a form of moral instruction—rather than *law* as we might understand that term. As biblical scholar Daniel Block suggests, "Treating [the Deuteronomic Code] primarily as 'law' and limiting 'law' to this section obscures its theological agenda and invites readers to expect legislation like that passed in our own modern legislatures. The entire book is 'Torah'—which is best understood as instruction in righteous living as defined by the spokesman (Moses) for the divine suzerain (Yahweh)."[6]

This example, which briefly discusses only a few considerations relating to one small part of the Bible, demonstrates how difficult, and even dangerous, it can be to use the Bible as a source for lawmaking today. Interpretation is never a straightforward matter of reading what the Bible "literally" says and applying the words directly to contemporary circumstances. We always must pay attention to the "world behind the text"—its historical context—the "world within the text"—its literary features—and the "world in front of the text"—the very different later his-

Elements of Biblical Exegesis: A Basic Guide for Students and Ministers (Grand Rapids: Baker Academic, 2008).

4. See "Rebellious Son," Jewish Virtual Library, https://tinyurl.com/y4zluu28.

5. See Daniel I. Block, "Deuteronomic Law," in Strawn, ed., *Oxford Encyclopedia of the Bible and Law*.

6. Block, "Deuteronomic Law."

torical circumstances, including our own, to which the text may relate.[7] As Christian interpreters, we also must remain sensitive to how the Holy Spirit may use the text, including through forms of reading that are more meditative or devotional than didactic, and including through new insights and applications that may not have been apparent to previous readers, as well as to the role the community of the church may play in shaping or constraining idiosyncratic interpretations. Embedded in this paragraph, of course, are enormous, intractable theological debates about the nature of biblical inspiration and authority, the role of tradition, reason, and experience as sources of theological authority, ecclesiology, pneumatology, and so on.

Addressing any of those debates in detail is far beyond the scope of this book. The best I can do is identify the approach I have chosen and try to connect it with my methodology for a constructive theology of law. My approach to Scripture here is narratival. As many contemporary biblical scholars and theologians have noted, the Bible can be read to suggest an overarching story involving "creation, 'fall,' Israel, Jesus, and the church" and the coming consummation.[8] As Richard Bauckham notes, "A narrative hermeneutic recognizes the way narrative creates its own world in front of the text and so interprets our world for us; how narrative opens up new possibilities of living that change us and our world; how we are given our identities by the narratives of our own lives and the wider narratives to which they relate."[9]

Of course, any such narrative scheme across the sprawling, diverse canon of Scripture could be contested and threatens to flatten the distinctiveness of any given text. There is a sense in which any narrative scheme for the canon is an imposition upon any given text—a problem, as Bauckham notes, of the relation between the "particular" details of any given text and the "universal" narrative.[10] The overarching narrative does not always spring so neatly from the particular texts as narrative theologians might like. I think, however, that the concept of a general canonical narrative fits with the notion of the "canon" itself. The canon, after all, was identified by the church well after its particular texts

---

7. See, e.g., Gorman, *Elements of Biblical Exegesis*; Joel B. Green, *Seized by Truth: Reading the Bible as Scripture* (Nashville: Abingdon, 2007).

8. See, e.g., N. T. Wright, *The Last Word: Beyond the Bible Wars to a New Understanding of the Authority of Scripture* (San Francisco: HarperSanFrancisco, 2005); N. T. Wright, *The New Testament and the People of God* (Minneapolis: Fortress, 1992); Craig G. Bartholomew and Michael W. Goheen, *The Drama of Scripture: Finding Our Place in the Biblical Story* (Grand Rapids: Baker Academic, 2004).

9. Richard Bauckham, *The Bible and Mission: Christian Witness in a Postmodern World* (Grand Rapids: Baker Academic, 2005), 12.

10. Bauckham, *Bible and Mission*, 11.

were composed based in significant part on the church's lived experience in the story of redemption, in particular through the "rule of faith" that places the life, death, and resurrection of Jesus Christ at the center of history.[11]

Indeed, the narratival approach to Scripture connects with another theological theme of this book, which is that a theology of "law" inevitably entails a theology of "history." The narrative of Scripture discloses God's purposes for creation, consummated in the life, death, and resurrection of Jesus Christ. "Law" as a feature of the biblical narrative, and as a feature of human history, plays an important, even central role in that narrative. If we wish to develop a constructive theology of law, and if we wish to reflect and act wisely and faithfully concerning law in our present moment in the divine drama, we must discern the times before (or if) we prioritize one kind of legal reform or another as an aspect of the church's mission in the world. My approach, then, both to Scripture, history, and the philosophy and theology of law, is to explore the age-old question of how the "universal" relates to the "particular."

LAW AND THE NARRATIVE OF SCRIPTURE: CREATION

At the start of the canonical biblical narrative, in Genesis 1–4, God creates the heavens and the Earth, and establishes humanity as stewards over the Earth.[12] At the climax of the Bible's first creation narrative in Genesis 1, on the sixth day, God creates humanity—הָאָדָם, hā'āḏām, the generic term "the adam"[13] (Gen 1:26–28). God tells humanity to "be fruitful and multiply, and fill the earth, and subdue it; and rule over the fish of the sea and over the birds of the sky and over every living thing that moves on the earth" (Gen 1:28 NASB). The Hebrew text uses the words פְּרוּ (p'rū), וּרְדוּ (ūr'ḏū), וּמִלְאוּ (ūmil'ū), and וּרְבוּ (ūr'ḇū), an interest-

---

11. See, e.g., Craig D. Allert, *A High View of Scripture? The Authority of the Bible and the Formation of the New Testament Canon* (Grand Rapids: Baker Academic, 2007).

12. Portions of this chapter are drawn from my article "Lex Machina Non Est: A Response to Lemley's 'Faith-Based Intellectual Property,'" *University of Louisville Law Review* 56, (2018): 219.

13. Most biblical scholars agree that the creation narratives in Genesis 1 and Genesis 2 are different narratives, with a different order of events, and likely written by different authors—thus there is a "first" and "second" creation narrative in Genesis. The original redactors of the canonical text, of course, would have realized this, and made no apparent attempt to resolve the differences, suggesting that the purpose of including these two different texts side by side was to make subtly different, but complementary, theological points. See Russell R. Reno, *Genesis* (Grand Rapids: Brazos Press, 2010), 66–67; John Muddiman and John Barton, *The Oxford Bible Commentary* (Oxford: Oxford University Press, 2007), 41–44.

ing rhythmic pattern not noticed in English translation.[14] The rhythmic pattern sets up a sort of cadence within the text, suggesting a movement toward a crescendo. Indeed, the verb מלא, which is the root form of the term וּמִלְאוּ (ūmil'ū), can suggest accomplishment, completion, or fulfillment.[15] As many commentators have noted, God does not drop humanity into a static creation. God entrusts to humanity the *purpose* of engaging in fruitful, creative activity that will make the Earth into something even more beautiful than it was in the beginning. The human "cultural mandate," as theologians often call it, has a purpose, which is that humanity would "subdue" the Earth.[16] While God "rests" on the seventh day (Gen 2:2), humanity's creative work is just beginning.

So what would it mean for humanity to subdue the Earth? Commentators have long wrestled with this question, and unfortunately this concept has at times been used to justify practices that degrade the natural environment. Interestingly, some early commentators wondered why the Earth as originally created would have been "wild" or in need of "subduing," since Genesis 2 pictures humanity originally dwelling in the paradise of Eden. But most commentators now agree that the concept here is one of wise governance or stewardship.

The text suggests that God leaves to humanity the job of caring for the material creation, which includes humanity itself. The purpose of human creative activity is the flourishing of all of creation, including human flourishing. Humanity is not commanded to "be fruitful and multiply" just for the purpose of "more." The command to be fruitful and multiply is connected to the command to fill, subdue, and rule over the earth. In the biblical creation narratives, the end of human creative activity (including the most amazing creative activity of all, bringing new human life into the world) is that all of creation would become all that God intends for it to be.

In the framework of the Bible's creation theology, then, human cultural activity has a *purpose*, with embedded values and concepts of excellence—or, stated negatively, concepts of falling short or missing the mark. (In the New Testament, the Greek word translated "sin" in English is ἁμαρτία (hamartia), which literally means "to miss the mark.")[17]

14. For the Hebrew text, see *Biblia Hebraica Stuttgartensia* (Berlin: German Bible Society, 1997). The prefix ו, transliterated here as ū, is a waw–consecutive, which connects two words or phrases, often translated into English as "and." See Gary D. Pratico and Miles V. Van Pelt, *Basics of Biblical Hebrew* (Grand Rapids: Zondervan, 2007), chap. 5.

15. For lexical information on these terms, see Ludwig Koehler and Walter Baumgartner et al., *The Hebrew and Aramaic Lexicon of the Old Testament* (Boston: Brill, 1996).

16. See, e.g., Andy Crouch, *Culture Making: Recovering Our Creative Calling* (Grand Rapids: IVP Books, 2013).

17. For the Greek New Testament, see Kurt Aland and Matthew Black et al., eds., *The Greek*

In the Bible's second creation narrative, the first humans, Adam and Eve, live in the garden in harmony with God and the rest of creation, "naked and unashamed." In the garden are two trees: the tree of life and the tree of the knowledge of good and evil. God instructs Adam and Eve not to eat the fruit of the tree of the knowledge of good and evil. But, tempted by the serpent, Adam and Eve disobey God and are expelled from paradise and cursed with the toils of unrewarding work, the pains of childbirth, and the inevitability of physical death. Yet even as they are removed from the garden, God provides Adam and Eve with animal skins to clothe their nakedness—the first sacrifice for sin, and an immediate act of God's redemptive grace.

Jewish and Christian thinkers have debated the precise meaning of these chapters of Scripture for millennia. We do not need to delve too deeply into modern debates about the relationship between Scripture, theology, and science to note that many early Christian interpreters recognized numerous features of the "literal" sense of these chapters that suggested allegorical or typological meanings.[18] One of the most interesting questions raised by these texts is what the "trees" represent.

The tree of life appears at the end of Scripture—in Revelation—as well as in the beginning here in Genesis. In Revelation 22:2, the tree of life stands at the center of the New Jerusalem, and "its leaves are for the healing of the nations." Many Christian commentators have associated the tree of life with the "tree" of the cross: the tree of life in Revelation 22:2 is symbolic of the victory over sin and death Christ accomplished on the cross. That this tree also is present in the garden suggests the presence of Christ both at the beginning of creation and at its consummation, as mentioned in the famous first lines of John's Gospel: "In the beginning was the Word, and the Word was with God, and the Word was God" (John 1:1 NIV). It is significant that John's Gospel likely was written by the same person or community that produced the text of Revelation

New Testament, 4th rev. ed. (New York: American Bible Society, 2000). For lexical information, see Walter Bauer and Frederick William Danker, eds., *A Greek-English Lexicon of the New Testament and Other Early Christian Literature*, 3rd ed. (Chicago: University of Chicago Press, 2001).

18. In my view, these chapters are literary-symbolic texts, which reflect elements of the surrounding ancient Near Eastern culture, but which refer to unique events in the history of God's dealings with humanity. They are true and trustworthy forms of communication about humanity's status as a creature, our common rebellion against God, and God's gracious response to us. They do not function as modern "scientific" statements of origins. When I refer to "Adam" and "Eve" in this chapter I am not suggesting there must have been a "literal" genetic Adam and Eve, which would contradict human evolutionary biology, although perhaps there was a "literal" spiritual Adam and Eve. The interpreter's task, as I hope this chapter demonstrates, is to reflect carefully on the "literal" sense of the text in an effort to draw out various layers of meaning communicated in and through the text.

(which is also traditionally called "the apocalypse of John").[19] There is a theological similarity in these texts, both of which focus on the "cosmic" realities of creation and redemption.

But what about the tree of the knowledge of good and evil? One popular way of understanding this tree is that it refers to humanity's innocence before sin entered the world. Adam and Eve did not know the difference between "good and evil" because there was no "evil" in the garden. There is some support for this view in the serpent's deceptive suggestion to Eve that God was depriving Adam and Eve of secret knowledge that would enable them to become more wise and powerful. Indeed, some Jewish commentators have suggested that this tree and even the serpent's deception were *necessary* for Adam and Eve to grow into full, human, moral maturity.

While there is something important to these observations, it cannot be the case that Adam and Eve had no knowledge at all of right and wrong in the garden. First, they presumably understood that the terms "good" and "evil" had some identifiable meaning. Otherwise, the tree could just as well have been called the "tree of something unexplainable." Second, they presumably understood that God's *command* not to eat of this tree ought to be obeyed. Perhaps they did not understand anything beyond the consequence of disobedience—"you will surely die"—but they must have understood *at least* that God *ought* to be obeyed if one wishes not to "die." In fact, taking the two creation narratives in Genesis 1 and 2 together, it seems that they would have understood that God *inherently* ought to be obeyed, aside from particular consequences, simply because God is God. Third, the serpent's deception made an appeal based on moral content—that is, that God was hiding something and therefore could not be trusted—which would make no sense unless Adam and Eve already knew something about the difference between good and evil.

The point of this discussion is to suggest that, when human beings are living in right relationship with God, each other, and the rest of creation, we possess a natural, innate sense of what is good, beautiful, and true. Theologians sometimes call this *natural law* or the *sensus divinitatus*. There are enormously difficult debates among theologians and philosophers about whether there is any such thing as natural law, or even if there is such a thing, whether human beings can know it. In fact, the concept of natural law is out of favor in most modern legal scholarship.

19. Biblical scholars debate who exactly might have authored and edited the final canonical texts of the Gospel of John and Revelation. The precise details of these debates are not important for our purposes. There is no doubt that there are significant theological connections between these texts. See, e.g., René Kieffer, "John," in *The New Oxford Bible Commentary*, 960-61; Richard Bauckham, "Revelation," in *The New Oxford Bible Commentary*, 1288.

Nearly all Christian thinkers agree, however, that creation inherently is "good" because God, the creator, is good. Indeed, that affirmation is repeatedly evident in the creation hymn of Genesis 1 as God declares each element of creation "good" and the totality of creation "very good."

I believe there is a natural law, but I think the concept makes little sense outside explicitly articulated doctrines of God and creation.[20] I see little reason to accept the constraints of modernity against specifically "religious" or theological discourse in the public square, and I write on these subjects as a Christian theologian as well as a law professor. From the perspective of my hermeneutical approach, any concept of natural law requires a discussion of how that concept fits into the biblical *narrative* of God's activity as creator, sustainer, and redeemer of the cosmos.

Whether we human beings in our sinful state can know the natural law is another question. Some theologians, particularly in very strong versions of the Lutheran and Reformed traditions, have at times argued that sin has erased the human capacity for knowing the natural law apart from the regeneration of the Holy Spirit and the revelation of Scripture. And the great Swiss theologian Karl Barth famously argued that any kind of natural theology, including natural law theories, contradict the absolute freedom of God's self-revelation as well as the depth of human alienation. Even within these traditions, however, there is usually more room for some kind of natural law concept than might otherwise appear to be the case.[21] At the very least, there is a sense in most Christian thought that human beings ordinarily know something is missing, that we somehow are falling far short of an ideal, even if we might not be able to specify the positive content of the natural law in any detail.

"Law" matters, then, because there are principles of right relationship built into creation, and life contrary to those principles tends toward disorder, chaos, and violence. The man's exercise of the gift of free will to choose to eat of the "knowledge of good and evil," God warned, would lead to death—the ultimate destruction of beauty, food, life, and freedom.

20. There is a very important branch of legal philosophy called the "New Natural Law" school, led by John Finnis and others, that tries to establish a version of natural law on "neutral" philosophical grounds, and there are more libertarian-leaning scholars who argue for some kinds of "natural rights" (particularly rights in private property) based on the thinking of Enlightenment philosophers such as Immanuel Kant and John Locke. See John Finnis, *Natural Law and Natural Rights*, 2nd ed. (Oxford: Oxford University Press, 2011). In my view, this approach does not work without explicit reference to its religious foundations. See Russell Hittinger, *The First Grace: Rediscovering the Natural Law in a Post-Christian World* (Wilmington, DE: Intercollegiate Studies Institute, 2011).

21. See Thomas Joseph White, OP, ed., *The Analogy of Being: Invention of Antichrist or Wisdom of God?* (Grand Rapids: Eerdmans, 2010); Stephen J. Grabill, *Rediscovering the Natural Law in Reformed Theological Ethics* (Grand Rapids: Eerdmans, 2006).

An intimate acquaintance with evil, the kind of "knowledge" that arises from the sexual union of a man and wife, is a bondage to the dark nothing of death. Law is the boundary God set in the garden against nihilism. God's law, given in the garden, trains us to achieve the ends for which we were created.

FLOOD, NOAHIC COVENANT, AND BABEL

In the biblical narrative, as human society develops outside the garden, violence increases. Within ten generations after Adam, God nearly destroys the entire creation because there is no other way to check human violence (Gen 6:1–5).[22] The narrative of Noah's flood is shocking to modern ears: God destroys all life on Earth, save for the animals and eight humans aboard the ark. Modern critics overlook the cause of this divine judgment: in the narrative, humanity had become irrepressibly violent, and that violence threatened to undo the very fabric of creation.[23] Without the flood, everything would have been permanently

22. The biblical flood narrative, of course, like the creation narratives, also presents numerous exegetical and hermeneutical challenges, particularly for anyone seeking to understand the biblical revelation's relationship to the overwhelming evidence from the various physical sciences for the age of the earth, the apparent physical impossibility of a literally global flood, the geographic dispersion of species, the lack of a recent human population bottleneck, and so on. See, e.g., Davis A. Young and Ralph F. Stearley, *The Bible, Rocks and Time: Geological Evidence for the Age of the Earth* (Downers Grove, IL: InterVarsity, 2008). Like the Genesis 1 and 2 creation accounts, these texts probably should be understood as an effort to make sense of a pervasive cultural memory in the ancient Near East. The Epic of Gilgamesh and related texts suggest that the theme of a great flood ran deep through the cultures that produced these biblical texts. See James B. Pritchard, ed., *The Ancient Near East: An Anthology of Texts and Pictures* (Princeton: Princeton University Press, 2010). The biblical flood narrative, then, perhaps represents a literary representation of a memory grounded in an act of God in time, the "scientific" or "historical"—in the modern sense—parameters of which are lost to us. For the purpose of doing theology, we take these historical-critical considerations into account in order to avoid naive mistakes such as the Creation Museum and the Noah's Ark Park, but we nevertheless return to the text with a "second naiveté" in order to hear what God may be saying to the church in and through the text today in the light of Christ, particularly in light of the central Christian narrative identified in the rule of faith and the early creeds. See, e.g., Anthony C. Thistleton, *New Horizons in Hermeneutics: The Theory and Practice of Transforming Biblical Reading* (Grand Rapids: Zondervan, 1992); Nicholas Wolterstorff, *Divine Discourse: Philosophical Reflections on the Claim That God Speaks* (Cambridge: Cambridge University Press, 1995); Ellen F. Davis and Richard B. Hays, *The Art of Reading Scripture* (Grand Rapids: Eerdmans, 2003). This sort of reading, in fact, seems truer to the Fathers than modernist scientific readings, even if the Fathers generally would have had no reason to question the historical basis for the literal sense of the flood narrative. See Peter C. Bouteneff, *Beginnings: Ancient Christian Readings of the of the Biblical Creation Narratives* (Grand Rapids: Baker Academic, 2008).

23. Modern critics who argue that the flood narrative sanctions divine "genocide" also, ironically, read the text, like modern religious fundamentalists, primarily as a "literal" or "historical" document of events rather than primarily as a literary and theological text. There are a host

destroyed by human violence. By sending the flood, God gave both the animal world and humanity a chance at a new start. As Jewish and Christian commentators have long recognized, the flood was an act of grace as well as an act of judgment.[24] At the conclusion of the story, God establishes the famous "rainbow" covenant (בְּרִית *beriyth*) with Noah, a covenant that includes a promise to all of creation itself that the Earth will never again be destroyed by a flood (Gen 9:12–16). As the tree of life was the sign (sacrament) of God's blessing of the original creation, the rainbow was the sacrament of God's covenant with the renewed creation after the flood. It is a gift of re-creation, and that gift is accompanied by law. This includes a negative command:

> You must not eat meat that has its lifeblood still in it. And for your lifeblood I will surely demand an accounting. I will demand an accounting from every animal. And from each human being, too, I will demand an accounting for the life of another human being.
>
> Whoever sheds human blood,
>   by humans shall their blood be shed;
> for in the image of God
>   has God made mankind. (Gen 9:4–6)

It also includes a recapitulation of the positive command given in the garden: "As for you, be fruitful and increase in number; multiply on the earth and increase upon it" (Gen 9:7 NIV). Thus there was law when the waters of chaos receded after the flood and God reaffirmed his commitment to the creation.

The Noahic covenant has occupied an important place in some Christian theologies of law. Some scholars, particularly in the Reformed tradition, emphasize how the Noahic covenant facilitates the *preservation* of sinful humanity and the fallen creation. The primary role of positive law, emphasized in the covenant's apparent reference to capital punish-

---

of modern questions the text neither asks nor answers: Isn't it unfair for God simply to wipe people out, even if they were wicked? How did all those animals fit on the ark? And so on. In its ancient Near Eastern context, consistent with contemporary stories such as the Epic of Gilgamesh, the text simply assumes God's "right" to judge creation and is utterly unconcerned with the mechanics of the flood, the ark, and the animals. Critiques of the narratives on this score therefore are a category mistake. The overarching *theological* point of the Genesis flood narrative is that God both judges sin and violence and preserves his creation, including humanity, against its own destructive tendencies. See, e.g., Bill T. Arnold, *The New Cambridge Bible Commentary: Genesis* (Cambridge: Cambridge University Press, 2008); Tremper Longman III, John H. Walton, and Stephen O. Moshier, *The Lost World of the Flood: Mythology, Theology, and the Deluge Debate* (Downers Grove, IL: IVP Academic, 2018).

24. See Arnold, *Genesis*.

ment, is to preserve some minimum degree of civic order, and positive law otherwise plays no redemptive purpose. Other scholars do not see the covenant in such limited terms.

Not long after the flood, however, we find humanity at it again. The city of Babel, with its common language and its tower jutting with phallic assertion into the center of creation, is an act of cosmic rape. The famous story of the "tower of Babel" in the Hebrew Bible isn't only about a tower. The tower appears in the center of a "city," through which humanity, which shares a common language, seeks to reach into heaven, "make a name" for itself, and prevent the possibility of becoming "scattered abroad over the face of the whole earth" (Gen 11:1–9 NASB). God becomes concerned that, if humanity completes this city, "nothing which they purpose to do will be impossible for them" (Gen 11:6 NASB). God scatters humanity and causes different groups to speak different languages in order to foil humanity's plans (Gen 11:7–9).

The story has often been interpreted as a warning against the vices of cities, the sin of pride, or a Promethean theft of technological knowledge from God.[25] Those all may be legitimate readings, but the story's placement in the timeline of the biblical protohistory suggests another interpretation related to this essay's theme: it is a story about the violence of technocracy.

The story is situated in the generations following the great flood of Noah (Genesis 7–10). A project of this scale, of course, would require significant coordination—indeed, it would require all the resources of the population, and above all, it would require a hierarchy of human control. There were no friendly open source projects in the ancient Near East. We should imagine the society of Babel's tower builders as a world of single-minded zealots leading a deluded population. Babel's tower builders were the first technocrats. So, once again, in an act of judgment and grace, God acts, humanity's common language is confused, and human beings are scattered across the Earth.[26]

But God does not leave humanity scattered. From out of an ancient Near Eastern metropolis, the city of Ur, a man named Terah moved his

25. See Arnold, *Genesis*.

26. Like the Bible's creation and flood narratives, the Babel story is not considered "literal history" by most mainstream biblical scholars and theologians. The point of these stories is not to suggest a newspaper-like account of "what happened." Like many ancient narratives, whatever connection these accounts may have to distantly remembered events in time, they mean to connect us with prototypical human experience. We human beings are violent. We human beings want to impose a common, uniform vision upon the world and upon each other so that we can control all the outcomes. In the name of the universal, we destroy the particular: the strong over the weak, the many over the few, the useful over the beautiful, the quantifiable over the felt.

family to the town of Haran. Terah's son Abram prospers in Haran, but receives a call from God:

> Now the Lord [יְהוָה, *Yahweh*] said to Abram, "Go from your country, your people and your father's household to the land I will show you.
>   I will make you into a great nation,
>   and I will bless you;
>   I will make your name great,
>   and you will be a blessing.
>   I will bless those who bless you,
>   and whoever curses you I will curse;
>   and all peoples on earth
>   will be blessed through you." (Gen 12:1–3 NASB)

The narrative shift from the end of the Babel story to the call of Abram is jarring. There is a genealogy from Noah's son Shem to Terah (Gen 11:10–26), a brief account of Terah's migration from Ur (Gen 11:27–32), and the account of Abram's call (Gen 12:1–3), without any indication of how Abram had come to communicate with Yahweh.

As Abram continues on his travels, he ends up in Egypt during a famine. Apparently he is an influential visitor, because he is noticed in Pharaoh's court and gains further wealth and influence by deceptively giving his wife Sarah as a wife to Pharaoh, claiming that Sarah is only his sister—a bizarre detail not often commented on in sermons (Gen 12:10–20). Pharaoh angrily gives Sarah back and Abram departs Egypt and engages in some disputes and other issues with his nephew Lot (Genesis 13–14).

The narrative continues as God makes a promise to Abram: "Look up at the sky and count the stars—if indeed you can count them. . . . So shall your offspring be" (Gen 15:5 NASB). The text then tells us that "Abram believed the Lord, and he credited it to him as righteousness [צְדָקָה *tsedeqah*]" (Gen 15:6 NASB). The term צְדָקָה includes the sense of justice and loyalty. In the Septuagint, it is translated δικαιοσύνη (*dikaiosunē*), the same term used in relation to the concept of "justification" in the Pauline corpus. As with Noah, God seals his relationship with Abram with a בְּרִית (*beryith*), a legal covenant (Gen 15:18). Law and justice therefore are at the foundation of Israel's story just as they are at the foundation of creation itself.

Abraham wavers and has a son (Ishmael) with his servant Hagar, but God also gives Sarah a son, Isaac. Isaac has two sons with his wife Rebekah, Jacob and Esau, who are rivals. In a strange recapitulation of Abraham's time in Egypt, Isaac lives among the Philistines during a famine, tries to protect himself by claiming Rebekah is his sister rather than his wife, and is sent away wealthy (Genesis 25).

Jacob steals the blessing due from Abraham to Esau and flees to Haran, to the home of Laban, his mother Rebekah's brother (Genesis 27–28).[27] Jacob immediately falls in love with Laban's daughter Rachel, and Laban promises Rachel to Jacob in return for seven years of labor. At the end of the seven years, Laban tricks Jacob into marrying his less attractive daughter, Leah, and Jacob agrees to work for another seven years to obtain Rachel. Yahweh sees that Jacob loves Rachel and not Leah, and blesses Leah with four sons, while Rachel remains barren. Rachel gives Jacob her servant Bilhah as a wife, with whom Jacob has two more sons. Not to be left behind, Leah, who is no longer bearing children, gives her servant Zilpah to Jacob, who bears him two more sons (Genesis 29–30). Meanwhile, Leah's son Reuben finds some mandrake plants in the fields, and Rachel strikes a deal with Leah, giving Leah access to Jacob's bed in return for some of the mandrakes. The mandrake was viewed as an aphrodisiac and fertility booster in the ancient Near East.[28] Leah bears Jacob two more sons and a daughter, and Rachel bears another son, Joseph. Jacob now has eleven sons—eleven of the patrilineal heads of the future twelve tribes of Israel.

Jacob's wealth increases, Laban's sons become jealous. Jacob decides it is time to leave Laban's household, and tries to sneak away. As they are leaving, Rachel steals Laban's "household gods" (תְּרָפִים *teraphim*). These likely were small statuettes that served as good luck charms and tools for divination.[29] Laban is most upset that they are missing, nearly resulting in violence when he tracks down the fleeing Jacob, and Jacob is equally offended, since he did not know Rachel stole them. The day is saved only because Rachel sits on the saddle bag in which they are hidden, claiming that she cannot get up because she is having her period. Laban then makes a covenant with Jacob that allows Jacob and his household to depart peacefully: another example of law, a legal agreement, facilitating the narrative of the sending of Israel as a blessing to the nations (Genesis 31).

27. This is the same "Haran" where Terah settled. Returning to Haran allowed Jacob to marry within his own tribe, a common ancient Near Eastern custom. See Arnold, *Genesis*, 248.
28. Arnold, *Genesis*, 270.
29. Arnold, *Genesis*, 274.

SLAVERY, EXODUS

Jacob favors his first son through Rachel, Joseph. The other brothers plot to get rid of Joseph and sell him into slavery. Joseph ends up a slave in Pharaoh's court in Egypt. Joseph is unfairly imprisoned as a result of accusations by the wife of the captain of Pharaoh's guard, Potiphar, who tried to seduce Joseph. But Joseph is favored by God, and after showing a talent for interpreting dreams, he ends up in a high administrative position in Egypt—the text tells us he becomes second only to Pharaoh himself. Joseph interprets Pharaoh's dreams about a coming famine and leads Egypt's preparations for the crisis. Threatened by the famine, Jacob sends his sons to Egypt for grain. The brothers appear before Joseph, who at first tricks them before revealing his true identity and welcoming the family to take refuge in Goshen, a territory controlled by Egypt (Genesis 31).

Subsequent generations of the family prosper in Egypt and begin to take on a collective identity as Hebrews. A new pharaoh forgets Joseph's contribution and becomes jealous and suspicious of the Hebrews. The new pharaoh enslaves the Hebrews, requiring them to work on building crews. Pharaoh becomes so paranoid that he commands the Hebrew midwives to kill any male babies. They deceive Pharaoh and allow the babies to live. The baby Moses is born into this context, hidden by his mother in a basket by the banks for the river, where he is discovered and adopted by Pharaoh's daughter. Moses grows up in Pharaoh's court but is awakened to his Hebrew identity as a young man, ultimately setting up the conflict through which God delivers the Hebrews from Egyptian slavery. The conflict develops over the course of ten plagues God visits on Egypt, culminating with the death of every firstborn child. God spares the Hebrew children by providing a protective sign of lamb's blood and establishes an annual festival on the day of this "passover" as a "perpetual ordinance" (חֻקַּת, ḥuqqat, statute or ordinance [Exod 12:14]) for the Hebrew people (Exodus 1–12).

Law now begins to serve a function for the Hebrews relating to memory and national identity. Again and again in the subsequent narratives in the Hebrew Scriptures, God will remind his people that he delivered them from slavery in Egypt. This reminder is meant to induce faith in God's provision, to encourage fidelity to God against the temptations of idolatry, and to distinguish Israel from surrounding nations.

These themes are evident immediately after the Passover. After the devastation of the plague of the firstborn, Pharaoh lets the Hebrews leave Egypt but quickly has a change of heart and sends an army to destroy the Hebrews, who are pinned against the banks of the Red Sea. God parts the sea, allowing the Hebrews to cross, and closes it up again when the Egyptian army tries to follow. The Hebrews sing a song of victory that pictures the Egyptians engulfed by the waters: "The floods covered them; / They wound down into the depths like a stone" (Exod 15:5 NRSV).

The word translated "floods" here in the NRSV is תְּהוֹם (*tehom*), the same word used of the primeval waters in Genesis 1 and of the source of Noah's floodwaters in Genesis 7–8. By destroying the Egyptian army, God was judging an old world, and through the "perpetual ordinance" of the Passover on the opposite banks of the Red Sea, he was establishing a new world among the Hebrews.

The song is taken up by Miriam, Moses and Aaron's sister, described as "the prophetess" (נְבִיאָה *nebiya*), who proclaims, "with tambourines and with dancing," "Sing to the Lord, for he has triumphed gloriously; / horse and rider he has thrown into the sea" (Exod 15:20–21). The waters swallow Egypt so the new creation of Israel can prosper.[30] God delivers Israel from slavery in Egypt and establishes his people in unique covenantal relationship by giving them law.

FROM COMMON LAW TO THE DECALOGUE

In the narrative given in Exodus, after Moses leads the people out of Egypt, they wander in the desert on their way to the promised land. Along the way, Moses meets with his father-in-law, Jethro, priest of Midian, who observes that Moses serves as a kind of oracle and common law judge when the people have disputes (Exod 18:1–16). Jethro advises Moses to appoint lower judges to handle some of the caseload, which Moses arranges (Exod 18:17–26). Other than direct divination, it is unclear what sort of common law Moses and his judges applied.

On the first day of the third month after leaving Egypt, at the foot of Mount Sinai, Moses receives a summons from God, who tells Moses to prepare the people for a divine visitation. The visitation occurs on the morning of the third day of the month, accompanied by terrifying "thunder and lightning, with a thick cloud over the mountain, and a very loud trumpet blast" along with smoke, fire, and earthquake (Exod 19:16 NIV). Only Moses and his brother Aaron are permitted to meet with God on the mountaintop. God then verbally announces the commandments. The text is unclear whether God's speech is broadcast to the

30. Miriam's song might be echoed in the New Testament apocalyptic literature, which pictures "Babylon" as a "great millstone" being thrown into the sea (Rev 18:21).

entire people or delivered to Moses and Aaron as reporters for the people (Exod 19:23–20:17).[31] Exodus 21–23 include numerous additional laws beyond the Ten Commandments with which Moses was to instruct the people, including laws relating to personal injuries, property, servants, money lending, and a variety of other matters.

In Exodus 24, Moses, Aaron, Aaron's sons Nadab and Abihu, and seventy of the elders of Israel are summoned again to the mountain. As they wait at the foot of the mountain, these assembled leaders of Israel receive a vision of God, apparently standing or sitting on "something like a pavement made of lapis lazuli, as bright blue as the sky" (Exod 24:10 NIV). This is an astonishing, direct vision of God, marked as such in the text: "but God did not raise his hand against these leaders of the Israelites; they saw God, and they ate and drank" (Exod 24:11 NIV). The rarity of this vision demonstrates that God is about to do something of foundational significance for Israel. God summons Moses to ascend the mountain and receive "the tablets of stone with the law and commandments I have written for their instruction" (Exod 24:12). A cloud covers the mountain for six days while Moses waits, and on the seventh day Moses is called into the cloud—mirroring the seven days of creation and the cycle of work and Sabbath. Moses remains on the mountain for forty days and forty nights, mirroring the length of the Noahic deluge. The tablets of the Law establish Israel as God's people, and through Israel God begins to re-create the world. Exodus 25–31 contains detailed instructions about the tabernacle, the priestly garments, and other aspects of how God should be worshiped.

Exodus 32 recites the infamous incident of the golden calf, when even Aaron, impatient for Moses's return from the mountaintop, participated in idolatry. Upon seeing the people's revelry before the golden calf, Moses breaks the stone tablets inscribed with the Law into pieces (Exod 24:19). In Exodus 34, God renews his covenant with Israel to Moses and inscribes two new stone tablets with the Law.

Deuteronomy 5 offers another account of the Decalogue. The Deuteronomic narrative pictures Moses instructing the people after forty years of wandering in the desert, at the threshold of the promised land (Deuteronomy 1–4). Moses recounts the theophany at the mountain and recites the commands he received from God. The commands in Deuteronomy 5 are similar to those in Exodus but differ in some respects that appear to reflect a different social setting.[32]

Whatever history and textual tradition might lie behind these narra-

---

31. See Edward L. Greenstein, "The Decalogue," in Strawn, ed., *Oxford Encyclopedia of the Bible and Law*.

32. See Greenstein, "Decalogue."

tives, by the Second Temple period the Decalogue came to occupy a central place in Jewish liturgy.[33] Along with the *Shema*, the Decalogue served as a marker of ethical identity that bound the Jewish people to God.[34] The *Shema* is the prayer drawn from Deuteronomy 6:4–9, 11:13–21, and Numbers 15:37–41, which begins, "Hear O Israel: The Lord our God, the Lord is one." As we will see, the Decalogue also was centrally important for later Christian theologians writing about ethics, law, and political society, though Christian interpreters sometimes struggled to articulate how this central component of Judaism translated into different Christian contexts.[35]

As the additional laws in Exodus 21–23 suggest, the Decalogue is by no means the only seemingly "legal" document in the Old Testament. Large portions of Leviticus and Deuteronomy contain detailed laws for daily and cultic life. Leviticus, which follows Exodus in the canon, depicts God directing Moses to instruct the people about these laws while they are wandering in the wilderness between Egypt and the promised land (Lev 1:1). Deuteronomy pictures Moses instructing the people as they prepare to enter the promised land after forty years of wandering. Many of the laws in Leviticus and Deuteronomy dealing with issues such as sexual offenses, dishonesty, theft, murder, and property rights overlap significantly with other Mesopotamian and Hittite law codes.[36] Some commentators suggest that the laws in Leviticus and Deuteronomy mitigate some of the harsher components of typical ancient Near Eastern laws, and that the biblical laws reflect particular concern for the land, the poor, and the outsider in provisions such as the gleanings and jubilee laws.[37]

It is unclear whether or to what extent any of the specific laws in Leviticus and Deuteronomy were ever practiced in ancient Israel. Mainstream scholarship suggests that Leviticus is composed of a priestly source (P) and a later holiness source (H), which supplemented and revised the P material, and which also supplemented and revised parts of Deuteronomy.[38] Deuteronomy, mainstream contemporary scholarship

33. Greenstein, "Decalogue."

34. Greenstein, "Decalogue."

35. See Jeffrey P. Greenman and Timothy Larsen, ed., *The Decalogue through the Centuries: From the Hebrew Scriptures to Benedict XVI* (Louisville: Westminster John Knox, 2012).

36. See Roy E. Gane, "Leviticus," and Eugene E. Carpenter, "Deuteronomy," in John H. Walton, ed., *Zondervan Illustrated Bible Backgrounds Commentary* (Grand Rapids: Zondervan, 2009), 1:288, 420.

37. See, e.g., Christopher J. H. Wright, *Old Testament Ethics for the People of God* (Downers Grove, IL: InterVarsity, 2004); Joseph William Singer, *The Edges of the Field: Lessons on the Obligations of Ownership* (Boston: Beacon, 2000).

38. See "Leviticus," in *The New Oxford Annotated Study Bible* (Oxford: Oxford University

suggests, likely was composed in the seventh century BCE by another source (the Deuteronomist source, or D) and reflects the reforms of Josiah, King of Judah (2 Kings 22–23), discussed below.[39]

THE CONQUEST

After Moses reiterates the provisions of the law and covenant, he prepares to pass leadership to a new generation who will bring Israel into the promised land. Our narrative focus then quickly becomes immensely complicated because God instructs the people to engage in holy war (*herem*). Deuteronomy 6:4 recites what will become the first part of the *Shema*—"Hear, O Israel: The Lord our God, the Lord is one," and Deuteronomy 6:5 connects this with a law of love that, as we will see, Jesus will place at the center of his ethical teaching: "Love the Lord your God with all your heart and with all your soul and with all your strength." But Deutronomy 7 makes clear that the people who currently live in the promised land have no legal or moral rights: "When the Lord your God brings you into the land you are entering to possess and drives out before you many nations—the Hittites, Girgashites, Amorites, Canaanites, Perizzites, Hivites and Jebusites, seven nations larger and stronger than you—and when the Lord your God has delivered them over to you and you have defeated them, then you must destroy them totally. Make no treaty with them, and show them no mercy" (Deut 7:1–2 NIV).

Joshua leads the Israelites across the Jordan and into their first major battle at Jericho, where the city is miraculously delivered into their hands. According to Joshua 6:22, "They devoted the city to the Lord and destroyed with the sword every living thing in it—men and women, young and old, cattle, sheep and donkeys." The only people spared were Rahab the prostitute, who assisted Joshua's spies, and her family (Josh 6:17). One member of Joshua's army, Achan, kept some plunder for himself, and as a result he and his family were stoned and their bodies burned (Joshua 7).

The Israelites then marched to the city of Ai, where they left "neither

Press, 2018), 141. A "source" here is likely a group or school of writers and editors working over a period of time, not a single author. Some scholars suggest there were multiple different schools within the P source. For a more detailed discussion, see Rolf Rendtorff and Robert A. Kugler, eds., introduction to *The Book of Leviticus: Composition and Reception* (Leiden: Brill, 2003). For a discussion of source criticism of the Pentateuch generally, see G. I. Davies, "Introduction to the Pentateuch," in John Barton and John Muddiman, ed., *New Oxford Bible Commentary: The Pentateuch* (Oxford: Oxford University Press, 2010).

39. "Deuteronomy," *New Oxford Bible Commentary*, 247.

survivors nor fugitives" (Josh 8:24 NIV). The text tells us that "twelve thousand men and women fell that day—all the people of Ai" (Josh 8:25 NIV). To celebrate this victory, "Joshua read all the words of the law—the blessings and the curses—just as it is written in the Book of the Law. There was not a word of all that Moses had commanded that Joshua did not read to the whole assembly of Israel, including the women and children, and the foreigners who lived among them" (Josh 8:34–35 NIV). Through the book of Joshua, with occasional twists and turns, the conquest marches on. Makkeedah: "He put the city and its king to the sword and totally destroyed everyone in it. He left no survivors" (Josh 10:28). Libnah: "The city and everyone in it Joshua put to the sword. He left no survivors there" (Josh 10:30). Lachish: "The city and every-one in it he put to the sword, just as he had done to Libnah. Meanwhile, Horam king of Gezer had come up to help Lachish, but Joshua defeated him and his army—until no survivors were left" (Josh 10:32–33). Eglon, Hebron, Debir—all the same (Josh 10:34–39). In a summation of this campaign, the text tells us, "Joshua subdued the whole region, includ-ing the hill country, the Negev, the western foothills and the moun-tain slopes, together with all their kings. He left no survivors. He totally destroyed all who breathed, just as the Lord, the God of Israel, had com-manded" (Josh 10:40).

The Israelites then faced "a huge army" of coalition troops from tribes throughout the region (Josh 11:1–5). Again, the text says, "Joshua took all these royal cities and their kings and put them to the sword. He totally destroyed them, as Moses the servant of the Lord had com-manded. . . . The Israelites carried off for themselves all the plunder and livestock of these cities, but all the people they put to the sword until they completely destroyed them, not sparing anyone that breathed" (Josh 11:12–14). To emphasize the point, Joshua 12 provides a list of thirty-one kings Joshua defeated. Even then, the conquest was not yet com-plete, and God instructed Joshua, now an old man, to begin dividing the conquered lands among the tribes of Israel (Joshua 13–22).

The conquest narrative is deeply troubling for modern readers on many levels. These texts, and others like them, led some in the early church to argue that the God depicted in the Old Testament is a different God that that depicted in the new—a position called Marcionism, asso-ciated with Marcion of Sinope (c. 85–160 CE), which was eventually rejected by other church leaders as a heresy. Others argue that the narra-tives represent only what the unduly violent Israelites *thought* God com-manded, or that the narratives were constructed whole-cloth during the exile as a kind of fictional polemic against Babylon, and should be interpreted by Christians in spiritual terms relating to our struggle against the powers of evil—a reading that combines modern historical-critical scholarship with the spiritual exegesis of some early church figures such as Origen of Alexandria.[40] Another traditional reading of this narrative is that God's ways are simply beyond human ways. A related reading is that the Canaanite nations were irredeemably wicked and that God's military judgment on them was an act of grace that open a path for a renewed humanity in Israel. A somewhat moderated traditional view is that God progressively reveals himself in Scripture and accommodates himself to historical circumstances. God's revelation of himself to the ancient Hebrews in the context of ancient Near Eastern holy war, then, differed from his fuller revelation of himself in Christ on the cross.

Some contemporary scholars have attempted to blunt the force of these narratives by suggesting that the "cities" were actually relatively small military garrisons with few or no women or children present.[41] These "military garrison" arguments tend to be mounted by conservative evangelical scholars who feel they need to defend a particular view of biblical inerrancy and historicity against the archaeological evidence as well as diffuse criticisms of the text's facial violence. While relatively few biblical scholars accept these rationalizations whole cloth, it is true that archaeological evidence has not disclosed anything corresponding to the massive military campaigns depicted in the text, and at some key sites such as Jericho, the evidence seems to contradict strongly any single sudden military destruction of the city in any timeline that would make sense of the narrative.

Many mainstream scholars therefore do agree that the actual "conquest" was really more a longer pattern of settlement, assimilation, and occasional tribal skirmishes, and that the Joshua narratives are largely or at least partly fictitious. Indeed, many mainstream scholars suggest that the entire biblical narrative of Israel from Abraham through the Egyptian captivity and exodus to the conquest is at best a highly exaggerated story forged in late preexilic or postexilic times for polemical purposes, reflecting a much more complex and gradual process by which some tribal groups developed a national identity as Israel—although all of this is hotly debated within the fractious world of biblical archeology.[42]

40. See, e.g., Douglas S. Earl, *The Joshua Delusion? Rethinking Genocide in the Bible* (Eugene, OR: Wipf and Stock, 2010).

41. See, e.g., Richard S. Hess, "The Jericho and Ai of the Book of Joshua," in *Critical Issues in Early Israelite History*, ed. Richard S. Hess, Gerald A. Klingbeil, and Paul J. Ray (Winona Lake, IN: Eisenbrauns, 2008); Paul Copan and Matt Flannagan, *Did God Really Command Genocide? Coming to Terms with the Justice of God* (Grand Rapids: Baker Books, 2014).

42. For a summary of different models modern scholars have used to discuss the "conquest,"

Whatever we make of the historical-critical scholarship, however, from a canonical and narratival perspective, we must first confront these texts in all their jarring strangeness.[43] The traditional reading that the conquest actually occurred as stated is consistent with the theme of fall, judgment, and redemption in the biblical protohistory, including the expulsion from Eden, the Noahic flood, and the judgment of Babel. This part of the Hebrew Scriptures simply is not concerned with modern notions of justice, much less with modern concepts of the international laws of war or prohibitions against genocide. Indeed, the notion of "genocide" is a construct of the modern law of war, not a concept that would even have been available to ancient Near Eastern people.[44]

One immediate point this suggests is the danger of taking any particular biblical text to represent "the biblical view" of law. The modern international law of war cannot be derived directly from the Bible, and certainly not from the conquest narratives. This does not mean the modern international law of war is mistaken or that Christians should support genocide—though, sadly, Christians throughout history have at times used the conquest narratives to support genocide, including, ironically and tragically, genocidal pogroms against the Jews. It shows that contemporary reflection on questions such as the legal limitations on warfare require the resources of reason, tradition, and experience, as well as the resources of Scripture.

Another point is that we should understand the conquest narratives within the broader narratives of God's righteous demands and his gracious provision of new opportunities for humanity. Concerning our theme of "law," the text repeatedly depicts the Law, the Torah, as the centerpiece of this provision. By displacing the Canaanites, God makes room for a new society governed by a new law.[45] In addition, the Hebrew Scriptures do not stop at the conquest narratives. The conquest narratives frame what comes next in the historical books. We will eventually learn that Israel *loses* the land, just as the Canaanites did, as a result of God's judgment against oppression and injustice. Finally, from

---

see Koert Van Bekkum, *From Conquest to Coexistence: Ideology and Antiquarian Intent in the Historiography of Israel's Settlement in Canaan* (Leiden: Brill, 2011), chap. 1.

43. See Karl Barth, "The Strange New World within the Bible," in *A Map of Twentieth Century Theology: Readings from Karl Barth to Radical Pluralism*, ed. Carl E. Braaten and Robert W. Jenson (Minneapolis: Augsburg Fortress, 1995), 21–30.

44. To be clear, I think the condemnation of genocide in the modern law of war is entirely correct and important. The point is that reading these ancient narratives in light of such modern concepts is anachronistic.

45. Again, this is how the narrative presents itself. The fact that much of the Levitical and Deuteronomic law actually borrows from surrounding ancient Near Eastern law codes is for this purpose beside the point.

the perspective of a Christian interpreter thinking about a constructive Christian theology of law and justice, we must keep reading into the New Testament, and in particular to the teachings, death, and resurrection of Christ.

As we will see, in the Sermon on the Mount and in his other ethical teachings, and in his self-giving death, Jesus demonstrates that the real *herem* warfare occurs in the spiritual realm, against the powers of violence and oppression in the world, and against the powers of sin and death within our own souls. In this respect, modern readings that combine historical-critical scholarship about the later polemical purposes of the conquest narratives, combined with traditional patristic spiritual and christological interpretations of these texts, help us understand that these texts are not roadmaps for contemporary law and policy but rather serve as pointers toward the prophetic judgment against the failure of any society—whether Canaanite, Israel, or Christian—to keep God's law.

CONQUEST TO JUDGES

After the conquest narratives, Joshua leads a ceremony in which the people reaffirm their covenant with Yahweh, during which Joshua "reaffirmed for them decrees and laws. And Joshua recorded these things in the Book of the Law of God. Then he took a large stone and set it up there under the oak near the holy place of the Lord" (Josh 24:25–26). After Joshua dies, in a pattern that will become familiar, the generation following this great and faithful leader did not finish the task he began. The remaining Canaanite nations were not removed from the land, and the people "took [Canaanite] daughters in marriage and gave their own daughters to [Canaanite] sons, and served [Canaanite] gods," and "forgot the Lord their God and served the Baals and the Asherahs" (Judg 1:1–3:5). When the people revert to their evil ways, God punishes them through military subjugation to Canaanite leaders; the people cry out and God appoints a מוֹשִׁיעַ—a *mōwōšîaʿ*, a "deliverer" or "savior" (Othniel and Ehud, Judges 3), or, remarkably (again, as with Miriam), a נְבִיאָה *nebiah*, "prophetess" (Deborah, Judges 4) and then a אִישׁ נָבִיא *ish nabiy'*, literally a "man prophet" (Gideon, Judges 6). These leaders and their associates rescue the people through assassinations and miraculous military victories. Among the more colorful episodes, Ehud kills King Eglon of Moab with a hidden sword, and, the text tells us, "even the handle sank in after the blade, and his bowels discharged. Ehud did not pull the sword out, and the fat closed in over it" (Judg 3:22). And Jael, wife of Heber the Kenite, kills Sisera, commander of a Canaanite army, while he sleeps: she "picked up a tent peg and a hammer and went quietly to him while he lay fast asleep, exhausted. She drove the peg through his temple into the ground, and he died" (Judg 4:21). There is a bad leader, Abimelek (Judges 9), leaders who pass with only incidental comment (Tola, Judg 10:1–2), and Jair, who, in what sounds like an echo from a children's folk song, had thirty sons who rode thirty donkeys and controlled thirty towns (Judg 10:3–5); other good leaders (Jephtah, Judges 10:6–11:7); and more leaders who pass without much comment (Ibzan, Elon, and Abdon—again, with references to numbers of offspring and donkeys [Judg 11:8–13]); and the famous story of the strongman Samson (Judges 13–17).

Following these narratives are two stories that begin, "In those days Israel had no king" (Judg 18:1; 19:1). The first involves an idolater, Micah (not the later prophet), who receives his comeuppance at the hands of some men from the tribe of Dan, who become idolaters themselves (Judges 17–18). The second involves a Levite who allows his concubine to be abused by some Benjamites and then cuts her dead body into twelve pieces and delivers them to each of the areas of Israel, resulting in massive violence between the other tribes and the Benjamites (Judges 19–21). Although there is some reconciliation after the violence (involving the abduction of women to serve as wives for the surviving Benjamites [Judg 21:20–23]), the book of Judges concludes as these two episodes began, with an ominous note that sums up a history of civil instability and violence: "In those days Israel had no king; everyone did as they saw fit" (Judg 21:25).

The theological problem of violence in the Judges narratives is similar to that raised by Joshua, though perhaps on a smaller scale. From a historical-critical perspective, Judges, likely compiled by Deuteronomist editors in the late seventh and sixth centuries BCE, seems to have been intended to explain why Israel was exiled.[46] From our narrative perspective, Judges introduces the theme of a deliverer, savior, or prophet who cleanses the nation of impurity and recalls it to allegiance to Yahweh and his law. Judges also includes the theme of the brave, cunning, righteous woman who acts on the people's behalf. Finally, Judges displays the chaos that results when "everyone does as they see fit"—that is, when there is no rule of law.

46. "Judges," *New Oxford Annotated Study Bible*, 355.

FROM JUDGES TO KINGS

The prophet Samuel serves as a sort of transitional figure between the period of the judges and the period of the kings. When Samuel was a priest in training, "the word of the Lord was rare in those days; visions were not widespread" (1 Sam 3:1). As Samuel grows into his role as a priest and prophet, a seafaring tribe that will continue to serve as Israel's nemesis, the Philistines, raid Israel and capture the ark of the covenant, a terrible catastrophe for Israel. The ark, however, causes the Philistines to fall ill, and under Samuel's leadership, the Philistines were defeated, and the ark was returned (1 Sam 4:1–7:11).

When Samuel grows old, he appoints his sons Joel and Abijah to serve as judges, but true to form, they "did not follow in his ways, but turned aside after gain; they took bribes and perverted justice" (1 Sam 8:3 NASB). They people then demand a king, "like other nations," instead of prophets and judges (1 Sam 8:5). This suggests that the people's desire for a king is a rejection of Yahweh as king (1 Sam 8:7). Through God's guidance, Samuel finds Saul and anoints him as king, inaugurating the period of the monarchy (1 Sam 9:17–10:1).

Saul, however, is rejected by God when he usurps Samuel's role as prophet before an important battle (1 Sam 13:8–15). The narrative in 1 Samuel here is terse and the nature of Saul's sin is unclear, but it appears that Saul views his kingship as a license to control God or to control a religious function that did not belong to him. After some significant twists and turns, this leads to Samuel's anointing of David as the future king (1 Sam 16:13).

David becomes the prototypical king at the outset of a golden age. Eventually, after the exile, Israel's prophets will look for the restoration of the Davidic throne, and the Gospel writers will connect Jesus with the line of David. David at times fails greatly, particularly in his adultery with Bathsheba and his murderous scheme to ensure that Bathsheba's husband, Uriah the Hittite, is killed in battle (1 Sam 11:1–12:1). But the Bible's historical books and the psalms that are attributed to David ultimately portray him as a righteous and blessed king. For our purposes we can focus on one of the most famous of those texts, Psalm 19.[47]

The first section of Psalm 19 is a *locus classicus* for various kinds of natural theology, including for later views about the natural law:

47. Although the psalm is attributed to David, these notations are not part of the Psalms themselves, and we do not know who or when the various psalms in the canonical collection were first composed. See, e.g., "Psalms," *New Oxford Annotated Study Bible*, 773. It is likely, however, that at least some of the Psalms were collected for use in worship prior to the exile. See John Goldingay, *Psalms 1–41* (Grand Rapids: Baker Academic, 2006), 21.

The heavens declare the glory of God;
　　the skies proclaim the work of his hands.
Day after day they pour forth speech;
　　night after night they reveal knowledge.
They have no speech, they use no words;
　　no sound is heard from them.
Yet their voice goes out into all the earth,
　　their words to the ends of the world.
In the heavens God has pitched a tent for the sun.
　　It is like a bridegroom coming out of his chamber,
　　like a champion rejoicing to run his course.
It rises at one end of the heavens
　　and makes its circuit to the other;
　　nothing is deprived of its warmth. (Ps 19:1–6 NIV)

The second section of Psalm 19 completes this picture of creation's witness to God with a hymn to the law (*torah*):

The law of the Lord is perfect,
　　refreshing the soul.
The statutes of the Lord are trustworthy,
　　making wise the simple.
The precepts of the Lord are right,
　　giving joy to the heart.
The commands of the Lord are radiant,
　　giving light to the eyes.
The fear of the Lord is pure,
　　enduring forever.
The decrees of the Lord are firm,
　　and all of them are righteous. (Ps 19:7–9 NIV)

In the third section of the psalm, the speaker—presumptively King David as the psalm's author—and through his words the worshipers who sing or recite the psalm, seek to apply the Torah to themselves:

They are more precious than gold,
　　than much pure gold;
they are sweeter than honey,
　　than honey from the honeycomb.
By them your servant is warned;
　　in keeping them there is great reward.
But who can discern their own errors?
　　Forgive my hidden faults.
Keep your servant also from willful sins;

may they not rule over me.
Then I will be blameless,
    innocent of great transgression. (Ps 19:10–13 NIV)

The concluding stanza invites the worshiper to take the Torah deeply to heart: "May these words of my mouth and this meditation of my heart be pleasing in your sight, Lord, my Rock and my Redeemer" (Ps 19:14 NIV).

The biblical picture of King David, then, as emphasized in Psalm 19, imagines a time when the nation and its leadership, though flawed, sought to uphold the law embedded in creation and spoken to the nation by God.

The golden age continues, at least for a time, under David's son Solomon. Solomon, 1 Kings tells us, "loved the Lord, walking in the statutes of his father David; only, he sacrificed and offered incense at the high places"—that is, at Canaanite shrines (1 Kgs 3:3). We see here a hint of Solomon's later troubles, as he seeks both to follow YHWH and to please numerous wives and concubines who serve foreign gods. Offered a blessing from God, Solomon chooses wisdom, and becomes the prototype of the wise person in the Bible's wisdom literature, emphasized in the famous "splitting the baby" judgment (1 Kgs 3:1–28). "God gave Solomon very great wisdom, discernment, and breadth of understanding as vast as the sand on the seashore," the text of 1 Kings tells us, "so that Solomon's wisdom surpassed the wisdom of all the people of the east, and all the wisdom of Egypt" (1 Kgs 4:29–30 NASB). Indeed, "people came from all the nations to hear the wisdom of Solomon; they came from all the kings of the earth who had heard of his wisdom" (1 Kgs 4:34 NASB).

As one of his crowning achievements, Solomon builds a spectacular temple for YHWH in Jerusalem (1 Kings 6–7). Although this is presented as a great and righteous achievement, the text notes that Solomon "conscripted forced labor out of all Israel; the levy numbered thirty thousand men" (1 Kgs 5:13). As Walter Brueggemann argues, this oppression sowed the seeds for Israel's fall.[48] And even with all his wisdom and great achievements, Solomon "loved many foreign women" in violation of God's commands (1 Kgs 11:1)

As a result of Solomon's failures, after Solomon's death, God divides the kingdom between Solomon's son, Rehoboam, and the man Solomon had appointed as a supervisor of forced laborers, Jeroboam. Rehoboam's advisors suggest he ease the burden of forced conscription—perhaps

---

48. Walter Brueggemann, *The Prophetic Imagination*, 2nd ed. (Minneapolis: Fortress, 2001).

knowing that Jeroboam could garner the support of the laborers in a coup—but Rehoboam refuses (1 Kgs 12:1–15).

In an echo of Pharaoh's responses to Moses, Rehoboam tells the laborers, "My father made your yoke heavy, but I will add to your yoke; my father disciplined you with whips, but I will discipline you with scorpions" (1 Kgs 12:14). The resulting dispute leaves the kingdom divided between the northern kingdom of Israel, led by Jeroboam, and the southern kingdom of Judah, led by Rehoboam. The Bible's historical books then recount events under twenty succeeding kings of Judah and nineteen succeeding kings of Israel, replete with intrigue, assassinations, and wars.[49] Among these kings there were some who followed God's law and sought reform, but most, in the texts' repeated refrain, "did evil in the sight of the Lord."

FALLEN KINGS, CONQUEST, AND EXILE

As a result of the persistent evil of Israel and Judah's kings, God allows the powerful nations of Assyria and Babylon to dominate the kingdoms of Israel and Judah. One of the reforming kings, Josiah, seeks to rescue the southern kingdom of Judah from Assyrian influence. Assyria had defeated the northern kingdom of Israel and had made the southern kingdom of Judah essentially a vassal state when King Ahaz and then King Hezekiah of Judah reached agreements with Assyria nearly a hundred years before Josiah's reforms.[50]

Josiah's reform effort proves short-lived. According to 2 Kings 23:29–30, Josiah is killed in a battle against Pharaoh Necho of Egypt, who had allied with Assyria. (The text of 2 Kings here mentions a source that sadly is lost to history, the "annals of the kings of Judah." See 2 Kgs 23:28.) Josiah's son Jehoahaz assumes the throne and cooperates with

---

49. For a list of the kings mentioned in the historical books, see John H. Walton, *Chronological and Background Charts of the Old Testament* (Grand Rapids: Zondervan, 1994), 30–31. There are many differences in chronology and detail between the books that recount most of these episodes, 1–2 Kings and 1–2 Chronicles, as well as various historical-critical questions about the events they narrate. The historical and theological reasons for these differences, and the details of debates between "minimalists" and "maximalists" about the literal historicity of the texts, is beyond the scope of this book. For a review of the "minimalist vs. maximalist" debate, see William G. Dever, "Hershel's Crusade, No. 2: For King and Country: Chronology and Minimalism," *Biblical Archeology Review* 44, no. 2 (2018). For one thoughtful approach from a conservative evangelical perspective, see Iain Provan, V. Phillips Long, and Tremper Longman III, *A Biblical History of Israel*, 2nd ed. (Louisville: Westminster John Knox, 2015).

50. See Provan, Long, and Longman III, *Biblical History of Israel*; 2 Kgs 16–17; Iain Provan, "2 Kings," in Walton, ed., *Zondervan Illustrated Bible Backgrounds Commentary*, 177–211.

Pharaoh Necho, only to be displaced by his brother Jehoiakim, who apparently becomes Necho's new favorite.

Both Jehoahaz and Jehoiakim are listed among the evil kings of Judah (2 Kgs 23:31–37). During Jehoiakim's reign, the Babylonian King Nebuchadnezzar invaded Judah (2 Kgs 24:1–2). Jehoiakim at first becomes Nebuchadnezzar's vassal but then rebels and is displaced (2 Kgs 24:1–2). Jehoiakim dies, and his son Jehoiachin takes the throne. Nebuchadnezzar besieges Jerusalem and "carried all Jerusalem into exile: all the officers and fighting men, and all the skilled workers and artisans," including Jehoiachin himself, and installs Jehoiachin's uncle Zedekiah as a vassal king in Jerusalem (2 Kgs 24:15–17).[51] In his most devastating act for Israel's self-identity, Nebuchadnezzar "removed the treasures from the temple of the Lord and from the royal palace, and cut up the gold articles that Solomon king of Israel had made for the temple of the Lord" (2 Kgs 24:13). Zedekiah also rebels, and Nebuchadnezzar again besieges the city, executes all of Zedekiah's sons, blinds and enslaves Zedekiah, and burns the city to the ground, including Solomon's temple and the royal palace (2 Kgs 25:1–26).[52]

The Babylonian exile was a defining event for the self-identify of the Jewish people. The legal texts in Leviticus and Deuteronomy, along with other parts of the Torah, likely were edited into their canonical form during the Babylonian exile.[53] The entire Torah therefore represents a theological history leading to the possibility of an ideal society under God's law that was never fully realized in practice.

As Calum Carmichael has argued, the Torah's place in biblical history shows that the biblical law codes are embedded in a thick narrative about what Israel was and what Israel should be, a narrative shaped by the experience of exile.[54] And as Rolf Rendtorff suggests, whatever else textual criticism might say about the sources underlying a text like Leviticus, the canonical text "is part of the story of Israel at Sinai, which itself is part of Israel's journey from Egypt to the borders of the promised land, which in turn is closely connected with the story of the creation of the world, the Flood, the calling of Abraham and the history of his fam-

---

51. Zedekiah's name originally was "Mattaniah" and was changed by Nebuchadnezzar as an act of control.

52. For some historical context relating to these texts, see Provan, "2 Kings," 202–11.

53. See "Deuteronomy," *New Oxford Annotated Study Bible*, 247–48.

54. Calum M. Carmichael, *Illuminating Leviticus: A Study of Its Laws and Institutions in the Light of Biblical Narratives* (Baltimore: Johns Hopkins University Press, 2006). One need not accept all of Carmichael's conclusions about the historical development of the biblical legal tradition to grant his conclusion about the relationship between law and idealized historical narrative.

ily up to their moving to Egypt."[55] As G. I. Davies notes, the Pentateuch is "the product of a long process of tradition" in which individuals or schools of theologians within Israel's history shaped and reshaped the diverse texts in a way that "bears witness to the whole history and life of Israel, and not just to the period which it purports to describe."[56] The failure to realize this ideal society under the law, in the vision of the biblical prophets, resulted in the Assyrian conquest and the Babylonian exile as God's judgment on the nation. But the prophets also offered the hope that a surviving remnant of faithful Israel would return to the law and that Israel would one day be restored.

PROPHETIC LAMENT

In addition to the redaction of the Torah and the histories, the exile and the events leading up to it also prompted the creation of the Hebrew Bible's prophetic literature, a key source for any constructive theology of law. In the exilic and postexilic literature, when Israel's prophets sought to explain the nation's defeat by Assyria and Babylon, the central reasons for this disaster were idolatry and the failure to live by the law's requirements for justice, conditions that were closely linked. This is the cry of the prophet Micah:

Hear this, you leaders of Jacob,
    you rulers of Israel,
who despise justice
    and distort all that is right;
who build Zion with bloodshed,
    and Jerusalem with wickedness.
Her leaders judge for a bribe,
    her priests teach for a price,
    and her prophets tell fortunes for money.
Yet they look for the Lord's support and say,
    "Is not the Lord among us?
    No disaster will come upon us."
Therefore because of you,

---

55. Rolf Rendtorff, "Is It Possible to Read Leviticus as a Separate Book?" in *Reading Leviticus: Responses to Mary Douglas*, ed. John F. A. Sawyer and Mary Douglas (Sheffield: Sheffield Academic Press, 1996), 23. For some criticisms of Rendtorff's approach, see Davies, "Introduction to the Pentateuch," 48–49. My point here is not to enter into debates among biblical scholars about different types of critical methods or the details of dating, which I am not qualified to assess, but rather to note that the legal materials in the Old Testament can plausibly be read as part of a broader canonical narrative.

56. Davies, "Introduction to the Pentateuch," 52.

Zion will be plowed like a field,
Jerusalem will become a heap of rubble,
    the temple hill a mound overgrown with thickets.[57] (Mic 3:9–12 NIV)

In particular, the center of this collapse was the failure to take the law deeply to heart, as evidenced by mistreatment of the poor, the widow, and the stranger. The prophet Jeremiah offered this indictment: "Also on your skirts is found the lifeblood of the innocent poor" (Jer 2:34 NASB).[58] Not merely superficial acknowledgment of the law, but the internalization of its principles, was what God desired of the nation:

This is what the Lord Almighty, the God of Israel, says: Reform your ways and your actions, and I will let you live in this place. Do not trust in deceptive words and say, "This is the temple of the Lord, the temple of the Lord, the temple of the Lord!" If you really change your ways and your actions and deal with each other justly, if you do not oppress the foreigner, the fatherless or the widow and do not shed innocent blood in this place, and if you do not follow other gods to your own harm, then I will let you live in this place, in the land I gave your ancestors for ever and ever. But look, you are trusting in deceptive words that are worthless.

Will you steal and murder, commit adultery and perjury, burn incense to Baal and follow other gods you have not known, and then come and stand

57. The historical context of Micah's speeches is unclear. See David H. Master, "Micah," in *Zondervan Illustrated Bible Backgrounds Commentary*, vol. 5, ed. John H. Walton (Grand Rapids: Zondervan, 2009). Micah 1:1 states that Micah received his call "during the days of Jotham, Ahaz and Hezekiah, kings of Judah" (Mic 1:1 NASB). Some scholars suggest Micah may have lived during the last years of Jeroboam II in the north and the early years of Jotham in Judah (Master, "Micah," 122). Others relate Micah's oracles to the Syro-Ephraimite war of 735–734 BCE, the destruction of Samaria in 722/21 BCE, or events connected with King Hezekiah in 712 or 701 BC (Master, "Micah," 122–23). In any event, it is clear that Micah was written during a period of significant political and economic upheaval. Master suggests that "as the Phoenicians began their push westward across the Mediterranean, they created enormous trading networks enhanced by increasingly efficient transportation strategies. Throughout the eighth century, the Phoenician desire for agricultural produce for trade drove famers throughout the region to adopt 'more efficient' (and likely more ruthless) methods" (Master, "Micah," 123). Thus, for Master, Micah's oracles may represent a call for justice and mercy for those affected by these massive social and economic changes.

58. As Steven Voth has noted, "Jeremiah was born into a world of violent changes and intense power struggles." Steven Voth, "Jeremiah," in *Zondervan Illustrated Bible Backgrounds Commentary*, vol. 4, ed. John H. Walton (Grand Rapids: Zondervan, 2009). The context of Jeremiah is the fall of Jerusalem to the Babylonians in 586 BCE. This event produced "a profound and irreversible scar in the life and identity of ancient Israel" (Voth, "Jeremiah," 230). As Richard Hays suggests, the trauma of this event, along with the hope expressed by Jeremiah at the very end of his prophetic text (Jeremiah 31), echo through the texts of the Gospels: "The echo of Jeremiah 31 offers comfort, beckoning God's people to lean forward into the hope of the days that are surely coming when God—in the person of Jesus—will have *mercy*, bringing back the exiles, and write the Law on their hearts." Richard B. Hays, *Reading Backwards: Figural Christology and the Fourfold Gospel Witness* (Waco: Baylor University Press, 2014), 43.

before me in this house, which bears my Name, and say, "We are safe"—safe
to do all these detestable things? Has this house, which bears my Name,
become a den of robbers to you? But I have been watching! declares the
Lord. (Jer 7:3–11 NIV)

The consequence of this departure from God and his law was a
de-creation, a return to the primal chaos, an abolition of humanity:

I looked on the earth, and behold, it was formless and void;
And to the heavens, and they had no light.
I looked on the mountains, and behold, they were quaking,
And all the hills moved to and fro.
I looked, and behold, there was no man,
And all the birds of the heavens had fled.[59] (Jer 4:23–25 NASB)

The Bible's prophetic literature is filled with this sort of concern for justice and law, in particular on behalf of the poor and oppressed.[60] It is a
sad irony that the most vocal expositors of "Bible prophecy" today adopt
the chiliastic dispensationalist approach, which fuels the culture wars, as
discussed in the conclusion to this book. The Bible's "prophetic" literature, in fact, is more concerned with "forth-telling" than "foretelling."
It does contain hopes for the future—in the Old Testament, that Israel
would be revived by a messianic figure, and in the New Testament, that
history will be consummated at Jesus's future return. But it offers these
hopes through comparison to the current state of things. The rhetorical
purpose is to exhort hearers to change and to persevere.

Indeed, the Bible, and the Jewish tradition, often speak of "the law
and the prophets" in one breath. Jesus said he had not come to abolish
"the Law or the Prophets" but to fulfill them (Matt 5:17) and summarized
"the law and the prophets" with the love command (Matt 22:40). The
law, the Torah, described how God's people were supposed to live. The
"prophets" exposed the consequences of failure to keep the Torah and
called the people back to covenant faithfulness. In discussions of Jesus,
the law, and the gospel, we often miss that Jesus, like all Jews, held the
law and the prophets together.

Another good example of the prophetic attitude is found in Isaiah 1.
The writer laments over the condition of Israel:

59. The reference to the earth as "formless and void"—_tōhū wābōhū_—is a quotation from Gen
1:2. For a beautiful musical rendition of this passage, see the _accompagnato_ in Part One of Han-
del's _Messiah_.
60. For a classic study of this theme, see Walter Brueggemann, _The Prophetic Imagination_, 2nd
ed. (Minneapolis: Fortress, 2001).

Your country is desolate
    your cities burned with fire;
your fields are being stripped by foreigners
    right before you,
    laid waste as when overthrown by strangers. (Isa 1:7 NIV)

The prophet then speaks on behalf of Yahweh, comparing Israel to Sodom and Gomorrah, and explaining that external piety is inadequate—indeed is detestable—without justice:

Hear the word of the Lord
    you rulers of Sodom;
listen to the law of our God,
    you people of Gomorrah!
"The multitude of your sacrifices—
    what are they to me?" says the Lord.
"I have more than enough of burnt offerings,
    of rams and the fat of fattened animals;
I have no pleasure
    in the blood of bulls and lambs and goats." (Isa 1:10–11 NIV)

Yahweh is displeased with these offerings in part because they are mingled with idolatrous practices relating to other gods:

When you come to appear before me,
    who has asked this of you,
    this trampling of my courts?
Stop bringing meaningless offerings!
    Your incense is detestable to me.
New Moons, Sabbaths and convocations—
    I cannot bear your evil assemblies. (Isa 1:12–13 NIV)

Yahweh tells Israel he will not hear its prayers because of their guilt:

When you spread out your hands in prayer,
    I will hide my eyes from you;
even if you offer many prayers,
    I will not listen.
Your hands are full of blood;
    wash and make yourselves clean. (Isa 1:15–16 NIV)

Yahweh's speech here evokes the image of a priest at the altar, cutting the veins of a sacrificial animal and lifting his bloodied hands in prayer. The inherent violence of this sacrificial act, of course, cannot be the cause of offense, because the Torah requires such sacrifices and says God will delight in them. The reason for Yahweh's revulsion at the hands bloodied with sacrifices is that the religious syncretism connecting that worship with other gods is also related to social injustice. The blood of sacrifices at the altar is mixed and defiled with the blood of the oppressed population. The solution Yahweh provides is starkly simple:

> Take your evil deeds out of my sight!
> Stop doing wrong,
> learn to do right!
> Seek justice [מִשְׁפָּט mishpat], defend the oppressed.
> Take up the cause of the fatherless,
> plead the case of the widow. (Isa 1:16–17 NIV)

Yahweh concludes this address with a compelling appeal:

> "Come now, let us settle this matter,"
> says the Lord.
> "Though your sins are like scarlet,
> they shall be as white as snow;
> though they are red as crimson,
> they shall be like wool.
> If you are willing and obedient,
> you will eat the best from the land;
> but if you resist and rebel,
> you will be devoured by the sword."
> For the mouth of the Lord has spoken. (Isa 1:18–20 NIV)

This eschatological vision of this part of Isaiah includes the famous image of beating "swords into plowshares" (Isa 2:4). The full eschatological context of this image involves the judgment of disputes under the rule of God's law rather than through war:

> "In the last days
> the mountain of the Lord's temple will be established
> as the highest among the mountains;
> it will be exalted above the hills,
> and all nations will stream to it. . . .
> He will teach us his ways,
> so that we may walk in his paths.
> The law will go out from Zion,
> the word of the Lord from Jerusalem.
> He will judge between the nations
> and will settle disputes for many peoples.

They will beat their swords into plowshares
   and their spears into pruning hooks.
Nation will not take up sword against nation,
   nor will they train for war anymore.
Come, descendants,
   let us walk in the light of the Lord. (Isa 2:3–5 NIV)

This kind of image is the heart of the Bible's prophetic literature: a community of diverse nations living at peace together under God's law.

JESUS, PROPHECY, LAW, AND HISTORY

Covenant, law, and justice are closely linked from the Bible's proto-history, through the patriarchs, and into the eras of the judges and the kings. The prophetic mission is required because the nation failed to satisfy the law's requirement of justice. This failure produced the judgment of exile.

The hope of fulfilling the prophetic appeal, such as the one from Isaiah above, fueled the return from exile and threaded through the diverse streams of Judaism during the Second Temple period. The intertestamental literature, particularly the books of the Maccabees, apocalyptic texts such as 1 and 2 Enoch, and the Qumran documents, testify to the enduring sense that, even as the Second Temple is built in Jerusalem, the nation remains in exile because of its failure to keep Torah.[61] This is the background into which Jesus of Nazareth was born and began his ministry.

Jesus, like the prophets before him, defined the true observance of the law as an inward transformation that issues in worship of God and regard for others: "Hear, O Israel! The Lord our God is one Lord; and you shall love the Lord your God with all your heart, and with all your soul, and with all your mind, and with all your strength" and "You shall love your neighbor as yourself" (Mark 13:29–31 NASB). It is often suggested that Jesus upset the "legalism" of strictly observant Jews (including the Pharisees) by flaunting rules like the restriction on harvesting food or healing people on the Sabbath. But Jesus stood in the tradition of the Hebrew prophets and of other Second Temple Jewish reformers in emphasizing that the central focus of the Torah was the reformation of the heart reflected in the basis for the entire law, the *Shema*.

---

61. See Shaye D. Cohen, *From the Maccabees to the Mishnah*, 2nd ed. (Louisville: Westminster John Knox, 2006); George W. E. Nicklesburg, *Jewish Literature between the Bible and the Mishnah* (Minneapolis: Fortress, 2011).

This is evident most centrally in the Sermon on the Mount, in which Jesus, as the new Moses, interprets the Torah through the foundational law of love. The Sermon on the Mount represents a major fault line in political theology and, consequently, in our discussion of law. A "perfectionist" stream of interpretation running from some of the church fathers, notably Tertullian, through the radical Reformers and into today's Anabaptist-influenced movements, takes the Sermon as Jesus's restatement of the divine command, presently applicable to individuals, civic institutions, and governments alike.[62] Some elements of the Sermon are not inconsistent with the temporal positive law and in fact simply reflect sound advice in any age. When Jesus says, "Settle matters quickly with your adversary who is taking you to court" (Matt 5:25 NIV), any good lawyer should nod her head in agreement—better to settle if possible than to waste time and money on litigation. But Jesus's sharp rejection of the *lex talonis*, if taken literally, is another matter: "Do not resist an evil person. If anyone slaps you on the right cheek, turn to them the other cheek also. And if anyone wants to sue you and take your shirt, hand over your coat as well" (Matt 5:39–40 NIV).

If the perfectionist interpretation of these parts of the Sermon is correct, any participation by followers of Jesus in any elements of the temporal positive law must be radically called into question, if not quickly rejected. Jesus seems to say here that his followers should refuse to enforce their basic legal rights, including rights of personal integrity against assault and their property rights. Extended more broadly to the law of nations, this would suggest a nation should tolerate terrorism, invasion, and war by hostile persons or nations without any police or military defense. For followers of Jesus, then, the temporal positive law would represent a doomed relic of the present age, and the only hope of freedom or justice would lie in the (imminent) eschaton.

Because of these difficulties, a "realist" stream, influenced by Augustine, running through the magisterial Reformers and into modern political theology influenced by Reinhold Niebuhr, takes the Sermon as the statement of an eschatological ideal that is impossible to realize fully in this life. For some within the "realist" stream, the Sermon's commands

---

62. See, e.g., Glen A. Stassen, *Living the Sermon on the Mount: A Practical Hope for Grace and Deliverance* (New York: Josey-Bass, 2009). As Jennifer Herdt has noted, salvation in the Sermon "apparently comes not through faith or through grace of the cross, but through obedience to a higher standard of righteousness. It is thus not surprising that the Sermon on the Mount often lies at the heart of radical and restorationist movements within Christianity, movements that stand in judgment on the failure of the church to live up to gospel demands." Jennifer A. Herdt, "Rain on the Just and the Unjust: The Challenge of Indiscriminate Love," *Studies in Christian Ethics* 22, no. 1 (2009): 34–47; Richard A. Burridge, *Imitating Jesus: An Inclusive Approach to New Testament Ethics* (Grand Rapids: Eerdmans, 2007), 61.

are beyond the capacity of both individuals and societies, while others take the commands as requirements for life in the church but not for secular political institutions.[63] Under a realist interpretation, an individual Christian or a political state might properly assert some legal rights to personal integrity, property, or state security, even backed by force, if the individual's or state's internal motivations were based in love, particularly love for vulnerable people in the broader political community.

Some contemporary exegetes have tried to develop a perfectionist approach that takes the concerns of the realists seriously. Glen Stassen, for example, argues that the command not to resist an evil person entails resisting an evil person "by evil means,"[64] an argument further developed in Stassen and David Gushee's book *Kingdom Ethics*. Gushee and Stassen note that the Sermon's commands would not necessarily prohibit recourse to the temporal law, because they in fact require followers of Jesus to "resist evil by taking an action to oppose injustice, to stand up for human dignity, and to invite to reconciliation."[65]

Further, as Richard Burridge has emphasized in his recent work on New Testament ethics, Jesus's prophetic stance is also evidenced in the Gospel narratives of Jesus's words and deeds.[66] As Burridge argues, this does not reflect an indifference to the law. Faithful Jews who wished to follow the Torah, Burridge notes, "Believed that a teacher's example was as important as his words."[67] A rabbi's actions could provide a *ma'aseh*, a precedent, for the correct interpretation and application of the Torah.[68] Thus, we must consider not only Jesus's words in the Sermon on the Mount and in his other sayings but also Jesus's actions. Most notably, Burridge suggests, Jesus radicalized the command to love God and neighbor by requiring that his followers also love their enemies.[69] Burridge notes that "Jesus's ethical teaching is not a separate and discrete set of moral maxims, but part of his proclamation of the kingdom of God as God's reign and sovereignty are recognized in the here and now."[70] Jesus lived this ethical teaching in particular by welcoming in

---

63. See Hans Dieter Betz, *The Sermon on the Mount: A Commentary on the Sermon on the Mount, Including the Sermon on the Plain* (Minneapolis: Augsburg Fortress, 1995), 11–42 (providing an extensive history of exegesis of the Sermon since Augustine).

64. Stassen, *Living the Sermon on the Mount*; David P. Gushee and Glen H. Stassen, *Kingdom Ethics: Following Jesus in Contemporary Context*, 2nd ed. (Grand Rapids: Eerdmans, 2016), 98–102.

65. Gushee and Stassen, *Kingdom Ethics*, 99.

66. Burridge, *Imitating Jesus*.

67. Burridge, *Imitating Jesus*, 73.

68. Burridge, *Imitating Jesus*, 73.

69. Burridge, *Imitating Jesus*, 51.

70. Burridge, *Imitating Jesus*, 61.

the community of his followers those people who had been rejected by the broader society, both by the Roman empire and by the religious leaders. While Burrdige does not treat the Sermon in as much detail as Gushee and Stassen, this suggests that the Sermon is part of a pattern of welcome for the outcast.

These insights from Stassen, Gushee, and Burridge suggest fruitful ways to think about the Sermon in connection with a constructive theology of law, particularly in relation to our narratival perspective on Scripture. Jesus's commands in the Sermon *do* apply to how individual Christians and political communities should think about the positive law, but they are *not* impossible prescriptions that require individuals and states to accept violence and evil passively while waiting for the eschaton. Instead, the Sermon, and more broadly the life and teachings of Jesus, show that a new time has arrived, a time of renewal when the concerns of the prophets for the poor and oppressed are brought into the focus of God's action in history.

LAW FROM JESUS TO PAUL

As Christianity began to separate from Judaism in the first century, and particularly as more non-Jews became Christians, the early church confronted the problem of how to interpret and apply the Torah.[71] Factions developed concerning whether gentile Christians were required to observe the Torah's rules concerning circumcision and diet, as reflected in Acts 15. Jesus's saying in Matthew 5:17–19 seems to represent the sentiments of the pro-Torah faction:

> Do not think that I have come to abolish the Law or the Prophets; I have not come to abolish them but to fulfill them. For truly I tell you, until heaven and earth disappear, not the smallest letter, not the least stroke of a pen, will by any means disappear from the Law until everything is accomplished. Therefore anyone who sets aside one of the least of these commands and teaches others accordingly will be called least in the kingdom of heaven, but whoever practices and teaches these commands will be called great in the kingdom of heaven.[72]

However, as church historian John McGuckin notes, even Matthew's Gospel knocks against the legalism of the Pharisees in favor of "a new

---

71. See John A. McGuckin, *The Ascent of Christian Law: Patristic and Byzantine Formulations of a New Civilization* (Crestwood, NY: St. Vladimir's Seminary Press, 2012), 17–18.

72. Matthew 5:17–19 (NIV). See commentary on this text in *The Jewish Annotated New Testament* (Oxford: Oxford University Press, 2011).

philosophy of law."[73] In both Matthew and Mark's Gospels, McGuckin suggests, "the old law of external observances is . . . contrasted with a new spirit of seeking the inner intentionality of law: access to God's will and the implementation of behavior that is acceptable."[74] Thus, says McGuckin, "The Church of the first century became a strong movement to call for a radical reconstitution of the Torah, giving primacy to the *scholia* of Jesus himself as now collected in the Gospel texts, affording him a far higher status as Law-Giver than Moses."[75]

Still, McGuckin notes, the early church understood that the law is not abrogated in Jesus but rather is "radical[ly] renovated."[76] First-century Christians asserted "that Jesus was the heart and center of all law . . . the Church elevate[d] Jesus as its Lawgiver in preference to Moses."[77] This new philosophy of law, McGuckin believes, led to the church's separation of the "ceremonial" and "moral" law (reflected, for example, in Paul's letter to the Galatians) and its prioritization of the sayings of Jesus as the hermeneutical lens for reading Israel's Scriptures—a "new constitution" in Christ.[78] But this new constitution was of the *living* Christ, "a living and ongoing principle, not merely a dead reference to a body of literature."[79] McGuckin discerns here "a specifically Aristotelian principle in relation to the interpretation of law: that the 'mind of the Lawgiver'

---

73. McGuckin, *Ascent of Christian Law*, 18.

74. McGuckin, *Ascent of Christian Law*, 18–19.

75. McGuckin, *Ascent of Christian Law*, 19. See also Robert Louis Wilken, *The Spirit of Early Christian Thought* (New Haven: Yale University Press, 2003). As Wilken notes, "Early Christian thought . . . was as much an attempt to penetrate more deeply into the mystery of Christ, to know and understand what was believed and handed on in the churches, as it was to answer the charges of critics or explain the faith to outsiders" (Wilken, *Spirit of Early Christian Thought*, 3).

76. McGuckin, *Ascent of Christian Law*, 19. One way in which this occurred, which is not emphasized by McGuckin, was in Justin's supposed separation of the ceremonial and moral law, and in the allegorizing of the Old Testament law in relation to the witness of the Old Testament prophets. See Jaroslav Pelikan, *The Christian Tradition: A History of the Development of Doctrine*, vol. 1, *The Emergence of the Catholic Tradition (100–600)* (Chicago: University of Chicago Press, 1971), 15–21. Pelikan suggests that "although the law and the prophets belonged together in the language of Jewish theology, Christian theology identified its cause with that of the prophets against the law" (18). Nevertheless, Pelikan observes, "the most important early heresies were not Jewish, but anti-Jewish in their inspiration" (71). The early church therefore rejected Marcion's efforts to deny that the Old Testament law was part of Scripture (71–81). Marcion's followers had even attempted to amend Matt 5:17 to read, "I have not come to fulfill the law but to abolish it" (76).

77. McGuckin, *Ascent of Christian Law*, 19.

78. McGuckin, *Ascent of Christian Law*, 19–20. See also Pelikan, *Emergence of the Catholic Tradition*, 71–81.

79. McGuckin, *Ascent of Christian Law*, 20. As Wilken notes, for the early church, "the Christian gospel was not an idea but a certain kind of story, a narrative about a person and things that had actually happened in space and time" (Wilken, *Spirit of Early Christian Thought*, 15).

must be consulted in all matters of legal interpretation and development of first principles."[80]

Indeed, the New Testament literature outside the Gospels illustrates the ongoing application of this narrative in the life of the developing Christian church and provides further gloss on Jesus's life and teachings. In its first centuries the church did not produce any extensive written law codes. This is not surprising, given the church's initial position as an apocalyptic movement often subject to persecution by the Roman authorities.[81] As McGuckin notes, "To have told any writer of the New Testament that the icon of the Lord would be set up in the imperial palace would have drawn out merely disbelieving laughter."[82] Nevertheless, some of the early epistolary literature in the New Testament, particularly the deutero-Pauline epistles, as well as some of the very early patristic literature, begin to establish rules for conduct in the church that represent a sort of internal law.[83]

An interesting example of this process is 1 Timothy, probably composed in Paul's name within a Pauline Christian community sometime after Paul's death.[84] The introduction to 1 Timothy criticizes a group of troublemakers who have deviated from instruction based in "love that comes from a pure heart, a good conscience, and sincere faith" (1 Tim 1:5 NRSV).[85] The false teachers have "turned to meaningless talk, desiring to be teachers of the law, without understanding what they are saying or the things about which they make assertions" (1 Tim 1:6–7 NRSV). They "occupy themselves with myths and endless genealogies that promote speculations" instead of offering "the divine training that is known by faith" (1 Tim 1:4 NRSV).[86]

80. Wilken, *Spirit of Early Christian Thought*, 15.
81. McGuckin, *Ascent of Christian Law*, 21.
82. McGuckin, *Ascent of Christian Law*, 21.
83. McGuckin, *Ascent of Christian Law*, 21–25.
84. See, e.g., Richard Hays, *The Moral Vision of the New Testament: A Contemporary Introduction to New Testament Ethics* (New York: HarperCollins, 1996); Introduction to 1 Timothy, *The Jewish Annotated New Testament* (Oxford: Oxford University Press, 2011); Luke Timothy Johnson, *The Writings of the New Testament*, 3rd ed. (Minneapolis: Fortress, 2010), 375–83, 389–95; Douglas A. Campbell, *Reframing Paul: An Epistolary Biography* (Grand Rapids: Eerdmans, 2014), 367–68.
85. Luke Timothy Johnson suggests that the opponents of Pauline teaching addressed in 1 Timothy likely probably represent "the sort of elitist esoteric groups we so often encounter in the religiosity of the Hellenistic world," for example, Gnostics. Johnson, *Writings of the New Testament*, 390. Risto Saarinen similarly notes that the "myths" of the false teachers "may refer to many kinds of Hellensistic myths, for instance, pagan gods, stories of the origin of the world, esoteric and gnostic teachings in both Judaism (Titus 1:14) and other circles." Risto Saarinen, *The Pastoral Epistles with Philemon and Jude* (Grand Rapids: Brazos, 2008), 33.
86. Saarinen suggests that "the apostle's warning against myths and genealogies is directed against the intellectual and imaginative stimulation they provide: one should not believe in

The problem, the author says, is not the law, but manner in which the false teachers use the law:

> Now we know that the Law is good, if one use it lawfully, And we know this: that Law is laid down not for an upright person, but for the lawless and disorderly, for the impious and sinful, for the unholy and profane, for parricides and matricides, for killers of men, For the whorish, for men who couple with catamites, slave-dealers, liars, perjurers, and for whatever else opposes sound teaching, In keeping with the good tidings of the glory of the blissful God with which I was entrusted.[87] (1 Tim 1:8–11)

Here it sounds like the "law" has nothing but a negative role, although the reference here seems to be to the Torah and not to the Roman civil law in general.[88] But the author then recites principles of right order that mirror Roman household codes, including prayer for the civil authorities: "First of all, then, I urge that supplications, prayers, intercessions and thanksgivings be made for everyone, for kings and all who are in high positions, so that we may lead a quiet and peaceable life in all godliness and dignity. This is right and is acceptable in the sight of God our Savior, who desires everyone to be saved and to come to the knowledge of the truth" (1 Tim 2:1–4).

The civil authorities, it seems, are thought to have some positive role in facilitating good order, although this also might consist primarily in restraining evil people. Civil order will facilitate churchly order, includ-

imagined stories, but had better trust the sound doctrine handed over by reliable witnesses" (Saarinen, *Pastoral Epistles*), 33.

87. As translated by David Bentley Hart in *The New Testament: A Translation* (New Haven: Yale University Press, 2017). I am employing Hart's fascinating and occasionally controversial translation for this passage because it is the only modern English translation I am aware of that attempts to specify the word *arsenokoitais* beyond the generic "practicing homosexuality" (NIV), "homosexuals" (NASB), or "sodomites" (NRSV). Hart suggests that this term "would not mean 'homosexual' in the modern sense, for the simple reason that the ancient world possessed no comparable concept of a specifically homoerotic sexual identity; it would refer to a particular sexual behavior, but we cannot say exactly which one" (416nb). Hart offers a "guess" that the term "is based simply upon the reality that it the first century the most common and readily available form of male homoerotic sexual activity was a master's or a patron's abuse of young male slaves." Richard Hays (*Moral Vision*, 379–89), in contrast, argues somewhat convincingly that the term derives from the Septuagint's translation of Leviticus 18:22. I highlight this not to take a position here about the broader debate about homosexuality and Christian ethics but simply to acknowledge the debate and the translation issue.

88. See *The Jewish Annotated New Testament*, text note to 1 Tim 1:7–8. Richard Hays sounds a similar note about the author of this text: "It is hard to avoid the impression that the vision of the Christian life in 1 Timothy is characterized by conformity to fixed convention of respectable, law-abiding behavior. The characteristic Pauline themes of freedom, suffering with Christ, costly love for the sake of the community, and living in the creative tension between the ages have been drastically deemphasized, if not entirely abandoned. In their place we find the modest, mundane virtues of the orderly household" (Hays, *Moral Vision of the New Testament*, 70).

LAW AND THEOLOGY 57

ing modesty in dress, the subordination of women to male authority, the roles of bishops and deacons, respect for elders, the maintenance of a widow's list (under very specific conditions), and slaves' respect for their masters.[89]

New Testament scholars note that the deutero-Pauline 1 Timothy contrasts in some ways with the theology of law in the clearly authentic Pauline letters of Romans and Galatians. Both in Romans and Galatians, Paul pictures the Torah as a negative propaedeutic that leads to a new kind of freedom.[90]

For example, in Romans 3:19, Paul says, "Now we know that whatever the law says, it speaks to those who are under the law, so that every mouth may be silenced, and the whole world may be held accountable to God" (Rom 3:19 NRSV).[91] Similarly, in Galatians 3:2–3, Paul poses an exasperated question to the Galatian Christians: "The only thing I want to learn from you is this: did you receive the Spirit by doing the works of the law or by believing what you heard? Are you so foolish? Having started with the Spirit, are you now ending with the flesh?" (Gal 3:2–3 NRSV). In fact, Paul tells the Galatians, "all who rely on the works of the law are under a curse" (Gal 3:10).[92] The law "was added because of

---

89. See 1 Tim 2–6. Hays suggests that "perhaps the moral vision of the pastorals was inevitable (and even necessary) for the church at the end of the first century to achieve social cohesion and to survive external pressures" (Hays, *Moral Vision of the New Testament*, 71). Douglas Campbell argues that 1 Timothy's emphasis on law and household order represents a response, in part, to Marcionism (Campbell, *Reframing Paul*, 368).

90. See Hays, *Moral Vision of the New Testament*, 70.

91. Frank Thielman notes that "Paul's use of the term *law* in the argument in Romans is perhaps the most perplexing element in a notoriously complex letter." Frank Thielman, *Paul and the Law: A Contextual Approach* (Downers Grove, IL: InterVarsity, 1994), 165.

92. Thielman states that "when Paul says that those who rely on works of the law are under a curse, he is not saying anything particularly controversial to a Jew" (Thielman, *Paul and the Law*, 127). At least some contemporary Jewish interpreters disagree. The *Jewish Annotated New Testament*, for example, states that "Paul's negative assessment of the Torah and those who follow it is striking: he insists that the Torah does not come from God (3:19–20); no longer has a salvific role, and perhaps never did (3:21–22); and its observance is akin to the worship of the Greek gods (4:9–10)" (332). Johnson, however, consistent with many contemporary interpreters of Paul, notes that Paul's focus is not on faith in Christ in contrast to observance of Torah but on the adequacy of Christ as the faithful one who fulfilled Torah (Johnson, *Writings of the New Testament*, 296). Johnson says that, for Paul in Galatians, Torah "is both *annulled* and *fulfilled* by the Messiah. It is annulled as an absolute norm for God's activity and human righteousness. If the only measure of righteousness is Torah, then Jesus cannot be the source of God's life. This is because Jesus is unrighteous according to that norm: He is a 'sinner,' one who is 'cursed by God' because he 'hangs on a tree' (Deut. 21:23)" (296). But, Johnson continues, "because it was always more than law—being God's revelation and wisdom—Torah is also fulfilled in the Messiah. Paul cannot even speak of righteousness without using Torah's narratives and prophecies. . . . God did something new in Jesus's death: he revealed righteousness outside the norm of Torah. This calls for a new response of faith, which shows that Torah as the bearer of promise is also fulfilled."

transgressions, until the offspring would come to whom the promise had been made" (Gal 3:19).

But, Paul continues in Romans, the law is not abolished, but is fulfilled by the "law of faith" (Rom 3:27).[93] "Do we then overthrow the law by this faith?" Paul asks, to which he responds, "By no means [μὴ γένοιτο]! On the contrary, we uphold the law" (Rom 3:31).[94] Likewise, in Galatians, Paul says, "Is the law then opposed to the promises of God? Certainly not [μὴ γένοιτο]!" The law was a "disciplinarian [παιδαγωγὸς] until Christ came, so that we may be justified by faith" (Gal 3:24). The Greek term παιδαγωγὸς, *paidagōgos*, refers to a pedagogue, a tutor hired by the head of a household to instruct young boys in life and morals.[95] But now, Paul tells the Galatians, we are no longer young boys in the household, who are "no better than slaves" (Gal 4:1). "As many of you as were baptized into Christ," he says, "have clothed yourselves with Christ," and thus "there is no longer Jew or Greek, there is no longer slave or free, there is no longer male or female; for you are all one in Christ Jesus" (Gal 4:28).[96]

Yet Paul does not advocate antinomian freedom. "What should we say? That the law is sin?" he asks rhetorically, to which he offers his familiar refrain: "By no means [μὴ γένοιτο]!" The law demonstrated to Paul the depth of his sin, but his sin was his own, within himself, and not inherent in the law (Rom 7:13–25). In response to this dilemma, Paul offers his great *cri de coeur*:

93. In his commentary on Romans, Karl Barth characterized Paul's teaching in this chapter as a dialectic that drives us away from any sort of self-reliance. Karl Barth, *The Epistle to the Romans*, 6th ed. (London: Oxford University Press, 1968), 110. As Barth notes, "The man who boasts that he possesses something which justifies him before God and man, even if that something be his own insecurity and brokenness, still retains confidence in human self-justification." N. T. Wright, perhaps influenced by Barth's later work on the doctrine of election, suggests that Paul's theology, particularly as expressed in Romans 3:27–4:25, centers on "the redefinition, in and around Jesus the Messiah, of the Jewish doctrine of election, rooted in the covenant theology of Genesis and Deuteronomy and worked out through Jesus's saving death and resurrection." N. T. Wright, *Paul and the Faithfulness of God*, 2 vols. (Minneapolis: Fortress, 2013), 2:846.

94. N. T. Wright suggests that Paul's "covenantal perspective on election, and its redefinition through Jesus the Messiah, provides the larger category within which 'juridicial' and 'participationist' categories can be held together in proper Pauline relation" (Wright, *Paul and the Faithfulness of God*, 2:846).

95. See *Strong's Concordance*, 3807.

96. N. T. Wright notes that Paul's theology concerning the relation of Jews and gentiles and the role of Torah is rooted in monotheism. "Paul returns," Wright says, "to the most foundational confession of the Jewish faith, the *Shema*: since God is one, he is God of Gentiles as well as Jews. Monotheism undergirds not only election, but also the christologically redefined election: this God will justify circumcision on the basis of *pistis* [faith], and uncircumcision through *pistis*" (Wright, *Paul and the Faithfulness of God*, 2:848).

So I find it to be a law that when I want to do what is good, evil lies close at hand. For I delight in the law of God in my inmost self, but I see in my members another law at war with the law of my mind, making me captive to the law of sin that dwells in my members. Wretched man that I am! Who will rescue me from this body of death? Thanks be to God through Jesus Christ our Lord! So then, with my mind I am a slave to the law of God, but with my flesh I am a slave to the law of sin. (Rom 7:21–25)

In fact, then, there is no conflict in Paul's theology of law between "law" and "freedom."[97] The pedagogue of the law moves him to understand his own sin, his own inner rejection of the fundamental law of love, which paradoxically frees him to take on the nature of the only one who was able to fulfill the law: Christ.

This is why Paul says to the Galatians, "Do not use your freedom as an opportunity for self-indulgence, but through love become slaves to one another. For the whole law is summed up in a single commandment: 'You shall love your neighbor as yourself'" (Gal 5:13–14). A person who is "led by the Spirit" is "not subject to the law" but displays the "fruit of the Spirit": "love, joy, peace, patience, kindness, generosity, faithfulness, gentleness, and self-control" (Gal 5:22–23). "There is no law against such things," Paul says (Gal 5:23). Yet, a person who does the "works of the flesh," which Paul says are "obvious"—"fornication, impurity, licentiousness, idolatry, sorcery, enmities, strife, jealousy, anger, quarrels, dissensions, factions, envy, drunkenness, carousing and things like these"—"will not inherit the kingdom of God" (Gal 5:19–21).[98]

97. As the notes above on Paul's discussion of Torah suggest, I am broadly sympathetic to the "New Perspective" reading of Paul that centers on God's election of a people for participation in his mission of redemption—the Jews, first, through Torah, and the gentiles as well, through Christ's faithful fulfillment of Torah. See generally N. T. Wright, *Paul and the Faithfulness of God*, 2:846–48. My appreciation for the "New Perspective," however, supplements, rather than supplants, more "existential" readings of Paul, in particular by Barth but also by Augustine and, to a degree, Calvin and Luther.

98. Augustine noted the tension in this section of Galatians between law and human freedom. "People think that the apostle here denies that we possess free will. They do not perceive what he is saying to them: If they refuse to hold fast to the grace they have received, through which alone they are able to walk in the Spirit and avoid fulfilling the desires of the flesh, they will not be able to do as they wish. . . . It is love that 'fulfills the law.' But 'the wisdom of the flesh' by following temporal goods opposes spiritual love. How can it be made subject to the law of God (that is, freely and obediently fulfill righteousness and not be opposed to it) when even as it tries it must be vanquished?" Augustine, *Commentary on the Epistle to the Galatians*, in *Ancient Christian Commentary on Scripture VIII*, ed. Mark J. Edwards (Downers Grove, IL: InterVarsity, 2014), 81.

THE GOSPELS, PAUL, LAW, AND NARRATIVE

As this survey suggests, the notion of "law" in the Gospels and in Paul is complex and has engendered much debate throughout history, particularly since the Reformation. Martin Luther commented on this in Galatians 2:2–3 with characteristic starkness:

> Right here we have one more difference between the Law and the Gospel. The Law does not bring on the Holy Ghost. . . . The Law and the Gospel are contrary ideas. They have contrary functions and purposes. To endow the Law with any capacity to produce righteousness is to plagiarize the Gospel. The Gospel brings donations. It pleads for open hands to take what is being offered. The Law has nothing to give. It demands, and its demands are impossible.[99]

Augustine, in contrast, commenting on this passage, distinguished the "moral" and "ceremonial" law: "so that this question may be carefully treated and no one may be deceived by ambiguities, we must first understand that the works of the law are twofold: for they reside partly in ceremonial ordinances and partly in morals."[100] Augustine argued that the Jewish ceremonial law had become incomprehensible and therefore brought confusion. But the Christian sacrament, Augustine claimed, "when it is understood . . . produces spiritual joy and is celebrated gladly and in due season [and] is applied either to the contemplation of truth or to good morals."[101] For Augustine, "The contemplation of truth is founded in the love of God alone, good morals in the love of God and the neighbor, and on these two precepts depend the whole Law and the Prophets."[102]

Luther was certainly correct over Augustine in recognizing that Torah cannot arbitrarily be divided into "ceremonial" and "moral" components, and Augustine's claim that the Christian sacraments are somehow more accessible than the Jewish "ceremonial" law is an obvious case of special pleading. Nevertheless, Augustine's focus on the *internal* in contrast to the *external* role of Torah and sacrament is on point, and permits also a more favorable reading of Luther: no one is justified by external adherence to the law, but rather, as a person by faith is drawn into right worship of God, he or she experiences transformative grace

---

99. Martin Luther, *Commentary on Galatians*, trans. Theodore Graebner, Christian Classics Ethereal Library, https://tinyurl.com/yxrptq7v.

100. Augustine, *Galatians*, 35.

101. Augustine, *Galatians*, 35.

102. Augustine, *Galatians*, 35.

that provides the freedom to live an authentically human life. Consistent with this theme, N. T. Wright aptly hears this in a narrative key:

> Paul's overall point, throughout Galatians 3 and 4, is *narratival*. . . . Once you understand how the story works, the great covenant story from Abraham to the messiah, you can see (a) that the Torah was a necessary, God-given thing, with its own proper role within that story, and (b) that the God-given role of Torah has now come to a proper and honourable end—not that there was anything "wrong" with it, but that it was never designed to be permanent. The latter is what Paul specially needs to stress, but the former point is vital (despite the long and loud chorus of dualistic readers) to avoid any slide towards Marcionism. . . . Galatians 3 is not, then, an argument hinging on the theological contrast between "grace" and "law," or even the psychological contrast between the struggle to please a legalistic God and the delight of basking in the undeserved pleasure of a gracious one. Those contrasts are indeed present as resonances, and later theologians were not wrong to draw out such implications. But the point at which those extra meanings took over and became central, displacing the actual argument Paul was mounting, was the point at which the exegetes ceased to listen to him and began to listen instead to the echo of their own voices bouncing off the text.[103]

In contrast to the hard distinctions found in some later Christian theologies, particularly in the Lutheran strand of the Reformation, then, contemporary biblical scholarship generally recognizes that both Jesus and Paul were thoroughly Jewish and that neither of them rejected Torah.[104] Jesus's "fulfillment" of Torah in the Sermon on the Mount, says Jonathan Klawans, represents rabbinic tradition that sought the meaning of Torah beyond its plain literal sense.[105] And Paul, Mark Nanos tells us, "saw himself wholly within Judaism, as one who was assigned a special role in the restoration of Israel and the nations."[106] Paul "was a reformer," Nanos says, "one who sought to redress what he believed to be an oversight . . . he was not the founder of a new religion, even if things turned out otherwise."[107] Early Christianity and rabbinic Judaism after the destruction of Herod's temple began to part ways over the universality of this claim for gentiles who did not observe all the requirements of Torah, and this is evident in the Acts and the Pauline and Petrine epistles as they wrestle with the problem of table fellowship.[108]

103. Wright, *Paul and the Faithfulness of God, Book II,* 2:863.

104. See, e.g., "The Law" and "Paul and Judaism," in *The Jewish Annotated New Testament.*

105. *Jewish Annotated New* Testament, 516.

106. *Jewish Annotated New* Testament, 552.

107. *Jewish Annotated New* Testament, 552.

108. See "Food and Table Fellowship," in *The Jewish Annotated New Testament;* McGuckin, *Ascent of Christian Law,* 17–18.

Nevertheless, both Jesus and Paul advocated a theology of Torah that was shared by other pious Jews: the Torah should not be understood as a set of arbitrary rules but rather as a teacher, a pedagogue, that facilitates inner transformation and a culture of *shalom*.[109] N. T. Wright suggests that Paul's "covenantal perspective on election, and its redefinition through Jesus the Messiah, provides the larger category within which 'juridicial' and 'participationist' categories can be held together in proper Pauline relation."[110] Law as a means of "participation" in God's life —in God's mission—in fact was central to subsequent Christian theologies of law.

CIVIL RESPECT OR CIVIL DISOBEDIENCE?

Paul's difficult discussion of the Torah relates primarily to how followers of Jesus should live within the community of the church. Paul also addressed how the church should live in relation to the broader society. One of these texts, Romans 13:1–7, is a *locus classicus* for political theology:

> Every person is to be in subjection to the governing authorities. For there is no authority except from God, and those which exist are established by God. Therefore whoever resists authority has opposed the ordinance of God; and they who have opposed will receive condemnation upon themselves. For rulers are not a cause of fear for good behavior, but for evil. Do you want to have no fear of authority? Do what is good and you will have praise from the same; for it is a minister of God to you for good. But if you do what

109. In light of current scholarship about Jesus, Paul, and Judaism, I would not draw such sharp distinctions as McGuckin regarding first-century Christian understandings of Torah. McGuckin agrees that "it is not an abrogation of the law that is actually taking place here," but he thinks the early Christians undertook "a radical renovation of the Law by those who felt empowered to compose a new constitutional arrangement of it" (McGuckin, *Ascent of Christian Law*, 19). Although McGuckin is correct to note that Christians were unique in placing Jesus at the center of the Torah's fulfillment, the notion that Torah was not about the code itself so much as the inner transformation wrought by the code was a thoroughly rabbinic one. McGuckin suggests that part of the subtle shift concerning law and order between the authentic Pauline epistles of Romans and Galatians and the deutero-Pauline epistle of 1 Timothy reflects the growing influence of Roman ideals on the late first and early second century church as it became further distinguished from rabbinic Judaism (65). The household codes so emphasized in 1 Timothy and other deutero-Pauline epistles reflect the Roman jurisprudential idea of *auctoritas*: a legal principle bears moral authority "by virtue of its own logic, by virtue of its inherent rightness, and by virtue of the high standing of the person who voiced the argument" (66). *Auctoritas*, McGuckin notes, was distinct in Roman legal theory from *potestas*, the "power to be able compel others to one's will." True law is grounded in *auctoritas* and not merely in *potestas*. The same broadly held true, McGuckin shows, in the development of Christian synodical and conciliar practices through the fourth century (62–94).

110. Wright, *Paul and the Faithfulness of God*, 2:846.

is evil, be afraid; for it does not bear the sword for nothing; for it is a minister of God, an avenger who brings wrath on the one who practices evil. Therefore it is necessary to be in subjection, not only because of wrath, but also for conscience' sake. For because of this you also pay taxes, for rulers are servants of God, devoting themselves to this very thing. Render to all what is due them: tax to whom tax is due; custom to whom custom; fear to whom fear; honor to whom honor. (Rom 13:1–7 NASB)

This text seems to contradict other places in which the New Testament calls the temporal governing authorities into question. Another *locus classicus* of political theology, Acts 5:12–27, shows the response of Peter and the other apostles, who have been arrested because the "signs and wonders" they were performing were attracting many followers. An angel freed them from prison and commanded them to continue preaching the gospel. The religious authorities confronted them, stating that "we gave you strict orders not to continue teaching in this name," to which the apostles responded, "we must obey God rather than man" (Acts 5:28 NASB). And the entire text of Revelation is a call to stand firm and resist the totalitarian power of Rome, referred to in vivid apocalyptic symbols as a dragon, a demonic beast, a ravenous whore, and the like.[111]

This tension has not been lost on interpreters through the ages. In his commentary on Romans, written in an age when the church was still sometimes persecuted by Roman authorities, Origen of Alexandria asked, "Is even that authority that persecutes God's servants, attacks the faith, and subverts religion, from God?"[112] Origen responded that political authority is given by God to punish evil and praise good, but that if political leaders misuse their power, they are no longer acting on God's behalf.[113] Therefore, Origen concluded, Paul "is not speaking about those authorities that instigate persecutions against the faith; for in such cases one must say, 'It is necessary to obey God rather than men.'"[114]

As a modern example, in his *Römerbrief*, Karl Barth suggested that Romans 13 was in fact *subversive* of human political authority by placing all such authority under God.[115] For Barth, God's authority over political rule "means that all human consciousness, all human principles and

111. For a discussion of the political imagery in Revelation, *see*, e.g., Michael J. Gorman, *Reading Revelation Responsibly: Uncivil Worship and Witness: Following the Lamb into the New Creation* (Eugene, OR: Wipf & Stock, 2010); Richard Bauckham, *The Theology of the Book of Revelation* (Cambridge: Cambridge University Press, 1993).

112. Origen, *Commentary on the Epistle to the Romans, Books 6–10*, ed. Thomas P. Scheck, Fathers of the Church (Washington, DC: Catholic University of America Press, 2002), 7.26.

113. Origen, *Romans* 7.26.

114. Origen, *Romans* 9.27.

115. Barth, *Romans*, 481–85 (emphasis in original).

axioms and orthodoxies and –isms, all *principality and power and dominion*, are AS SUCH subjected to the destructive judgment of God. *Let every man be in subjection* means, therefore, that every man should consider the falsity of all human reckoning as such."[116] A person who instigates a political rebellion, Barth said, "may be justified at the bar of history; but he is not justified before the judgment-seat of God."[117]

We will come back to Origen, who personally suffered severe persecution under Roman rule, and to other Christian theologians who thought about law and politics, in chapters 2 and 3 and in part 2 of this book, "Praxis." For now, we note that both civil disobedience and civic compliance are part of the New Testament narrative concerning the church's life in the world.

We should not examine that contrast in a vacuum, however, because Paul also gave practical advice for how the church should live in this world. In Romans 12, for example—preceding the exhortation to be subject to the ruling authorities—Paul instructs the Roman Christians as follows:

> Bless those who persecute you; bless and do not curse. Rejoice with those who rejoice, and weep with those who weep. Be of the same mind toward one another; do not be haughty in mind, but associate with the lowly. Do not be wise in your own estimation. Never pay back evil for evil to anyone. Respect what is right in the sight of all men. If possible, so far as it depends on you, be at peace with all men. Never take your own revenge, beloved, but leave room for the wrath of God, for it is written, "Vengeance is Mine, I will repay," says the Lord. "But if your enemy is hungry, feed him, and if he is thirsty, give him a drink; for in so doing you will heap burning coals on his head." Do not be overcome by evil, but overcome evil with good. (Rom 12:14–21)

We can see in these practical instructions, including the instruction to respect lawful temporal authorities, an echo of Jesus's practical instructions in the Sermon on the Mount.

APOCALYPTIC CONSUMMATION

In Acts and in the Pauline and pseudo-Pauline epistles, we can discern an emphasis on living within the bounds of the law established by temporal rulers, but with a subversive twist that radically relativizes temporal rule under the reign of God. The most subversive part of this social

116. Barth, *Romans*, 485–86, emphasis original.
117. Barth, *Romans*, 482.

ethic, perhaps, is hope in Christ's final victory over sin and death, which empowers the church to endure hardship with humility, kindness, and patience as a form of quiet civil disobedience. This ethic also maintains the possibility of overt civil disobedience, particularly if the temporal authorities demand that the church stop ministering the gospel, including both the proclamation of Christ and the enactment of "signs and wonders" of God's reign—the healing and wholeness that flow from the life of the community of Jesus's followers. The New Testament's apocalyptic literature, particularly the book of Revelation, continues this theme in a more strident key and further points toward the final act of the drama of history—the consummation of an ideal political community in the heavenly city embodying the law of love under the reign of the risen Lamb.

The text of Revelation's judgment on Roman rule is complete and unyielding. When God unleashes his judgment, "the kings of the earth, the princes, the generals, the rich, the mighty, and everyone else, both slave and free" hide in terror (Rev 6:15 NIV). Revelation 13 depicts the power of Rome as a demonic beast that fights against God's people. As Richard Bauckham notes, "Revelation itself allows no neutral perception: either one shares Rome's own ideology, the view of the Empire promoted by Roman propaganda, or one sees it from the perspective of heaven, which unmasks the pretensions of Rome."[118] Roman power, however, is overcome by the "Lamb," the crucified Christ, who restores the true law and draws all the nations to himself.

The picture of the Lamb's victory involves legal judgment by rightful powers who are able to recognize that the suffering, oppressed followers of the Lamb are truly righteous, in contrast to the oppressive political powers of Rome (e.g., Rev 20:4). It culminates in the establishment of a glorious city, a New Jerusalem, illumined by the glory of God. The "nations" walk by the city's light, "the kings of the earth will bring their glory into it," "its gates will never be closed," and "the glory and the honor of the nations" will be brought into the city (Rev 21:22–27).

This final picture of restorative judgment by higher powers, and of the "kings" and "nations" entering the city and bringing "glory" and "honor" into it, seems to contrast starkly with the texts' previously unflinching hostility toward Rome. It reflects, however, the eschatological vision of the Old Testament prophets, and thereby connects the New Testament narrative with that of the Old Testament. The divine judgment is not against human society as such, or human law as such, or human history as such. Rather, the divine judgment restores the oppressed through the

118. Bauckham, *Theology of the Book of Revelation*, 35.

suffering of the Lamb and the perseverance of the church, unmasking the evil of oppression personified by Rome, and establishing a new community flourishing under the law of love.

2.

Law and History

INTRODUCTION

As chapter 1 shows, "law" is central to the biblical narrative, both in the Old and New Testaments. The "natural law" is built into creation; legal relationships between people, tribes, and nations help secure peace; and God establishes his people through a legal code after they have been freed from the injustice of Egyptian slavery. God judges his people when they ignore the law, particularly the law's requirement of justice for the poor and oppressed. Jesus fulfills the law and restores justice for the community of Israel, and Paul explains how that justice extends not only to Israel but the gentiles and the whole cosmos.

This does not mean the Bible's treatment of "law" is always consistent or unproblematic. Some of the specific laws in Leviticus and Deuteronomy, read naively at face value, seem strange and harsh to modern ears. The narratives of the conquest of Canaan in the Old Testament are difficult to understand in light of what we might think about natural law, justice, and international law today. The New Testament's critique of the Roman Empire seems to counsel withdrawal from the world, including from any sanguine assessment of the positive law, except for Paul's otherwise strange and perhaps subtly subversive admonition to respect the ruling authorities in Romans 13. These complications counsel us to exercise caution about using any specific biblical text as a proof text for positive law today. Nevertheless, the broad narrative arc of the canon of Scripture suggests that "law" is central to the *missio Dei*.

Given this scriptural theme, it is not surprising that law also matters to the story of the church. The story of the church matters to a constructive theology and praxis of law because the biblical narrative does not exist in a vacuum. Scripture is a set of living texts through which the Holy Spirit speaks to and through the church in the changing circumstances of history. Theologians usually speak of Scripture, tradition, reason, and experience as sources of authority. We might debate the relationship of these different sources of authority to each other, but at the very least, the way in which the church historically has heard Scripture is an important part of our process for discerning what the Spirit says to the church through Scripture today.[1]

The sketch of the biblical narrative concerning law offered in chapter 1 suggests significant continuity between the Old and New Testaments. At the same time, we noted at least one important place of apparent discontinuity: the Old Testament's endorsement of holy war compared to Jesus's ethic in the Sermon on the Mount and Paul's practical instructions about patience and humility.

HISTORY AND CONTINUITY

The first-century church faced other questions about the continuity of the Torah, which bitterly divided the church and occupy a central place in the New Testament canonical literature following the Gospels. The dispute is discussed in Acts 15: "Certain people came down from Judea to Antioch and were teaching the believers: 'Unless you are circumcised, according to the custom taught by Moses, you cannot be saved.' This brought Paul and Barnabas into sharp dispute and debate with them" (Acts 15:1–2 NIV). Paul and Barnabus traveled to Jerusalem to discuss the question with other church leaders, in particular Peter. At Jerusalem, "some of the believers who belonged to the party of the Pharisees stood up and said, 'The Gentiles must be circumcised and required to keep the law of Moses'" (Acts 15:3–5). The apostles and elders met and reached a compromise in a meeting that later came to be called the "Jerusalem Council," resulting in a kind of legal judgment in the form of a brief circular letter limiting the gentile believers only as follows: "It seemed good to the Holy Spirit and to us not to burden you with anything beyond the following requirements: You are to abstain from food sacrificed to

---

1. For some good discussions of these principles, see, e.g., John R. Franke, *The Character of Theology: A Postconservative Evangelical Approach* (Grand Rapids: Baker Academic, 2005); Trevor A. Hart, *Faith Thinking: The Dynamics of Christian Theology* (Eugene, OR: Wipf and Stock, 2005); Joel B. Green, *Seized by Truth: Reading the Bible as Scripture* (Nashville: Abingdon, 2010); John Webster, *Holy Scripture: A Dogmatic Sketch* (Cambridge: Cambridge University Press, 2003).

idols, from blood, from the meat of strangled animals and from sexual immorality. You will do well to avoid these things" (Acts 15:28–29).

Peter's openness to this compromise seems to have been rooted in his prior experience with mission to the gentiles. Peter, a good Jew, believed he should not associate with gentiles—notwithstanding the time he had spent with Jesus in ministry to others, such as Samaritans, who were considered unclean (Acts 10:28). But, in a hunger-induced trance, Peter received a mystical vision from God about eating unclean food that convinced him he should associate with gentiles (Acts 10:9–23). This led Peter to preach in the house of Cornelius, a Roman centurion, and to baptize the household—not something the Torah's holiness codes or the narratives of Joshua, Judges, or the historical books would seem to approve (Acts 10:24–48).

Acts 11 tells us that the Jewish apostles and believers in Judea at first criticized Peter but then gladly accepted Peter's actions after he told the story of his vision and his experience in Cornelius's house (Acts 11:1–18). As Acts 15 suggests, however, the matter was not settled for many of the Jewish Christians by this first meeting with Peter. Indeed, Paul's letter to the Galatians seems to suggest that Peter was much less accommodating than Luke's account in Acts 15 indicates, that the dispute between Paul and Peter was much more intense, and that Peter continued to have reservations about eating with gentiles (Galatians 1–2).

Whatever the relationship between the accounts in Acts and Galatians, it is clear that Paul continued to confront claims by Jewish Christians that gentile Christians must keep the entire Torah, including the mark of circumcision. Other texts in the New Testament also suggest ongoing tensions about what aspects of the Jewish purity codes (particularly concerning food sacrificed to idols) or rules about rituals and special observances should apply to gentile believers, and broader tensions between Paul's mission to the gentiles and the more "traditional" and Jewish perspectives of Peter and James (cf. Acts 15:29; Romans 14; 1 Corinthians 8–10; 1–2 Peter; James). Indeed, James seems to contradict directly Paul's central message of justification by faith—"You see that a man is justified by works and not by faith alone" (Jas 2:24)—which led Martin Luther effectively to excise it from the canon.[2]

As suggested in our extended discussion of Paul above, the true extent of theological tension between the epistles attributed to Peter and James

2. It is doubtful that the apostle Peter wrote the epistles attributed to him in the New Testament canon. Many scholars also doubt whether the traditional attribution of the Epistle of James to James the brother of Jesus, though some scholars argue for James's authorship. See Rainer Riesner, "James," in *The Oxford Bible Commentary*, 1256; Eric Eve, "1 Peter," in *The Oxford Bible Commentary*, 1263; Jeremy Duff, "Peter," in *The Oxford Bible Commentary*, 1271.

and the Pauline corpus is debatable, particularly in light of contemporary scholarship about Paul's essentially Jewish view of the Torah, and also in light of the enigmatic epistle to the Hebrews, which also may have been written by Paul or a disciple of Paul. The New Testament literature from Acts through these letters does, however, illustrate the immediate problem of how the developing gentile community of Jesus followers would relate to the first generation of Jewish Christians. In light of the Hebrew Scriptures—the only Scriptures available at the time—the Jewish followers of Jesus in the first century were presumptively *right* to express grave concerns about fellowship with gentiles who refused circumcision and who ignored most of the Torah's rules about ceremonies, food, and the like. Peter's openness to gentiles in Acts, based only on a personal experience and an idiosyncratic mystical vision rather than on what is written in the Torah, seemed to them like precisely the kind of syncretism condemned in the law and the prophets. Paul's turn toward interiority, focused on a circumcision of the heart rather than external observance, was consistent with Jewish pietism but also understandably seemed to many Jewish Christians to go too far.

For the purposes of this chapter, the most significant aspect of this tension relates to the relationship between "Israel" and "the church." The Old Testament's vision of Israel, from the protohistory through the prophets, was of an immanent political society accountable under its law directly to God. "Religion" and "law" were not separate categories because the minute details of the positive law in Leviticus and Deuteronomy, no less than the broad principles of the Decalogue, entailed fidelity to God. This is why, in the Old Testament, when a leader—a judge or a king—is unfaithful to the law, the nation faces God's judgment. The hope in the prophets is that God will restore the nation under a righteous ruler as a political society among the nations. The New Testament assumes that all kings and nations are under immanent judgment and that a new age of resurrection will soon arrive in which the church, a transnational community, will rule over a new creation directly under the risen Christ.[3]

This revised and reworked eschatological vision in the New Testament does not necessarily imply supercessionism—a *replacement* of Israel by the church—but it does suggest that the church's role in the present age, unlike the Old Testament's vision for Israel, is not immanent polit-

3. See, e.g., Richard Bauckham and Trevor Hart, *Hope against Hope: Christian Eschatology at the Turn of the Millennium* (Grand Rapids: Eerdmans, 1999); N. T. Wright, *Surprised by Hope: Rethinking Heaven, the Resurrection, and the Mission of the Church* (New York: HarperOne, 2008); Richard B. Hays, *The Moral Vision of the New Testament: A Contemporary Introduction to New Testament Ethics* (New York: HarperCollins, 2013).

ical rule.⁴ Positive law, therefore, does not *define* the church's mission. The church exists within political communities and therefore will interact with, and be concerned with, the positive law, but the church's mission is not to bring about God's kingdom in or through any historical nation. Indeed, in the eschatological consummation of history, the nations and kings, without any apparent priority or preference, will be brought into the new Jerusalem. The question of how the church should live under and relate to the positive law became more and more difficult as decades, centuries, and millennia passed without the parousia of Jesus anticipated in the New Testament.

A central part of this eschatological tension involves the extent to which the kingdom of God breaks into present history as part of the church's participation in God's mission in the world. The *missio Dei* involves the reign of God, which is the reign of peace, or *shalom*. George Hunsberger notes that

> shalom envisions the full prosperity of a people of God living under the covenant of God's demanding care and compassionate rule. In the prophetic vision, peace such as this comes hand in hand with justice. Without justice, there can be no real peace, and without peace, no real justice. Indeed, only in a social world full of a peace grounded in justice can there come the full expression of joy and celebration.⁵

The biblical vision of *shalom* is of a universal social peace within the context of particular human *nations*. As Richard Bauckham suggests, "The social or, we could say, numerical movement of the biblical narrative is from the one to the many, from Abraham to the nations, from Jesus to every creature in heaven, on earth and under the earth. Socially, then, *mission is a movement that is always being joined by others, the movement, therefore, of an ever-new people.*"⁶ Christopher J. H. Wright demonstrates that this social movement involves *nations*:

> God's mission is to bless all the nations of the earth. But for that universal aim he chose the very particular means—the people of Israel. Their uniqueness was for the sake of God's universality. . . . Their unique stewardship of God's *redemption* was so that ultimately the law of God could go forth from

---

4. For some issues relating to the problem of supercessionism, see, e.g., Carl E. Braaten and Robert W. Jenson, eds., *Jews and Christians: People of God* (Grand Rapids: Eerdmans, 2003).

5. George Hunsberger, "Called and Sent to Represent the Reign of God," in Darrell Guder, *Missional Church: A Vision for the Sending of the Church in North America* (Grand Rapids: Eerdmans, 1998), 91.

6. Richard Bauckham, *The Bible and Mission: Christian Witness in a Postmodern World* (Grand Rapids: Baker Academic, 2005), 15 (emphasis in original).

them to the nations and the ends of the earth. And their unique structure of social, economic, and political *ethics* was designed to show what a redeemed community of humanity should (and eventually will) look like under the reign of God.[7]

The church, however, is not a nation but rather embedded within the nations. The mission of Israel as a nation extends into the mission of the church as a transnational reality *within* the nations. As Stephan Bevans and Roger Schroeder suggest, "The church is not about the church. It is about what Jesus called the Reign of God. We are most the church not when we are building up the church, but when we are outside of it: being good parents, being loving spouses, being diligent and honest in our workplace . . . sharing our resources with the needy, standing up for social justice. . . . At the same time, while the church is not the mission, 'the mission has a church.'"[8]

As the title of Bevans and Schroeder's book *Prophetic Dialogue* suggests, the church's presence in any particular society is not to provide religious or spiritual warrant for elements of that society that conflict with the reign of God. The church's witness is always dialogical and prophetic because no human society yet embodies the peace of God's reign. The church comes into a society humbly and gratefully, as if entering someone else's garden. It embraces both "the spirituality of the outsider," which enables the church to "speak out" in the process of "letting go" of perceived certainties brought into a new culture, and the "spirituality of the insider," the cultural native who can perceive and address places where the local culture might need to change.[9]

These ideas about inculturation, prophetic dialogue, and the universal social scope of the *missio Dei* are the lifeblood of any theology of mission. They suggest, I think correctly, that the church should not prioritize its institutional "rights" within a society, as though the church were yet one more self-interested party fighting for scarce resources, striving to perpetuate itself in a great social Darwinian struggle. At the same time, if the church does speak prophetically within a society, if it is engaged from within as a cultivator of the society's resources, if it advocates for the oppressed, if it embodies the spirituality of both the outsider *and* the insider, it will take on at least some characteristics of a *citizen* of that society and necessarily will engage in conversations about its relation-

---

7. Christopher J. H. Wright, *The Mission of God* (Grand Rapids: Zondervan, 2013), 462.

8. Stephen B. Bevans and Roger P. Schroeder, *Prophetic Dialogue: Reflections on Christian Mission Today* (Maryknoll, NY: Orbis, 2011), Kindle loc. 316, 361.

9. Bevans and Schroeder, *Prophetic Dialogue*, chaps. 6–7.

ship to the society's law and governance. For this reason the relationship between "church and state" is historically deep and important.

CHURCH, "STATE," AND LAW

I have used the common phrase "church and state" in the preceding section, but from a historical and theological perspective, *state* is something of an anachronistic term. The notion of a "state," in the modern sense of a nation with sovereign rights to establish its own legal system and to develop its own religious and cultural identity within a community of other sovereign nation-states interconnected by international law, conventionally is traced back to the Peace of Westphalia, which ended the Thirty Years' War in 1648.[10] The modern nation-state therefore is seen as a stepchild of the Protestant Reformation. At that time religious freedom meant a nation's political rulers—the prince or king—could choose whether the nation would officially be Catholic, Calvinist, or Lutheran, and the extent to which dissenters would be tolerated.

There was no question even immediately after the Westphalian settlement of a European nation without an established, governmentally favored Christian church body. The more radical idea of separation of church and state as we understand it today was a product of many influences, including the Puritan/Parliamentarian faction of the English Civil War (1642–1651) and related Puritan movements (including the group led by John Winthrop that landed at Plymouth Rock in 1620); the role of newly emerging dissenting and "free church" groups such as the Quakers and Baptists in the American Colonies; roiling enthusiasm and resulting church divisions of the First Great Awakening in the 1730s and 1740s; and the liberal Enlightenment political philosophy that became popular in the seventeenth and eighteenth centuries and that informed the revolutionary era, including the American and French Revolutions. But even these modern notions are rooted in the far more ancient, and equally contested, concept of the relationship between temporal and spiritual power.[11]

10. See Peter H. Wilson, *Europe's Tragedy: A New History of the Thirty Years War* (New York: Penguin, 2009), chap. 21.
11. See, e.g., Sidney Z. Ehler and John B. Morrall, eds., *Church and State through the Centuries: A Collection of Historic Documents with Commentaries* (Westminster: The New Man Press, 1954), chaps. 5–7; John Witte Jr., *God's Joust, God's Justice: Law and Religion in the Western Tradition* (Grand Rapids: Eerdmans, 2006), chaps. 1–3, 5–8.

CHRISTIAN THOUGHT ABOUT LAW BEFORE
CONSTANTINE: CLEMENT, ORIGEN, TERTULLIAN

Like parts of the biblical narrative, the story of the church's relationship to "law" is long, complex, and often troubling. It is true, as many ecclesial ethicists today note, that particularly after Constantine the church often lost its sense of prophetic distance from temporal power. Whether this was a massive "Constantinian shift" or a "Constantinian moment" rather than a major shift is something historians and theologians continue to debate.[12] Nevertheless, both prior to and after Constantine, Christian thinkers understood that "law" is an important theological category and that the church must in some way relate to the temporal authorities. In this, they were trying to interpret the biblical narrative in their own times.

One of the intellectual centers of early Christianity was the catechetical school of Alexandria, which was led by Clement of Alexandria in the late second century, only a few generations after the apostles. Clement, one of the "Greek Fathers," was a pagan convert to Christianity who was deeply conversant with Greek philosophy. One of his efforts within the catechetical school of Alexandria was to demonstrate how Christianity was consistent with, and surpassed, the Greek philosophy that underpinned Hellenistic Roman society.

In his *Stromata* ("Miscellanies"), written from 198–203 CE, among many other topics (as the title suggests), Clement addressed the relationship between Christianity and pagan concepts of law and governance.[13] Clement first argued at length that the law and philosophy of Moses contained in the Old Testament predated Greek philosophy and that the Greeks in fact borrowed from Moses.[14] No scholar today would argue that Plato borrowed from Moses, but Clement's effort demonstrates his belief that all truth, including in law and politics, comes from God. In

---

12. Cf. Peter J. Leithart, *Defending Constantine: The Twilight of an Empire and the Dawn of Christendom* (Downers Grove, IL: IVP Academic, 2010); Oliver O'Donovan, *The Desire of the Nations: Rediscovering the Roots of Political Theology* (Cambridge: Cambridge University Press, 1996); John Howard Yoder, *The Priestly Kingdom: Social Ethics as Gospel* (South Bend, IN: University of Notre Dame Press, 1984); Stanley Hauerwas and William Willimon, *Resident Aliens: Life in the Christian Community* (Nashville: Abingdon, 2014). For an interesting discussion of Constantine's effort to "Christianize" the law, see Alan Kreider, *The Patient Ferment of the Early Church: The Improbable Rise of Christianity in the Roman Empire* (Grand Rapids: Baker Academic, 2016).

13. Clement, *Stromata*, in *Ante-Nicene Fathers*, vol. 2, ed. Alexander Roberts, James Donaldson, and A. Cleveland Coxe, trans. William Wilson (Buffalo, NY: Christian Literature, 1885), https://tinyurl.com/6oh9g9p.

14. Clement, *Stromata* 1.23–25.

particular, Clement argued, Plato's concept of law and legislation derived from Moses.[15] The Greek philosophers, Clement said, were like "children" learning about law and justice at the knee of Moses.[16]

According to Clement, both Moses and Plato recognized that good governance ultimately comes from the Creator, who endows humans with the capacity to organize society through laws.[17] Law provides punishments that can be necessary for "the correction of the soul."[18] Since law is related to the health of the soul, it is connected to God's deeper purposes in creation. The first lawgiver, who established the laws of creation, was the Son, "who unveiled the bosom of the Father."[19] Therefore, Clement said, "let no one . . . run down the law, as if, on account of the penalty, it were not beautiful and good."[20] This included, for Clement, not only the natural law but the positive law as well. The law's penalty works like a surgery or bad-tasting medicine—painful and unpleasant, but necessary for healing. Even the death penalty, according to Clement, though it destroys and does not heal the convicted, saves the rest of society from becoming infected by wickedness.[21] The "very function of the law" is "the highest and most perfect good," which is "to lead back anyone from the practice of evil to virtue and well-doing."[22]

Clement was succeeded as a teacher at the catechetical school in Alexandria by a towering intellect of the early church, Origen of Alexandria. In 202 CE, when Origen was seventeen, the church in Egypt was severely persecuted by Emperor Septimius Severus.[23] Origen's father, Leonides, a Christian and a literary professor in Alexandria, was imprisoned and beheaded, and the family's financial resources were confiscated.[24] When he was eighteen, Origen was appointed as a teacher of catechumens in Alexandria and subsequently developed into a well-known philosopher.[25] He once may even have participated in a religious debate or colloquium sponsored by Julia Mammaea, the mother of Emperor Alexander Severus, and later attracted wealthy patrons to the

15. Clement, *Stromata* 1.25.
16. Clement, *Stromata* 1.29.
17. Clement, *Stromata* 1.29.
18. Clement, *Stromata* 1.29.
19. Clement, *Stromata* 1.29.
20. Clement, *Stromata* 1.27.
21. Clement, *Stromata* 1.27.
22. Clement, *Stromata* 1.27.
23. John Anthony McGuckin, "The Life of Origen (ca. 186–255)," in *The Westminster Handbook to Origen* (Louisville: Westminster John Knox, 2004).
24. McGuckin, "Life of Origen," 7.
25. McGuckin, "Life of Origen," 7–9.

school in Alexandria.[26] Julia and Alexander welcomed Christians, and Julia herself may have been a Christian. Origen subsequently took on duties as a presbyter in Palestine and founded another school for Christian philosophy in Casarea amid claims by some rivals that his teachings were heretical.[27]

In 235 CE, military leaders murdered Julia and Alexander and mounted a revolt, sparking a new persecution against Christians.[28] Times became exceptionally turbulent, featuring invasions, civil war, military coups, plague, and twenty-six claimants to the imperial purple over fifty years—six in 238 CE alone. For a period during the reign of Philip the Arab (244–249 CE), a Christian-friendly emperor who may himself have been a Christian, Origen's career flourished again.[29] Philip, however, was killed during fighting against his erstwhile supporter in the senate, Decius, in September 249 CE. This coincided with a severe outbreak of plague, which may have killed as many as five thousand people a day in Alexandria alone, and which Decius blamed on the Christians.[30] Decius then embarked on one of the most severe of the Roman persecutions of Christians. Origen, among the most famous of Christian philosophers, was arrested and tortured repeatedly over the course of two years with iron collars and the rack in the hope that he would publicly recant.[31] He survived the Decian persecution, but his body was devastated by the torture, and he died sometime after Decius was assassinated.[32]

The purpose of reciting these details of Origen's life here is twofold. First, it illustrates that the story of the church prior to Constantine was not merely one of minority status and persecution. At times, Christian intellectuals were highly regarded and mingled freely with non-Christians. At other times, Christians were viciously persecuted. Second, it illustrates that Origen was not one to trade his understanding of Christian faith for political power.

Origen's thoughts about law are located primarily in his apologetic work, *Against Celsus*.[33] This text responds to arguments made by the pagan philosopher Celsus in his book *The True Word*, which is now

---

26. McGuckin, "Life of Origen," 11–12.

27. McGuckin, "Life of Origen," 15–17.

28. McGuckin, "Life of Origen," 19.

29. McGuckin, "Life of Origen," 22.

30. See Kyle Harper, *The Fate of Rome: Climate, Disease, and the End of an Empire* (Princeton: Princeton University Press, 2017).

31. McGuckin, "Life of Origen," 22.

32. McGuckin, "Life of Origen," 22–23.

33. Origen, *Contra Celsum*, in *Ante-Nicene Fathers*, vol. 4, ed. Alexander Roberts, James Donaldson, and A. Cleveland Coxe, trans. Frederick Crombie (Buffalo, NY: Christian Literature, 1885), https://tinyurl.com/6evm9m.

known to us only through Origen's response.[34] Many of Celsus's charges were familiar kinds of scapegoating: Christians undermine the social order because they refuse to worship the old gods, observe the old social conventions, or honor the emperor. The heart of the question, as Origen quoted from Celsus, was this: "You surely do not say that if the Romans were, in compliance with your wish, to neglect their customary duties to gods and men, and were to worship the Most High, or whatever you please to call him, that he will come down and fight for them, so that they shall need no other help than his. . . . What would happen if the Romans were persuaded to adopt the principles of the Christians, to despise the duties paid to the recognised gods and to men, and to worship the Most High?"[35] In other words, if everyone became Christians, society would fall apart, and the barbarians would destroy Rome.

Origen did at times sound like a radical separatist in response to these charges: "We do not render the honor supposed to be due to those who, according to Celsus, are set over the affairs of the world," Origen said, because Christians cannot serve both God and mammon.[36] If the "law of God and the law of mammon, are completely opposed to each other," the Christian is bound to obey God's law.[37] Further, Origen suggested, Christians "are to despise ingratiating ourselves with kings or any other men, not only if the favor is to be won by murders, licentiousness, or deeds of cruelty, but even if it involves impiety towards God, or any servile expressions of flattery and obsequiousness, which things are unworthy of brave and high-principled men."[38] Yet, at the same time, Origen noted that Scripture instructs Christians to be subject to the ruling powers (quoting Rom 13:1), countering Celsus's argument that Christians must always disobey the emperor's commands. Even with this concession, Origen suggested that some rulers "reign cruelly and tyrannically, and . . . make the kingly office the means of indulging in luxury and sinful pleasures," and noted that Christians cannot make oaths based on the emperor's authority if that authority is constituted by demons.[39]

Origen's ultimate response to Celsus was eschatological: "It will surely come to pass," he says, "that all who are endowed with reason shall come under one law."[40] It seemed impossible that the warring factions of "Asia, Europe, and Libya, as well Greeks as Barbarians," would come to peace

---

34. Origen, *Contra Celsum* 1.
35. Origen, *Contra Celsum* 8.69.
36. Origen, *Contra Celsum* 8.56.
37. Origen, *Contra Celsum* 8.56.
38. Origen, *Contra Celsum* 8.65.
39. Origen, *Contra Celsum* 8.65.
40. Origen, *Contra Celsum* 8.72.

and agreement, Origen acknowledged, "and perhaps such a result would indeed be impossible to those who are still in the body, but not to those who are released from it."[41]

Another key figure who wrote about law in the pre–Constantinian era was Tertullian. In his defense of Christians against the charges of atheism, cannibalism, incest, and the dissolution of the bonds of the Roman empire, the *Apologeticum*, Tertullian called the Roman judicial system to task for not affording Christians and Christianity a fair hearing.[42] Tertullian's concept of justice emphasized fair and neutral procedures regardless of the nature of the charge or the accused:

> Supposing it to be true that we are criminals of deepest dye, why are we treated differently by you from our fellows, I mean all other criminals, since the same guilt ought to meet with the same treatment? When others are called by whatever name is applied to us, they employ both their own voices and the services of a paid pleader to set forth their innocence. They have every opportunity of answering and cross-questioning, since it is not even legal that persons should be condemned entirely undefended and unheard. But the Christians alone are not permitted to say anything to clear themselves of the charge, to uphold the truth, to prevent injustice in the judge.[43]

These procedural omissions, Tertullian argued, were tied to a substantive failure. The Roman authorities were not interested in whether the charges against Christians were true. Rather, "the one thing looked for is that which is demanded by the popular hatred, the confession of the name, not the weighing of a charge."[44] The Roman magistrates never determined "how many slaughtered babes each had already tasted, how many times he had committed incest in the dark, what cooks, what dogs had been present (on the occasion)."[45] Instead, the corrupt system

41. Origen, *Contra Celsum* 8.72.

42. See public domain translation available at https://tinyurl.com/yd4xhg9.

43. Tertullian, *Apologeticum* 2. In some ways consonant with contemporary missional theologies, such as that of N. T. Wright mentioned in the previous notes, Tertullian emphasized that Christian communities should be tolerated by the state because "God gave Christians as his gift to the world." Eric Osborn, *Tertullian, First Theologian of the West* (Cambridge: Cambridge University Press, 2003), 65. In Tertullian's economy, Christians' "innocence has tempered injustice in the world and their prayers have prevailed upon God for good" (Tertullian, *Apologeticum* 2).

44. Tertullian, *Apologeticum* 2.

45. Tertullian, *Apologeticum* 2. Osborn argues that "Tertullian's central idea is that the universe is made of opposites which must be harmonized and held together by reason. The persecution of Christians destroys this harmony and is therefore fundamentally wrong and due to demonic perversion. The balance of ethical opposites is necessary and anticipates God's final justice which will restore all things. The persecution of Christians undermines the moral fabric of the world. Tertullian's claim is strengthened by an insistence that the justice of the world is always proleptic and imperfect, whereas the final justice of God initiates the eschaton now" (Osborn, *Tertullian*, 67).

pressed for a confession or denial of "the name" of Christ, often through torture, and that confession or denial determined the entire case. His appeal therefore was to a higher concept of justice and what today we call "freedom of religion," rooted in fairness and truth, that transcended the raw power of the Roman state. Of course, Tertullian went on in the *Apologeticum* to refute these slanderous claims against the Christians, although it is unlikely his theoretical framework appealed to many patrician Romans, for whom the empire's success was indissolubly tied to the ancient pagan traditions (even if, for many of that class, the content of the pagan rituals was held as little more than superstition).

CHRISTIAN THOUGHT ABOUT LAW IN TRANSITION: LACTANTIUS

Lactantius, known as the "Christian Cicero," was another great early exponent of a Christian vision of law and justice. He had been an official in Diocletian's court and wrote his *Divine Institutes*, and particularly the section *On Justice*, in response to the great persecution under Diocletian.[46] Diocletian's was the last major Roman persecution of Christians, and among the most vicious.[47]

Lactantius also became a key advisor to Constantine and was instrumental in persuading Constantine to adopt a policy legally favoring Christianity. Lactantius thus serves as an interesting bridge figure who confounds any simplistic historiography of Constantinianism. He was an important thinker both in the persecuted church and in the Constantinian church.

Perhaps representing Lactantius as a "bridge" figure suggests that his thought is a key part of the Constantinian problem because Lactantius's thought on law and justice supplied the intellectual fuel for the Constantinian shift. There is some truth to this claim, but as usual, history is messier than a simple binary. First, Lactantius's arguments against the legal persecution of Christians in the *Divine Institutes* were entirely consistent with the natural law tradition of earlier Christian thinkers such as Clement, Tertullian, and Origen. By the time Lactantius wrote the *Divine Institutes*, there already was a rich tradition of Christian thought about law and justice derived from the Christian Scriptures in conversation with Greek philosophical sources. Second, Lactantius's argument in

46. McGuckin, *Ascent of Christian Law*, 110–12.
47. See Dale T. Irvin and Scott W. Sunquist, *History of the World Christian Movement, Volume 1: Earliest Christianity to 1453* (Maryknoll, NY: Orbis, 2001), 111.

the *Divine Institutes* was not that Christians should change society by the force of law but that the law should make space for Christians to follow Christ, which would inevitably benefit society.

A key aspect of Lactantius's argument related to an important aspect of classical Roman political thought that is often overlooked by contemporary thinkers who criticize Constantinianism: the prosperity of the empire rested primarily with the virtue of its citizens, not primarily with the power of the emperor. Rome's founding myth was that its political society was originally established as a republic of virtuous citizens with equal rights to govern. The absolute authority of the emperor was only later established through a (supposed) legislative act of the citizenry, meaning that the emperor's authority ultimately derived from the people.[48]

Lactantius's primary concern in *On Justice* was to demonstrate that the Christians, in fact, are the "true" Romans.[49] The Roman ideal was grounded in a sense of justice. As Lactantius noted, justice "is either by itself the greatest virtue, or by itself the fountain of virtue, which not only philosophers sought, but poets also, who were much earlier, and were esteemed as wise before the origin of the name of philosophy."[50] Without virtue, justice gives way to mere authority and power.

Lactantius recited portions of Aratus's poem *Phaenomena*—the same poem reference by the apostle Paul in Athens—which conjures a golden age of justice and virtue.[51] The golden age was lost, however, when people began to lust after power and possessions. When lust replaced virtue, law became separated from justice.[52] Now the governing authorities prevailed "as much by authority as by strength, or resources, or malice."[53] Having lost all traces of humanity, equity, and pity—which Lactantius

48. For a further discussion of this dynamic, see chap. 3.

49. Lactantius, *On Justice*, https://tinyurl.com/yxtxz96j.

50. Lactantius, *On Justice* 5.

51. Lactantius, *On Justice* 5, quoting Aratus, *Phaeonomena*, https://tinyurl.com/yy9rq747. The full paragraph from Aratus is compelling: "Her men called Justice; but she assembling the elders, it might be in the market-place or in the wide-wayed streets, uttered her voice, ever urging on them judgments kinder to the people. Not yet in that age had men knowledge of hateful strife, or carping contention, or din of battle, but a simple life they lived. Far from them was the cruel sea and not yet from afar did ships bring their livelihood, but the oxen and the plough and Justice herself, queen of the peoples, giver of things just, abundantly supplied their every need" (Aratus, *Phaeonomena* 101–7). As Elizabeth DePalma Digeser notes, "Although Hellenistic political theory had long put forward the idea that the just state was a reflection of the cosmos and that the monarch could somehow be the source of living law, Lactantius was among the first Christians to develop these notions within a Christian cosmology." See Elizabeth DePalma Digeser, *The Making of a Christian Empire: Lactantius and Rome* (Ithaca: Cornell University Press, 2000), 56–57.

52. Lactantius, *On Justice* 6.

53. Lactantius, *On Justice* 6.

identified as the "offices" of justice—the rulers instead "began to rejoice in a proud and swollen inequality, and made themselves higher than other men, by a retinue of attendants, and by the sword, and by the brilliancy of their garments."[54] But Christ, Lactantius argued, restored justice, and in the Christians the fruits of virtue that support the flourishing of the *civitas*, can be realized.[55]

Lactantius's appeal on behalf of the Christians was thus in part pragmatic: if the empire is to return to its golden age, Christians should be protected and not persecuted. But he also reached for a transcendent feature of justice: equality. "Although justice embraces all the virtues together," he said, "yet there are two, the chief of all, which cannot be torn asunder and separated from it—piety and equity."[56] Equity is inherent to human nature: "For God, who produces and gives birth to men, willed that all should be equal, that is, equally matched. He has imposed on all the same condition of living; He has produced to all wisdom; He has promised immortality to all; no one is cut off from His heavenly benefits."[57] This means that social distinctions are erased: "In His sight no one is a slave, no one a master; for if all have the same Father, by an equal right we are all children."[58] Lactantius admitted that such social distinctions persist even among Christians, but, he says, "we measure all human things not by the body, but by the spirit," so that "although the condition of bodies is different, yet we have no servants, but we both regard and speak of them as brothers in spirit, in religion as fellow-servants."[59]

Justice, then, for Lactantius, was closely connected to inward desire. A just man, he said, "is neither at enmity with any human being, nor desires anything at all which is the property of another."[60] Mere animals cannot be "just" because they cannot discipline their desires. In animals, Lactantius argued, "because they are destitute of wisdom, nature is the provider of supplies for itself. Therefore they injure others that they may profit themselves, for they do not understand that committing an injury is evil."[61] A man, however, "who has the knowledge of good and evil, abstains from committing an injury even to his own damage, which an

54. Lactantius, *On Justice* 6.
55. Lactantius, *On Justice* 7. DePalma Digeser suggests that "in asserting that piety and equity—as he defined them—were the first two principles of divine law, Lactantius expresses in Roman terms the two commandments on which the whole Christian Law is based . . . (Matt 22:36–40)" (DePalma Digeser, *Making of a Christian Empire*, 56).
56. Lactantius, *On Justice* 14.
57. Lactantius, *On Justice* 14.
58. Lactantius, *On Justice* 14.
59. Lactantius, *On Justice* 16.
60. Lactantius, *On Justice* 18.
61. Lactantius, *On Justice* 18.

animal without reason is unable to do; and on this account innocence is reckoned among the chief virtues of man."[62]

Lactantius's emphasis on piety and equity as the keys to justice undergirded his argument for religious freedom. If piety and virtue should be encouraged, and if all people are equal under the law, Lactantius asked, "who is so arrogant, who so lifted up, as to forbid me to raise my eyes to heaven? Who can impose upon me the necessity either of worshipping that which I am unwilling to worship, or of abstaining from the worship of that which I wish to worship?"[63] This, Lactantius claimed, is another way in which the Christians are the true harbingers of justice, the true Romans: "We, on the contrary, do not require that any one should be compelled, whether his is willing or unwilling, to worship our God, who is the God of all men; nor are we angry if any one does not worship him."[64]

Far from arguing that political power and positive law could establish the kingdom of God, then, Lactantius's claim was that the law should make space for the formation of virtue within the citizenry as they sought and found God. Real power came from the people, or more accurately, real power came from God working within the people, and it was a power related to classical, Stoic, Roman, and Christian virtues such as wisdom and forbearance, not a power of domination. At the same time, it is true that Lactantius thought the natural law governed individual, church, and state alike.[65]

---

62. Lactantius, *On Justice* 18.

63. Lactantius, *On Justice* 14.

64. Lactantius, *On Justice* 21.

65. As DePalma Digeser suggests, Lactantius's political theology eschewed any notion that the state should be subject to different standards than the church: "Lactantius intended his understanding of divine law to apply not merely to individuals but to the Roman state as a whole. . . . So long as evil existed (that is, until the second coming), there would be a need for the state, but the only legitimate government would be one that acknowledged the One God and treated its citizens with equity (*aequitas*). These arguments responded to the juridicial philosophy that had developed since Ulpian, in which Roman law was seen as a reflection not only of natural law but also of Roman Religion. No other Christian author before Lactantius had drawn so heavily on Cicero to attempt such a thoroughgoing discussion of justice or so clearly postulated a Christian empire whose foundation was based on a new understanding of natural law" (DePalma Digeser, *Making of a Christian Empire*, 58–59). Yet Alan Kreider notes that Lactantius urged Constantine to exercise patience in governing and that Constantine faltered when he diverged from Lactantius's advice. See Alan Kreider, *The Patient Ferment of the Early Church: The Improbable Rise of Christianity in the Roman Empire* (Grand Rapids: Baker Academic, 2016), 256–62.

THE PATRISTIC GIANT: AUGUSTINE

In our survey of the biblical narrative and law, we noted Psalm 19 as an example of "natural theology." Another locus of natural theology in the Bible is Romans 1, although Paul there suggests that people ignore the natural law. Unlike Clement, Origen, and Lactantius, most of the New Testament literature ignores the natural law element of Roman political thought. Tertullian, who famously asked what Jerusalem has to do with Athens, was also skeptical of what he saw as syncretism between pagan natural law concepts and biblical law. We might also offer a cynical eye—and there were no shortage of cynics in ancient Rome either—toward high-flying Roman rhetoric of virtue, wisdom, and forbearance in a society in which nearly half the population were slaves, and even free women held no political rights. In fact, we might say that this is a key aspect of the New Testament's theopolitical vision: it unmasks the pretense of "civil" society and exposes the infected rot at its core. It is a fair critique to suggest that Lactantius lacked an adequate sense of the constant tension between virtue and power.

But cynicism always oscillates between hope and nihilism. It may expose the infection so that it can be cleared out and the wound can begin to heal, or it may give up, seeing nothing but rot everywhere. Christian theology is grounded in hope, the hope that God eventually will restore all things. In Christian theology this is an *eschatological* question, a question of the end of history, connected with Christ's return. A key question is whether that peaceful resolution of history is entirely in the future or whether it is already breaking into history now. That question is central to the thought of the next thinker in our survey, Augustine.

Augustine's political theology, as expressed in his *City of God* and elsewhere, of course became a central pillar of Western Christendom.[66] Augustine, like Lactantius and Tertullian, understood that there is a spiritual or natural law built into the creation by God, which is the true source of righteousness. For example, he noted in the *Confessions* that, when he was a Manichean, he "did not know either that true inward righteousness takes as its criterion not custom but the most righteous law of almighty God, by which the morality of countries and times was formed as appropriate to those countries and times, while God's law itself

66. See, e.g., McGuckin, *Ascent of Christian Law*, chap. 6; Paul Weithman, "Augustine's Political Philosophy," in *The Cambridge Companion to Augustine*, ed. Eleanore Stump and Norman Kretzmann (Cambridge: Cambridge University Press, 2006).

has remained unchanged everywhere and always, not one thing in one place and something different elsewhere."[67]

If God's eternal law is unchanging, Augustine wondered, why are there obvious differences among the laws of various cultures throughout history? Is justice "fickle and changeable?"[68] No, Augustine answered, "but the epochs over which she rules do not all unfold in the same way, precisely because times change."[69] At various times and places, some particular applications of the eternal law might become more or less apparent and feasible.[70] Moreover, God's eternal law stands above the laws of any temporal king.[71] If God's law conflicts with the law of a human king, the human law should change. "As in the hierarchy of human society a more powerful official is placed above one of lesser rank and is to be obeyed," Augustine said, "so God stands above all."[72] To obey God's eternal law even if it conflicts with civil law does not undermine the community" but rather ultimately strengthens the community in its proper relation to God.[73]

At times God's law might seem opaque or confusing.[74] Yet God's law, for Augustine, was not merely an arbitrary decree. A breach of God's law does not harm God himself. "But how can our vices touch you, who are incorruptible?" Augustine asked rhetorically: "What crimes can be committed against you, who are immune from harm?"[75] His answer was that since the eternal law is part of God's good ordering of creation, breaches of that law destroy the human soul: "For even when people sin against you, they are maliciously damaging their own souls. Iniquity plays itself false when it corrupts and perverts its own nature, to which you gave life and order, or when it makes intemperate use of lawful things, or again when it burns with desire for other things not permitted, lusting to enjoy

---

67. Augustine, *Confessions* 3.13, trans. Maria Boulding, O.S.B. (San Francisco: Ignatius Press, 2012).

68. Augustine, *Confessions* 3.13.

69. Augustine, *Confessions* 3.13.

70. Augustine, *Confessions* 3.13. As Augustine notes, "Human beings live on earth for a brief span only, and they lack the discernment to bring the conditions of earlier ages, of which they have no experience, into the same frame of reference with those they know well; but they can easily perceive in one body or one day or one house what is appropriate for each limb, each period of time and all persons and places. Thus while they may be scandalized by the one, they readily submit to the other."

71. Augustine, *Confessions* 3.15.

72. Augustine, *Confessions* 3.15.

73. Augustine, *Confessions* 3.15.

74. Augustine, *Confessions* 3.15.

75. Augustine, *Confessions* 3.16.

them in a way contrary to nature."[76] The eternal law, built into the soul, therefore helps order human desires toward their proper end.

But if the rational soul inclines human beings to God, why do we end up with sin and violence? We think we have made ourselves free of the law, masters over it. But our quest for freedom binds us to slavery. This is why Augustine connected the need for a king—human law—to sin. Without sin, man would live by the divine law and would not become subject to other men. Because of sin, Augustine argued, men need the scourge of human law:

> And beyond question it is a happier thing to be the slave of a man than of a lust; for even this very lust of ruling, to mention no others, lays waste men's hearts with the most ruthless dominion. . . . And therefore the apostle admonishes slaves to be subject to their masters, and to serve them heartily and with good-will, so that, if they cannot be freed by their masters, they may themselves make their slavery in some sort free, by serving not in crafty fear, but in faithful love, until all unrighteousness pass away, and all principality and every human power be brought to nothing, and God be all in all.[77]

Human principalities, powers, and laws, for Augustine, were temporary restraints.[78] There is one path to freedom from this cycle of enslavement: love. For Augustine, the fulfillment of love, when God is all in all, marks the end of positive law. Love does not impose. Positive law, in contrast, is a relation of imposing power.

Nevertheless, for Augustine, at times the law must be coercive, since human desires are prone to distortion. If in our "curiosity" we twist our desires toward evil, the law operates to thwart those twisted desires and reign in such "curiosity":

> It is evident that the free play of curiosity is a more powerful spur to learning . . . than is fear-ridden coercion; yet in accordance with your laws, O God,

76. Augustine, *Confessions* 3.16.

77. Augustine, *City of God* 14.15, trans. Marcus Dods, *Nicene and Post-Nicene Fathers*, First Series, vol. 2 (Buffalo, NY: Christian Literature Publishing, 1887), available at newadvent.org/fathers/120119.htm.

78. Paul Wiethman notes that Augustine's view about the temporary nature of governance relates to his understanding of political authority as inherently coercive: "For Augustine, the most salient feature of political authority is just that feature an authority would have to have in order to govern a society of people all of whom are constitutionally prone to conflict: the authority to coerce them. This authority is common to those in positions of political power and the masters of slaves. Augustine also insists that subjection to political authority, like the subjection to a slave-master, is morally improving because both foster humility, particularly when the good are subjected to the bad. Thus political authority and the mastery of slaves both rely on coercion, and both teach humility to sinfully proud human beings" (Wiethmann, "Augustine's Political Theology," 240).

coercion checks the free play of curiosity. By your laws it constrains us, from the beatings meted out by our teachers to the ordeals of the martyrs, for in accord with those laws it prescribes for us bitter draughts of salutary discipline to recall us from the venomous pleasure which led us away from you.[79]

But here the sense of "law" employed by Augustine is largely internal: it is God's law that constrains us internally and the scourge of persecution that purifies us. We will see in a later section the problematic way in which Augustine applied his concept of positive law to religious dissent against the Donatists.

CONSTANTINIANISM, CHURCH, AND STATE

Our historical narrative so far suggests that Christian thought about natural law and positive law was remarkably consistent from the patristic era prior to Constantine through Augustine. Yet a conventional narrative among ecclesial ethicists is that the Christian church and the Roman state were separated prior to Constantine and were essentially unified after Constantine. The reality was much more complex than either one of continuity or one of radical discontinuity. In the period after Constantine and before the Reformation, church authorities and temporal rulers were engaged in constant struggles over their respective spheres of authority. These struggles were not primarily about whether the church could control the state. They were about whether the state could control the church. Further, these struggles were not uniform across various historical periods and places in Christendom. Disputes roiled between the Eastern and Western branches of the Catholic Church, not least over the spiritual jurisdiction of the Bishop of Rome (the Pope) in relation to the other bishops, including the Bishop in Constantinople, leading to the Great Schism between the Eastern and Western churches in 1054 CE.

A good touchstone for this discussion is a letter by Pope Gelasius I to the Emperor Anastasius, written in 494 CE.[80] The background of the letter was an early theological rift in the Eastern church over the mono-

---

79. Augustine, *Confessions* 14.23. On the theme of Augustine and "curiosity," see Joseph Torchia OP, *Restless Mind: Curiositas and the Scope of Inquiry in St. Augustine's Psychology* (Milwaukee: Marquette University Press, 2013); Paul Griffiths, *Intellectual Appetite: A Theological Grammar* (Washington, DC: The Catholic University of America Press, 2009).

80. See "Gelasius I," in *From Irenaeus to Grotius: A Sourcebook in Christian Political Thought*, ed. Oliver O'Donovan and Joan Lockwood O'Donovan (Grand Rapids: Eerdmans, 1999), 177–79.

physite controversy. The monophysite controversy was an outgrowth of the christological disputes that roiled the church in its early centuries.

The Council of Nicaea, called by the Emperor Constantine in 325 CE, had addressed the Arian controversy, which involved the relation of the Son to the Father. The question there was whether the Son had always existed as divine or had a temporal beginning as a divine person. In the broader terms, the question was whether Jesus was fully God. The history of this dispute written by the victors suggests that the Catholic party at the council, led by Athanasius, prevailed over the Arian party, resulting in the Nicene Creed, which states that Jesus is "Light of Light, very God of very God, begotten, not made, being of one substance [ὁμοούσιον, *homoousion*] with the Father." The reality was much more textured and complex.[81]

The Arian controversy continued to ferment after the council, and in addition, even among the those who supported the Nicene Creed, disagreements arose concerning the relationship between the incarnate Christ's human and divine natures. In the early fifth century the debate focused on the use of the title *theotokos*, "Mother of God," for Mary. This title was long used as a term of veneration for Mary as well as to signify that Jesus truly was divine, consistent with the Catholic Nicene view. The archbishop of Constantinople from 328–431, Nestorius, rejected the title *theotokos* in favor of *Christotokos* ("Christ-bearer"). Nestorius was responding to an ongoing theological dispute about the implications of Nicene Christology. If Jesus was fully divine, coeternal with the Father, how could it be that Mary was a "God-bearer"? This argument was associated with monks and clergy in Antioch, where Nestorius received his early training. In contrast, monks and clergy associated with the city of Alexandria, including Patriarch Cyril of Alexandria, adhered to the *theotokos* title.

Emperor Theodosius II supported Nestorius, but Pope Celestine supported Cyril. The pope instructed Cyril to excommunicate Nestorius. Nestorius convinced Theodosius to convene a council before the bull (legal order) of excommunication could be delivered. A council was called in Ephesus (the First Council of Ephesus in 431), but Nestorius was condemned as a heretic and deposed before the bishops from the east, including John I of Antioch, arrived at the council. The eastern bishops then convened their own council, at which Cyril was condemned and deposed. Both sides appealed to the emperor, who ordered

81. See Lewis Ayres, *Nicaea and Its Legacy: An Approach to Fourth-Century Trinitarian Theology* (Oxford: Oxford University Press, 2004); Rowan Williams, *Arius: Heresy and Tradition* (Grand Rapids: Eerdmans, 2001).

that both Nestorius and Cyril should be deposed and exiled. Over the next few years, however, Cyril returned from exile (after bribing some of Theodosius's courtiers), the Alexandrian/papal faction forced the removal of many Nestorian bishops, and Theodosius banished Nestorius to a monastery in Egypt that was under Cyril's jurisdiction. The Alexandrian/papal faction had prevailed, but a number of the eastern churches in Persia broke with the Catholic Church in what is today called the Nestorian Schism.

As this mention of the Nestorian Schism suggests, the First Council of Ephesus did not end all arguments about how to frame the relationship between Christ's divine and human natures. In the ongoing debate, "monophysites" argued that the incarnate Christ had one nature, derived from the separate divine and human natures; "diophysites" argued that the incarnate Christ was one person in two natures.[82] The monophysite position resulted from the views of an influential monk named Eutyches, who taught that the incarnate Christ had divine flesh that did not derive from Mary (notice how the *theotokos* issue continued to resurface). The monphysite controversy, then, can be viewed as an argument about whether the incarnate Christ was fully human, as well as an ongoing debate about how Christ's human nature related to his eternal divine nature.

At an initial synod, Eutyches's views were condemned by Archbishop Flavian of Constantinople. Eutyches appealed and in 449 CE, the Emperor Theodosius II called another council in Ephesus, from which one of Eutyches's chief theological rivals, Theodoret of Cyrus, was excluded. Pope Leo sent a letter (Leo's *Tome*) stating a view against Eutyches, but Leo's letter was not read to the council. When the meeting began, Archbishop Flavian was physically assaulted and later died of his injuries. The monophysite position was affirmed. Pope Leo denounced this as a "robber synod."[83]

The next year, Theodosius died after being thrown from his horse. His sister Pulcheria, who was sympathetic to the pope's position, took control of the government. Pulcheria entered into a politically expedient marriage with a military officer named Marcian, whom she crowned emperor. Pulcheria and Marcian then convened another church council, which met in 451 in Chalcedon. This council accepted Leo's *Tome* as

---

82. O'Donovan and Lockwood O'Donovan, *From Irenaeus to Grotius*, 177; Irvin and Sunquist, *History of the World Christian Movement*, 1:191–94.

83. Irvin and Sunquist, *History of the World Christian Movement*, 1:192.

orthodox and produced the Chalcedonian definition, an effort to bridge the competing theologies.[84]

Some groups within the Eastern churches, particularly associated with the Syrian, Persian, and Egyptian churches, however, rejected the Chalcedonian definition. Emperor Zeno (474–491) tried to construct a "union formula" that would unite the Chalcedonian and non-Chalcedonian churches in the East, but that formula was rejected at a synod in Rome by Pope Felix III in 484, resulting in schism between Felix and the Patriarch of Constantinople, Acacius. The "Acacian schism" endured for two generations. In 491 the Emperor Anastasius, who favored the monophysite position, took the Byzantine throne. This alarmed the Roman church leadership, which feared that the Eastern church might turn back against the Chalcedonian formula. Pope Gelasius attempted to stem the tide by asserting the universal jurisdiction of the Roman Pope above both the other bishops and the emperor.[85]

Gelasius's letter laid out the basic concept of "two powers"—church and crown—with different domains of authority and responsibility: "There are two powers, august Emperor, by which this world is chiefly ruled, namely, the sacred authority of the priests and the royal power."[86] According to Gelasius, the royal power must yield to the church in matters of religion:

> Of these that of the priests is the more weighty, since they have to render an account for even the kings of men in the divine judgment. You are also aware, dear son, that while you are permitted honorably to rule over human kind, yet in things divine you bow your head humbly before the leaders of the clergy and await from their hands the means of your salvation. In the reception and proper disposition of the heavenly mysteries you recognize that you should be subordinate rather than superior to the religious order, and that in these matters you depend on their judgment rather than wish to force them to follow your will.[87]

Gelasius conceded, at least in passing, that the church is subject to the temporal law of the crown as it relates to public order: "If the ministers of religion, recognizing the supremacy granted you from heaven in matters affecting the public order, obey your laws, lest otherwise they might obstruct the course of secular affairs by irrelevant considerations, with what readiness should you not yield them obedience to whom is

---

84. Irvin and Sunquist, *History of the World Christian Movement*, 1:193.
85. O'Donovan and Lockwood O'Donovan, *From Irenaeus to Grotius*, 177.
86. "Gelasius I on Spiritual and Temporal Power," in *Readings in European History*, trans. J. H. Robinson (Boston: Ginn, 1905), 72–73, https://tinyurl.com/y5ehy2gq.
87. "Gelasius I on Spiritual and Temporal Power."

assigned the dispensing of the sacred mysteries of religion."[88] Yet Gelasius further asserted that, in the domain of the church, the bishop of Rome—the pope—is the final authority, just as the emperor is the final authority in the temporal domain: "And if it is fitting that the hearts of the faithful should submit to all priests in general who properly administer divine affairs, how much the more is obedience due to the bishop of that see which the Most High ordained to be above all others, and which is consequently dutifully honored by the devotion of the whole Church."[89]

This history again illustrates that the "Constantinian shift" never was a simple matter of the fusion of church and empire. It is true that the religious and political elites of the time both envisioned a unified society under one emperor and one church. Church leaders often called on the emperor to intervene in theological and ecclesiastical disputes by convening counsels. But when emperors sought to assert their authority against the bishops, the bishops claimed an independence, and indeed a superiority, of the ecclesial authority over the temporal. This was particularly true of the increasingly influential bishop of Rome, the pope. Conflicts between crown and pope would continue through the medieval period, sometimes causing major social crises, including in the investiture controversy.[90]

The tension between the two domains of spiritual and temporal rule reached a crescendo in the investiture controversy in the eleventh century during the papacy of Gregory VII. As the language of "crescendo" suggests, the themes of this controversy had been sounding for centuries.

88. "Gelasius I on Spiritual and Temporal Power."
89. "Gelasius I on Spiritual and Temporal Power."
90. Another example of this dynamic is an infamous forgery, the "Donation of Constantine." The Donation purports to have been written by the Emperor Constantine after he was miraculously cured of leprosy after his baptism by Pope Sylvester. (In fact, Constantine never had leprosy, and was baptized on his deathbed by Bishop Eusebius of Nicomedia.) It gives to the See of Rome spiritual jurisdiction over the other principal sees in Christendom, Antioch, Alexandria, Constantinople, and Jerusalem, "as also over all the churches of God in all the world," and states that the Pope of Rome "shall be the highest and chief of all priests in the whole world." The Donation grants to Pope Sylvester and his successors the symbols of Constantine's political authority in the West, including "the diadem, which is the crown of our head; and the mitre; as also the superhumeral, that is, the stole which usually surrounds our imperial neck; and the purple cloak and the scarlet tunic and all the imperial robes; also the rank of commanders of the imperial cavalry." It then conveys to the Pope the imperial palace in Rome "and likewise all provinces, palaces and districts of the city of Rome and Italy and of the regions of the West . . . as a permanent possession to the holy roman Church." Finally, the Donation states that the capital of the empire should be moved to the East (presumably to Constantinople) "for it is not right that an earthly emperor should have authority there [in Rome], where the rule of priests and the head of the Christian religion have been established by the Emperor of heaven." See "The Donation of Constantine," in O'Donovan and Lockwood O'Donovan, eds., From Irenaeus to Grotius, 228–30.

The controversy involved who had the authority to appoint ("invest") bishops and other church officials such as the heads of monasteries. Churches and monasteries require land. In the early Middle Ages in Western Europe, the lands on which churches and monasteries sat often were controlled by feudal lords. Bishops, abbots, and other clergy took fealty oaths to these feudal lords, who in turn invested the churchmen with symbols of their authority.[91] Both the church and the large monasteries were powerful social institutions, and the noble families often sought to perpetuate their control by placing their own sons into key leadership roles through this power of investiture.[92] The nobility also frequently bought and sold clerical offices over which they had the power of investiture, a practice called simony.[93] These practices led to widespread corruption in the church. It was not uncommon, for example, for a clergy member to support multiple concubines (a practice called *nicolaitism*) as he and his extended family grew wealthy from control over the feudal lands.

In response, reforming popes sought to assert papal control over key church appointments. The dispute intensified when King Henry IV of Germany tried to appoint a new archbishop of Milan in 1075. Pope Gregory VII excommunicated Henry and proclaimed that all German nobility who had sworn loyalty to Henry were free of their oaths. This was a dramatic move by Gregory, because Henry had been attempting since the start of his reign to consolidate his power over the German nobility and put down a civil war. Gregory was staying at a castle in Canossa (in northern Italy) in late January on his way to meet the German nobility when Henry decided to seek absolution. Henry famously waited three days barefoot in the snow before Gregory offered absolution.[94]

It seemed that the church had obtained the advantage and secured the peace in Germany. However, civil war later erupted again, and Henry prevailed and eventually marched on Rome. Gregory was exiled, and Henry chose a different pope who granted Henry the title of emperor.[95]

Debates about investiture and wars among the nobility continued hand in hand for nearly fifty years until the Concordat of Worms

91. Ivrin and Sunquist, *History of the World Christian Movement*, 1:388.

92. For example, for a discussion of the power of the monastery at Cluny and its role in the tensions over investiture, see Uta-Renate Blumenthal, *The Investiture Controversy: Church and Monarchy from the Ninth to the Twelfth Century* (Philadelphia: University of Pennsylvania Press 1988), chap. 1.

93. Irvin and Sunquist, *History of the World Christian Movement*, 1:388.

94. Irvin and Sunquist, *History of the World Christian Movement*, 1:389. For a fuller description of these events, see Colin Morris, "The Discord of Empire and Papacy 1073–1099," in *The Papal Monarchy: The Western Church from 1050 to 1250* (Oxford: Oxford University Press, 1991).

95. Irvin and Sunquist, *History of the World Christian Movement*, 1:390.

between Pope Callixtus II and Holy Roman Emperor Henry V in 1122. In this agreement, the king's authority to invest clergy with temporal rights was recognized, while the canons of the cathedral, that is, the authorities within the head of the diocese, were entitled to elect the bishop.[96]

The Concordat of Worms did not by any means end all controversies over the relationship between temporal and spiritual power. Such controversies continued to roil European society throughout the Middle Ages. They reached another crescendo in 1295 when King Philip IV of France imposed a substantial tax on French churches and clergy to help pay debts incurred because of military activities.[97] When Pope Boniface VIII condemned this tax, Philip took actions against the church in France, including cutting off funding and arresting some of Boniface's allies in France.[98] This led Boniface to issue a bull entitled *Unam sanctum*, arguing that the church is a superior power to the crown. Boniface acknowledged that distinction between spiritual and temporal power but argued that spiritual power has the final say:

> Both, therefore, are in the power of the church, that is to say, the spiritual and the material sword, but the former is to be administered *for* the church but the latter *by* the church; the former in the hands of the priest; the latter by the hands of kings and soldiers, but at the will and sufferance of the priest. . . . However, one sword ought to be subordinated to the other and temporal authority, subjected to spiritual power.[99]

The year after issuing *Unam sanctum*, Boniface wrote a bull of excommunication against Philip. Before this document was issued, a group of Italian soldiers allied with Philip broke into Boniface's residence and beat him. They were trying to intimidate Boniface so that would resign, but not long after the beating, Boniface died.[100]

Philip then engineered the election of Pope Clement V, who was more sympathetic to France. Indeed, Clement's reliance on France, together with political instability in Italy, caused Clement to move the papal residence to Avignon in southern France.[101] This inaugurated a

96. See Colin Morris, "The Conflict Renewed: The Question of Investiture (1099–1222)," in *Papal Monarchy*.

97. Irvin and Sunquist, *History of the World Christian Movement*, 1:480.

98. Irvin and Sunquist, *History of the World Christian Movement*, 1:480.

99. His Holiness Pope Boniface VIII, *Unam sanctam*, November 18, 1302, trans. Bob Van Cleef, https://tinyurl.com/y38jncrl.

100. Irvin and Sunquist, *History of the World Christian Movement*, 1:481.

101. Irvin and Sunquist, *History of the World Christian Movement*, 1:481. For further discussion see John W. O'Malley, *A History of the Popes: From Peter to the Present* (Lanham, MD: Sheed & Ward, 2010), chaps 14–15.

sixty-seven-year period called the "Avignon Papacy," also sometimes called the "Babylonian Captivity of the Papacy," during which seven successive French popes resided in Avignon. At the conclusion of this period, in 1377, after encouragement from the mystic Catherine of Siena, Pope Gregory XI returned the papacy to Rome.[102]

Gregory died a year after his return to Rome. The next elected pope, Urban VI, immediately attempted to reform abuses in the curia, which offended the cardinals, who began to claim the election of Urban VI was invalid. They elected a new pope, Clement VII, while Urban elevated different bishops to cardinal, creating his own college of cardinals. France backed Clement VII, while England and Germany backed Urban VI, and other rulers in Spain and Italy vacillated.[103]

Debate over the divided papacy continued for more than twenty-five years, when in 1408, cardinals from both sides called for a council to resolve the dispute. Most of Europe's political leaders agreed with this plan, so the Council of Pisa was convened, and Pope Alexander V was elected. Urban VI and Clement VII, however, both retained substantial support, and both rejected Alexander's claim to the crown. At this point, there were three competing popes.[104]

When Alexander V died, the cardinals who supported him elected his successor, John XXIII, who moved his papal court to Germany. German king Sigismund persuaded John to call a general council, which met from 1414 to 1418 in Constance on Lake Geneva. At the end of the Council of Constance, all three of the existing popes were deposed, and a new pope, Martin V, was elected, ending the schism.[105]

The genesis of the papal schism in Pope Boniface VIII's dispute with King Philip IV over the relationship between temporal and spiritual power was one axis of a broader question of political theology. The other axis was the relationship between the pope and a general council. In 1054, the Eastern church, led from Constantinople, broke from the Western church, led from Rome, an event called the Great Schism. One of the underlying issues in the Great Schism was the authority of the Bishop of Rome in relation to the decisions of a general council. Although the Western church asserted papal supremacy over councils, some in the Western church were moving toward something like the Eastern position, particularly in light of the Western church's recent history of competing papal claims.[106] This movement of "conciliarism"

---

102. Irvin and Sunquist, *History of the World Christian Movement*, 1:482.
103. Irvin and Sunquist, *History of the World Christian Movement*, 1:483.
104. Irvin and Sunquist, *History of the World Christian Movement*, 1:483.
105. Irvin and Sunquist, *History of the World Christian Movement*, 1:483.
106. Irvin and Sunquist, *History of the World Christian Movement*, 1:483.

began to intersect with even more radical claims of early Reformers such as John Wycliffe and John Huss.[107]

THE MEDIEVAL ARISTOTELIAN SYNTHESIS: AQUINAS

Before arriving at the Reformation, however, we will make one final stop on this brief tour of patristic and classical Christian concepts of law to discuss one of the most important figures for "natural law" theorists: Thomas Aquinas. Aquinas and the later medieval scholastics attempted to forge a concept of social order that combined the newly rediscovered teleological ideas of Aristotle with classical Christian thought.[108]

Aquinas devoted a portion of his pedagogical treatise *Summa theologiae* to a "Treatise on Law," demonstrating how important the concept of law had become to Western Christian society. Aquinas most fully developed the link between "law" to the capacity for reason. He identified four kinds of law: eternal, divine, natural, and human.[109] As these four kinds of law suggest, law, for Thomas, was a means by which God instructs rational human creatures.[110] Thomas defined "law" as "a rule and measure of acts, whereby man is induced to act or restrained from acting."[111] The essential rule and measure for human action—the "law" of human action—for Thomas, was reason, "since it belongs to the reason to direct to the end, which is the first principle in all matters of action."[112]

At times, Thomas sounds like a modern positivist. Thomas agreed that positive law generally is unnecessary for virtuous people who seek to follow the light of reason, but that the bad person requires further dis-

---

107. Irvin and Sunquist, *History of the World Christian Movement*, 1:489–91.

108. See Denys Turner, *Thomas Aquinas: A Portrait* (New Haven: Yale University Press, 2014).

109. Aquinas, *Summa theologiae* I-II, 91, "On the Essence of Law" (hereafter *ST*), trans. Fathers of the English Dominican Province (1920), available at newadvent.org/summa/.

110. *ST* I-II, 90. Thomas contrasts "Law" to "Grace" in that "Law" is God's means of instruction and "Grace" is God's means of assistance. But in Thomas's system, "Law" and "Grace" are not antithetical concepts as they are in some Lutheran and Reformed theologies. Rather, for Thomas, "Law" and "Grace" are like two sides of the same coin. The literature on Aquinas and natural law theory is vast. For some good sources see Matthew Levering, *Biblical Natural Law: A Theocentric and Teleological Approach* (Oxford: Oxford University Press, 2012); Jean Porter, *Natural and Divine Law: Reclaiming the Tradition for Christian Ethics* (Grand Rapids: Eerdmans, 1999); Jean Porter, *Nature as Reason: A Thomistic Theory of the Natural Law* (Grand Rapids: Eerdmans, 2004); Russell Hittinger, *The First Grace: Rediscovering the Natural Law in a Post-Christian World* (Wilmington, DE: ISI, 2002); Paul E. Sigmund, "Law and Politics," in *The Cambridge Companion to Aquinas*, ed. Norman Kretzmann and Eleonore Stump (Cambridge: Cambridge University Press, 1993).

111. *ST* I-II, 90, art. 1.

112. *ST* I-II, 90, art. 1. Thomas here cites "the Philosopher," Aristotle.

cipline: "Men who are ill disposed are led willingly to virtue by being admonished better than by coercion; but men who are evilly disposed are not led to virtue unless they are compelled."[113] Yet Thomas clearly tied law to a transcendent end, which is embodied in statutes that are broadly applicable to the entire community.[114]

For Thomas, then, all true "law" was a participatory relation. "Law," he said, "is in all those things that are inclined to something by reason of some law: so that any inclination arising from a law, may be called a law, not essentially but by participation as it were."[115] This is true not only of the "natural law" that is built into the creation but also of positive law enacted at the command of a human sovereign. Thomas argued, "In order that the volition of what is commanded may have the nature of law, it needs to be in accord with some rule of reason. And in this sense is to be understood the saying that the will of the sovereign has the force of law; otherwise the sovereign's will would savour of lawlessness rather than of law."[116] The rule of reason, Thomas insisted, demonstrates that good or just laws must be directed toward the proper end of reason: the "common good," which is "universal happiness."[117] A putative law that is not directed toward the common good is "devoid of the nature of a law."[118]

The "common good" in the broadest sense—"the whole community of the universe"—in Thomas's thought, was governed by God.[119] Although God promulgates particular laws, "the end of the Divine government is God Himself, and His law is not distinct from Himself."[120] Moreover, all created things "partake somewhat of the eternal law," which is "imprinted on them" and which provides them with "their respective inclinations to their proper acts and ends."[121] Thomas noted that "even irrational animals partake in their own way of the Eternal Reason," but that only rational creatures participate in the Eternal Reason "in an intellectual and rational manner."[122] Therefore, Thomas said, "the participation of the eternal law in the rational creature is properly called a law,

113. *ST* I-II, 95, art. 1, ad 1.
114. See *ST* I-II, 95, art. 1, ad 2 (explaining why law governed by statute is superior to law enacted only by judges).
115. *ST* I-II, 90, art. 1, ad 1.
116. *ST* I-II, 90, art. 1, ad 2.
117. *ST* I-II, 90, art. 2. Here Thomas cites Aristotle's *Nichomachean Ethics*.
118. *ST* I-II, 90, art. 2.
119. *ST* I-II, 91, art. 1.
120. *ST* I-II, 91, art. 1, ad 3.
121. *ST* I-II, 91, art. 2.
122. *ST* I-II, 91, art. 2, ad 3.

since a law is something pertaining to reason."[123] Human law participates in divine law, in the life of God himself, to the extent that human practical reason concerning specific cases comports with speculative reason concerning the natural law imprinted on us as creatures.[124] The construction of positive law is a form of participation in God whereby the general principles of eternal law are applied to contingent cases through the exercise of practical reason.[125]

THE MAGISTERIAL REFORMERS: MARTIN LUTHER AND JOHN CALVIN

The roots of the Protestant Reformation are historically deep and complex.[126] Those roots included the history of conflicts between the temporal and spiritual power.

On January 9, 1520, Martin Luther was denounced by Pope Leo X in an edict titled *Exsurge Domine*.[127] Later that year, Luther wrote four extended pamphlets, *Treatise on Good Works*, *Address to the Christian Nobility of the German Nation Concerning the Improvement of the Christian Estate*, *The Babylonian Captivity of the Church*, and *The Freedom of a Christian*, as well as a refutation of papal authority titled *The Papacy at Rome*.[128]

In the *Treatise on Good Works*, Luther argued that a simple piety flows naturally from faith, in contrast to what he viewed as the overly elaborate and hypocritical piety of the Catholic religious leaders. The touchstone of this piety is the Ten Commandments, which Luther believed contained all the necessary principles for a moral life. In his discussion of the fifth commandment—"obey your father and mother"—Luther encompassed respect for the authorities within a household as well as for the church and the civil authorities. But Luther, with support from civil authorities, was disobeying the church and refusing the requirement in *Exsurge Domine* that he recant his allegedly heretical views. How did he square this with his discussion of the fifth commandment of respect for the church?

He did so by arguing that the obligation to obey church authorities

---

123. *ST* I-II, 91, art. 2, ad 3.

124. *ST* I-II, 91, art. 3, ad 1–3.

125. *ST* I-II, 91, art. 3, ad 3.

126. See, e.g., Diarmaid MacCulloch, *The Reformation* (New York: Penguin, 2004).

127. See Timothy J. Wengert, ed., *The Annotated Luther, Vol. 1: The Roots of Reform* (Minneapolis: Fortress, 2015), 261.

128. Wengert, ed., *Annotated Luther*, 257, 261.

applied only if they do not contradict the first three commandments against idolatry, taking God's name in vain, and requiring that the Sabbath be kept holy.[129] Here he contrasted disobedience to an unjust civil authority with disobedience to unjust church authorities.[130]

Civil authorities should always be obeyed even if they are unjust, Luther said, because they "cannot hurt the soul but only the body and what we possess."[131] Civil authority "is a small matter" to God "and is regarded by him as far too insignificant for a person—solely because of it (whether it acts justly or unjustly)—to oppose, disobey, or quarrel with it."[132] In contrast, spiritual authority "is a great, overflowing good and is regarded by God as much too precious, for even the humblest Christian to suffer in silence when it deviates from its own office by even a hair's breadth, not to mention when it completely violates its office as we observe almost every day."[133] If the spiritual authorities continue to fail in their responsibilities, Luther suggested, "the best and indeed the only remaining remedy would be for kings, princes, the nobility, cities, and communities to take the first step" in reforming Christendom.[134]

Luther expanded his discussion of the distinction in his *Address to the Christian Nobility*. In that text Luther said the "Romanists" hid from reform behind "three walls" of supposed papal authority: (1) that spiritual authority is above temporal authority and not subject to temporal jurisdiction; (2) that the pope alone can interpret the Scriptures; and (3) that only the pope can summon a council.[135] In response to this first "wall," Luther argued, "it is not proper for the pope to exalt himself above the secular authorities, except in spiritual offices such as preaching and giving absolution. In other matters, the pope is subject to the crown."[136] He was particularly concerned by *compositiones*, fees paid to the church under canon law through which people could buy dispensations from the ordinary rules of church life:

Here vows are dissolved; monks are granted freedom to leave their orders. Here marriage is on sale to the clergy. Here the children of whores can be legitimized. Here all dishonor and shame can be made to look like honor and glory. Here every kind of fault and blemish is knighted and ennobled. Here marriage with the forbidden degrees or otherwise forbidden is ren-

---

129. Wengert, ed., *Annotated Luther*, 337.
130. Wengert, ed., *Annotated Luther*, 342–47.
131. Wengert, ed., *Annotated Luther*, 343.
132. Wengert, ed., *Annotated Luther*, 343.
133. Wengert, ed., *Annotated Luther*, 343–44.
134. Wengert, ed., *Annotated Luther*, 342.
135. Wengert, ed., *Annotated Luther*, 371.
136. Wengert, ed., *Annotated Luther*, 415.

dered acceptable. O what assessing and fleecing take place there! It seems as though canon law were instituted solely for the purpose of setting a great many money traps from which anyone who wants to be a Christian must purchase his freedom.[137]

Luther's attack on canon law was consistent with his theology of salvation, which sharply distinguished "law" and "gospel." For Lutheran theology, in soteriological terms, "law" only condemns, while "gospel" announces the word of consolation.[138] Nevertheless, as the Lutheran 1577 Formula of Concord also noted, the law has three uses: to curb the sinful natures of both Christians and non-Christians; to mirror the purposes of God in creation; and to guide Christians toward living a more fruitful and joyful life.[139]

Therefore, although Luther's theology and later Lutheran theology clearly distinguished "law" and "gospel," Luther affirmed that the moral law and the temporal positive law continue to play important roles in history.[140] As we will see in the next section on the radical Reformers, others took Luther's views to suggest that the poor should rise up and break down the oppressive social order. In response, in one of his not-infrequent inflammatory moods, Luther wrote the pamphlet "Against the Robbing and Murdering Hordes of Peasants."[141] Luther thundered that

> I will not oppose a ruler who, even though he does not tolerate the Gospel, will smite and punish these peasants without offering to submit the case to judgement. For he is within his rights, since the peasants are not contending any longer for the Gospel, but have become faithless, perjured, disobedient, rebellious murderers, robbers and blasphemers, whom even heathen rulers have the right and power to punish; nay, it is their duty to punish them, for it is just for this purpose that they bear the sword, and are "the ministers of God upon him that doeth evil."[142]

The theology of the other great magisterial Reformer John Calvin differed from Luther's in many ways, but regarding the moral law, Calvin agreed with Luther that while the law does not save, it has the three uses

137. Wengert, ed., *Annotated Luther*, 405.

138. See The Book of Concord, art. 5.

139. The Book of Concord, art. 6.

140. For a good discussion of the nuances of Luther's thought on this question, see Lisa Sowle Cahill, *Blessed Are the Peacemakers: Pacifism, Just War, and Peacebuilding* (Minneapolis: Fortress Press, 2019), 183–90.

141. Martin Luther, "Against the Murderous, Thieving Hordes of Peasants," in *Martin Luther: Documents of Modern History*, ed. E. G. Rupp and Benjamin Drewery (London: Edward Arnold, 1970), 121–26.

142. Luther, "Against the Murderous, Thieving Hordes of Peasants," 121–26.

of a mirror (primarily of our sinfulness), a curb on sinners, and a guide for the elect.[143] Calvin also connected his understanding of the moral law to the role of the civil government. Calvin was concerned that "on the one hand, frantic and barbarous men are furiously endeavouring to over-turn the order established by God, and, on the other, the flatterers and princes, extolling their power without measure, hesitate not to oppose it to the government of God."[144] He argued that while the civil gov-ernment is temporary and imperfect, it plays an important role in God's providential work in history, including "to foster and maintain the exter-nal worship of God, to defend sound doctrine and the condition of the church, to adapt our conduct to human society, to form our manners to civil justice, to conciliate us to each other, [and] to cherish common peace and tranquility."[145]

Calvin's understanding of the temporal magistrate's authority might have been more extensive than Luther's because Calvin (who also studied law) thought the magistrate should enforce both tables of the law—that is, all of the Ten Commandments concerning worship and civil gover-nance—and that some form of law and political rule would characterize even humanity living within the kingdom of God.[146] Further, Calvin was personally involved in reforming the relationship between the civil and religious authority in the city of Geneva, which became deeply intertwined.[147] Calvin even infamously supported the execution of Michael Servetus, an accused heretic who was burned on a pile of his own books in 1553, though Calvin argued Servetus should be beheaded instead of burned. Nevertheless, even though he understood the tempo-ral and spiritual authority as perhaps more intertwined than did Luther, and even though he invested more weight in the temporal law than Luther, he still held the Augustinian view that there are two societies at work in history, one civil and one spiritual.[148]

RADICAL REFORMERS

Luther and Calvin each adopted some version of the traditional division between the temporal and spiritual powers and affirmed the authority of temporal rulers within their proper sphere. They are called the

143. John Calvin, *Institutes of the Christian Religion*, trans. Henry Beveridge (Edinburgh: The Calvin Translation Society, 1845), book 4.
144. Calvin, *Institutes* 4.20.
145. Calvin, *Institutes* 4.20.
146. Cahill, *Blessed Are the Peacemakers*, 202–6.
147. Cahill, *Blessed Are the Peacemakers*, 205–6.
148. Cahill, *Blessed Are the Peacemakers*, 203.

"magisterial" Reformers because they recognized a proper role for the temporal magistrate in relationship to the church. The radical reformers took the concepts of conscience and dissent further and began to argue that the church must exist apart from the temporal power. These radical reformers were the "frantic and barbarous men" whom Calvin believed were "furiously endeavouring to overturn the [civil] order established by God."[149]

A key point of tension here was the nature of baptism and its connection to a Christian citizen's political identity in the temporal commonwealth. Both Luther and Calvin advocated infant baptism within a state-sanctioned church. The baptized person was thus presumptively both a member of the church and a citizen of the Christian commonwealth in which the church was located. The commonwealth was still only a temporal power, with a limited function and jurisdiction, particularly in relation to the spiritual power of the church, but nevertheless membership in both the society of the church and of the state were linked by baptism of infants born into the community. This was also true, of course, in the Catholic jurisdictions. The radical Reformers began to challenge this arrangement by suggesting that baptism is only valid for adults who can make a conscious profession of faith. Some of the radical reformers began rebaptizing people who had been baptized as infants, earning the designation "*ana*baptists."

Rebaptism was a capital offense in the Catholic, Calvinist, and Lutheran territories alike.[150] In January of 1527, for example, the city council of Zurich executed Anabaptist leader Felix Manz by drowning, with support from the Reformer Ulrich Zwingli.[151] Zwingli himself was more radical in his views about the Eucharist than Luther and had engaged with Luther in bitter debate about that issue.

Some Anabaptist groups sought to withdraw from the temporal society altogether in order to form their own self-contained communities. One of these groups was the Hutterites, followers of a former milliner named Jakob Hutter. Seeking to follow the model of the early church in the book of Acts, the Hutterites were pacifists who taught that private property ownership was a sin and who shared all their property in common. Initially the Hutterites found a refuge, along with other Anabaptist groups in Moravia, where the local nobility had a history of supporting dissenters from the established church. When the leadership in Moravia

---

149. Calvin, *Institutes* 4.2.

150. See Dale T. Irvin and Scott W. Sunquist, *History of the World Christian Movement, Vol. 2: Modern Christianity from 1454–1800* (Maryknoll, NY: Orbis, 2012), 98.

151. Irvin and Sunquist, *History of the World Christian Movement*, 2:90.

changed, however, Hutter was tortured and burned at the stake, and his wife also eventually was executed.[152]

Not all the Anabaptists were pacifists. In fact, the massive energy unleashed by both the magisterial and radical reformations soon exploded into political and armed revolt. The German peasants' revolt, led by Thomas Müntzer, was spurred by Müntzer's apocalyptic vision that the world was about to end. It was brutally suppressed by the German princes, with support from Luther, and resulted in tens of thousands of deaths and Müntzer's execution in 1525.[153]

Another Anabaptist rebellion inspired by an apocalyptic vision took root in the city of Münster in 1534.[154] A farrier named Melchior Hoffman led a network of underground churches starting in Strasbourg. Hoffman believed the Holy Spirit was pouring out charismatic gifts on himself and his people in anticipation of the imminent end of history. When Hoffman was arrested and jailed, a baker from Amsterdam named Jan Matthijs became the leader of these communities. Matthijs believed he had received prophecies that the city of Münster would become the New Jerusalem at the heart of Christ's millennial kingdom. He left his wife for a woman named Divara van Haarlem and decamped to Münster. Matthijs won control of the city council, instituted a program of rebaptism in the churches, and enacted laws consistent with his political vision, including declaring that all property would be held in common. Citizens of Münster who dissented were exiled or executed.[155]

The Roman Catholic bishop of Münster worked with the prince to raise an army, which besieged the city. Matthijs encouraged his followers with the belief that Christ would return on Easter Sunday of that year. When Christ did not show up, Matthijs tried to break the siege and was killed. A tailor named Jan van Leiden then assumed leadership of the community, married Divara von Haarlem, declared that polygamy was God's will, married fifteen more women, and was proclaimed as a new King David, with Divara as his queen. The besieging army, however, entered the city in June of 1535. The city's entire remaining population was executed, except for the community's leaders, who were led around the country on a torture tour for over a year before being killed.[156]

Anabaptist communities elsewhere in Europe did not condone the excesses of the Münster rebellion but remained resolute in their

152. Irvin and Sunquist, *History of the World Christian Movement*, 2:97.
153. Irvin and Sunquist, *History of the World Christian Movement*, 2:94.
154. See Anthony Arthur, *The Tailor-King: The Rise and Fall of the Anabaptist Kingdom of Münster* (New York: St. Martin's, 1999).
155. Irvin and Sunquist, *History of the World Christian Movement*, 2:97.
156. Irvin and Sunquist, *History of the World Christian Movement*, 2:97–98.

convictions about adult baptism. A former Catholic priest named Menno Simons organized a new network of underground Anabaptist churches, which soon were called "Mennonite." Mennonites and other Anabaptist groups continued to be persecuted in Catholic, Calvinist, and Lutheran territories alike. Much of their piety came to embody the sense that they were the true form of the church, enduring suffering as Christ himself had suffered.[157]

CONCLUSION

This survey of some important figures in the history of Christian thought about law suggests some common themes and differences. Drawing from Scripture, history, and their contemporary experiences, all of these thinkers were concerned about the following themes:

- *Creation and natural law.* Is there a natural or moral law built into creation, and can human beings understand it?

- *History and eschatology.* Is there an overarching purpose to history, and can human beings discern it? What is the meaning of the present moment in history in relation to its purpose?

- *Temporal and spiritual power.* What is the relationship of the church to the temporal ruling authorities? When must Christians obey the ruling authorities, and when is dissent proper?

- *Civil society.* What is the nature of a good society? Is a good society possible at all in this world? Does a ruler have any obligation to seek the consent of the governed?

- *Positive law and its limits.* How does positive law relate to natural law? What can Christians expect the positive law to accomplish? Should Christians be involved in the formation and administration of the positive law?

Differences in historical circumstances and philosophical and theological presuppositions produced sometimes significantly different answers to these questions. The same questions and the similar kinds of answers remain with us today. In the next chapter, I offer some thoughts toward a constructive theology of law after modernity.

---

157. Irvin and Sunquist, *History of the World Christian Movement*, 2:98–99.

3.

A Constructive Theology of Law after Modernity

INTRODUCTION

The history of law and theology in chapter 2 ends at the Reformation in Western Europe. Political, religious, economic, and other differences in Western Europe led to what are popularly called the "wars of religion," including the Thirty Years' War. While some scholars question the extent to which this violent period was motivated by religious and theological differences, there is no doubt that it left deep wounds on the Western consciousness.[1] The Thirty Years' war may have claimed 15 to 20 percent of Europe's population, making it perhaps more destructive in terms of percentage of casualties than World War I or II.[2]

The war was concluded by the "Westphalian Settlement," which conventionally marks the beginning of the modern concept of sovereign nation-states bound by treaties and customary international law.[3] The Christian jurist Hugo Grotius (1583–1646) provided much of the intellectual heft behind the natural law theory of just war and international law for the Westphalian Settlement.[4]

1. See, e.g., William T. Cavanaugh, *The Myth of Religious Violence: Secular Ideology and the Roots of Modern Conflict* (Oxford: Oxford University Press, 2009).

2. Peter H. Wilson, *Europe's Tragedy: A New History of the Thirty Years War* (New York: Penguin, 2009).

3. See Wilson, *Europe's Tragedy*, chap. 21.

4. Oliver O'Donovan and Joan Lockwood O'Donovan, "Hugo Grotius," in *From Irenaeus to Grotius: A Sourcebook in Christian Political Thought* (Grand Rapids: Eerdmans, 1999), 787; Stanford Encyclopedia of Philosophy, "Hugo Grotius," July 28, 2011, https://tinyurl.com/y6zknk3n.

Grotius and the Westphalian Settlement stand at a historical divide. Some of Grotius's views augured modern ideas about law and authority, particularly in his statement that natural law would exist even without God.[5] Soon Western legal theory would begin to lose both the concepts of God and of natural law as sources of legal legitimacy. As Oliver and Joan Lockwood O'Donovan have noted, "Something dramatically new came to pass in the mid-seventeenth century, something of which [Thomas] Hobbes is a symbol, and which, for all its undeniable antecedents, marks a decisive break between the theological and rationalist traditions."[6] As the O'Donovans suggest, "Grotius, for all his embrace of the program of humanist science, was a true heir of the theological tradition; Hobbes, for all his wealth of theological opinion, broke with the structure of Christian political thought."[7]

Now, in our modern (or postmodern/hypermodern), post-Christian context, the church has lost its institutional authority in the governance of society, at least in the West. This could, ironically, be a good thing, or at least not as bad a thing, because it helps clarify the church's authentic mission in distinction from the temporal state—that is, it reverses the momentum of the Constantinian shift. But secularism also means that it has become difficult to articulate a distinctly Christian theology of law.[8]

LAW, DIVINE FREEDOM, AND POWER

The brief survey in chapters 1 and 2 of biblical and classical Christian sources shows that, in the Christian tradition, humanity is *homo juridicus*.[9] We are creatures of law. As legal historian Harold Berman notes in

5. See Michael P. Zuckert, "Natural Law without God? Considering Russell Hittinger's *The First Grace*," Jacques Maritain Center, https://tinyurl.com/y3d9mqhn.

6. O'Donovan and Lockwood O'Donovan, *From Irenaeus to Grotius*, 787.

7. O'Donovan and Lockwood O'Donovan, *From Irenaeus to Grotius*, 787.

8. For a good discussion of secularism, see Charles Taylor, *A Secular Age* (Cambridge: Harvard University Press, 2007).

9. In recent years, following on the formative work of Harold Berman, there has been an outpouring of scholarship on historical and contemporary Christian perspectives on the nature and purposes of positive law, which demonstrates, through diverse strands of the Christian tradition, similar themes to the survey of classical sources I outline in this chapter. See, e.g., Harold Berman, *Law and Revolution: The Formation of the Western Legal Tradition* (Cambridge, MA: Harvard University Press, 1983); Harold Berman, *Law and Revolution II: The Impact of the Protestant Reformations on the Western Legal Tradition* (Cambridge, MA: Belknap, 2006); Michael W. McConnell, Robert F. Cochran Jr., and Angela C. Carmella, eds., *Christian Perspectives on Legal Thought* (New Haven: Yale University Press, 2001); John Witte Jr., *God's Joust, God's Justice: Law and Religion in the Western Tradition* (Atlanta: Emory University Press, 2006); O'Donovan and Lockwood O'Donovan, *From Irenaeus to Grotius*; John Witte Jr. and Frank S. Alexander, eds., *The Teachings of Modern Christianity on Law, Politics and Human Nature*

his magisterial study *Law and Revolution*, early European Christian law was a means of reconciliation.[10] Law, he says, "was conceived primarily as a mediating process, a mode of communication, rather than primarily as a process of rulemaking and decision making. . . . Christianity treated even a king as a human being, subject like every other human being to punishment by God for his sins and only able to be saved by God's grace."[11] In contrast, the familiar refrain of the book of Judges highlights what happens when law's legitimacy is eroded: "In those days Israel had no king; everyone did as he saw fit" (Judg 21:25). Modern people are inclined to affirm this as good, but as the story of the Levite and his concubine in Judges 19 makes clear, the fruits of this circumstance are betrayal, rape, oppression, and violence.[12] The biblical witness and the classical Christian tradition affirm that law matters to the *missio Dei*.

In contrast to the biblical and classical sources, most modern legal philosophers look to legitimize law in sources other than God. These sources might include, for example, a consequentialist weighing of costs and benefits, a deontological rule extending to others the same rights one wants for one's self, or a social contract embodying broad public consent.[13] A few brash leaders have suggested that law is really only about power: as Chairman Mao quipped, "Political power begins at the end of the barrel of a gun."[14]

For Christian theology, all of these sources, except perhaps for raw power as such, can support law, but none of them supplies an adequate final source of law. Christian theology traditionally has conceived of a

(New York: Columbia University Press, 2006); John Witte Jr. and Frank S. Alexander, eds., *The Teachings of Modern Roman Catholicism on Law, Politics, and Human Nature* (New York: Columbia University Press, 2007); John Witte Jr. and Frank S. Alexander, eds., *The Teachings of Modern Orthodox Christianity on Law, Politics and Human Nature* (New York: Columbia University Press, 2007); John Witte Jr., *The Reformation of Rights: Law, Religion, and Human Rights in Early Modern Calvinism* (Cambridge: Cambridge University Press, 2008); John Witte Jr. and Frank S. Alexander, *Christianity and Law: An Introduction* (Cambridge: Cambridge University Press, 2008); Robert F. Cochran Jr. and David Van Drunen, eds., *Law and the Bible: Justice, Mercy and Legal Institutions* (Downers Grove, IL: IVP Academic, 2013).

10. Berman, *Law and Revolution*, 49–50.

11. Berman, *Law and Revolution*, 49–50.

12. See Stephen R. L. Clark, *Biology and Christian Ethics* (Cambridge: Cambridge University Press, 2000), 183–84.

13. For a good survey, see Isaak Dore, *The Epistemological Foundations of Law* (Durham: Carolina Academic Press, 2007).

14. "Problems of War and Strategy," in *Selected Works*, vol. 2, November 6, 1938, 224, https://tinyurl.com/y2tx5jdd. In this text, Mao argued that a proletariat revolution could not occur in China without an armed struggle against Japanese imperialism. He further noted that "our principle is that the Party commands the gun, and the gun must never be allowed to command the party." Thus, interestingly, even Mao recognized that violence cannot comprise the fundamental principle of society.

relation between God's being, the natural law, the laws of divine commands, and positive law. For Christian theology, then, positive law first derives its legitimacy from God's being.

There are some important and contested theological concepts to unpack in this claim. First is the relationship between God's being and God's will, and second is how the doctrine of creation follows from how we conceive of this relationship. What comes first, God's being, or God's will? Does God will as he is, or is God as he wills?

Some theologians and historians have argued that subtle but significant shifts occurred on this question starting in the late medieval/scholastic period. In the patristic and early medieval/scholastic period, these writers suggest, Christian theology said God's being precedes his will. In the later scholastic period, Christian theology moved toward "voluntarism," the notion that God's will precedes his being. The result, these theologians and historians argue, is that God began to seem more like an arbitrary, capricious, even sometimes monstrous force of sheer will, rather than the loving and gracious creator and sustainer of life. This trend, they suggest, intensified in some aspects of the Protestant Reformation, particularly in the thought of Martin Luther and John Calvin, and also influenced the neo-scholasticism of the Catholic Counter-Reformation. The fallout of the Reformation and Counter-Reformation, in turn, seeded modern political theory, with its focus on utilitarian calculations, deontological rules, social contracts, or raw power divorced from any metaphysically ultimate source of goodness.[15]

The historical outlines of this claim are hotly contested by other theologians and historians.[16] They suggest the later Catholic scholastics and the Protestant Reformers also emphasized God's being and were not merely stark voluntarists. Instead, these thinkers were trying to extricate God's divine freedom from the Aristotelian and Platonic straitjackets. Christian theology traditionally has asserted not only that God is the loving and gracious creator and sustainer of life but also that God is absolutely free, unconstrained by any higher power or principle. If God's

15. See, e.g., John Milbank, *Theology and Social Theory: Beyond Secular Reason*, 2nd ed. (London: Wiley-Blackwell, 2006); Michael Allen Gillespie, *The Theological Origins of Modernity* (Chicago: University of Chicago Press, 2008); Brad S. Gregory, *The Unintended Reformation: How a Religious Revolution Secularized Society* (Cambridge, MA: Harvard University Press, 2012).

16. See, e.g., John Hare, "Scotus on Morality and Nature," *Medieval Philosophy and Theology* 9 (2000): 15; "Editor's Introduction: John Duns Scotus and Modern Theology," *Modern Theology* 21 (2005): 539; Olivier Boulnois, "Reading Duns Scotus from History to Philosophy," *Modern Theology* 21 (2005): 603; Thomas Williams, "The Doctrine of Univocity Is True and Salutary," *Modern Theology* 21 (2005): 575; Nelson H. Minnich et al., "Forum Essay on *The Unintended Reformation*," *The Catholic Historical Review* 98 (2012): 503, 508–9.

being is described as a kind of abstract principle of "goodness" or "love," then God no longer seems free to act.

So is God's will constrained by "love"? Or, if not, is God's will merely arbitrary? Is "love" just a word without any real meaning, a kind of placeholder for the barrel of Mao's gun on a cosmic scale?[17] The dilemma raised here has deep roots in the Western philosophical tradition. It's referred to as the "Euthyphro dilemma" because a version of the question is found in a dialogue by Plato titled *Euthyphro*.[18] In Plato's typical fashion, the dialogue pictures Socrates pressing the limits of a problem by asking questions of an interlocutor, in this case Euthyphro. The key issue Socrates raises is "whether the pious or holy is beloved by the gods because it is holy, or holy because it is beloved of the gods."[19] The issue can be rephrased to ask whether (a) God wills or commands something because it is good, or (b) whether a thing is good because God wills or commands it.[20] If (a) is true, then it seems there is a "good" that is higher than God, which constrains God's freedom, and to which God's will or commands must conform. If (b) is true, then it seems God could will or command anything at all—murder, rape, the torture of babies—and call it "good," so that "good" doesn't have any real meaning. Is God "good," or is God "free"?

The best answer to this question—and the Euthyphro dilemma—for Christian theology is "yes." God is both "good" and "free." Whatever God commands or wills is truly, substantively, metaphysically "good," but God is not constrained to will or command, or not will or command, anything. "The good" does not exist in some way above or prior to God: God *is* the good, the transcendent ground of all being. This means, among other things, that "the good" is not an abstract, intellectual, impersonal principle. "The good," ultimately, is the Triune God, in his eternal relations within himself.

The discussion of biblical and historical Christian concepts of law in chapters 1 and 2 connected natural law with creation. This means natural law is *contingent* but not *arbitrary*. Creation is *contingent* because nothing required God to create this particular creation or to create at all.[21] We can imagine different kinds of plausible worlds, which means God exercised

---

17. This raises a concept that often is related to voluntarism: "nominalism." For further discussion of these questions, see David Bentley Hart, *The Experience of God: Being, Consciousness, Bliss* (New Haven: Yale University Press, 2013).

18. Plato, *Euthyphro*, https://tinyurl.com/5cyk58.

19. Plato, *Euthyphro*, https://tinyurl.com/5cyk58.

20. See Internet Encyclopedia of Philosophy, "Divine Command Theory," sec. 3, https://tinyurl.com/y4cvxj96.

21. For good discussions of these themes, see David Fergusson, *Creation* (Grand Rapids: Eerdmans, 2014) and Simon Oliver, *Creation: A Guide for the Perplexed* (London: T&T Clark, 2017).

some choice in creating this particular world. Moreover, God is complete in himself and did not need to choose to create at all. Absent creation, God's love and fellowship within his own Triune being would not diminish in any way. This means creation is utterly gratuitous. Creation is a gift God freely gives to created things. At the same time, creation is not *arbitrary* because it is God's gift and therefore flows from God's love. Creation's founding principle is love, not arbitrary power.[22] This means that the governing principles of creaturely existence, the natural law, could possibly have been different, but could never have been other than loving, good, and just. Since God is fully good, beautiful, loving, and just, he is not the author of evil. God's goodness, beauty, love, and justice must be "baked in" to creation itself. Creation itself *participates* in God's own goodness, beauty, love, and justice.

When we say creation "participates" in God's being in this way, of course, we must be careful to maintain the ontological distinction between God and creation. God is absolutely transcendent of creation. Creation is not part of God, nor is God part of creation. *Participate* is a word theologians have used to suggest that creation necessarily derives its being, including the characteristics of its being, from its source in God.

But if God is absolutely transcendent of creation, in what sense can we say creation participates in God's goodness, beauty, love, and justice? It is common to think of things like goodness, beauty, love, and justice, along with omnipotence, omniscience, and the like, as "attributes" of God. We might say, then, that God chose to create a universe containing things that also manifest those "attributes," even if to a lesser degree than does God himself.

There is something useful in this move, because it suggests the important theme of "gift." Nothing compelled or required God to create. God always was, is, and will be complete in himself. Creation was an act of love, a gift, a donation of God's goodness beyond himself. There is also something dangerous in this move, however, particularly for modern minds, because we tend to think of "attributes" as "things" that can be individually peeled off and separated from the person or item to which they are attached. We modern Western people are particularly prone to

22. This discussion of the contingency and order—or contingent order—of creation raises numerous interesting and thorny problems, including not least the problem of evil. If God could have chosen not to create, or created a different world, why did God create *this* world, with its excrescence of suffering and evil? Possible approaches to that problem are beyond the scope of this book. As my discussion above suggests, however, I do not find modern concepts that limit divine aseity, such as process theology, helpful. I also do not think theologies of creation rooted in divine glory are very helpful, unless we understand, as did the church fathers, that God's glory is always the vindication of God's love, not merely a display of God's power.

separate "essence" and "attributes" when we think about moral inclinations or sentiments.

Let's say Bob has always treated his business partners fairly. His negotiating style has been straightforward, he has never engaged in fraud, and if one of his suppliers or customers faced a problem with deliveries or payments, he tried his best to work with them toward a mutually acceptable solution before invoking his legal rights. We might say Bob is "fair" or "just." But let's also say midway through his career, Bob changed. He saw others growing rich through dishonesty, decided it was his turn to hit it big, and defrauded a major customer by siphoning hundreds of thousands of dollars from a contract into his personal bank account. We might say Bob is "dishonest," "greedy," or "unjust." We might even say Bob has become a "different person." But we would also say that the early-career Bob retains some kind of identity with the later-career Bob. When we say Bob has become a "different person," in common usage, we do not mean that literally.

I say "in common usage" here because this question of identity over time is philosophically very difficult and raises enormous metaphysical questions that have vexed philosophers and theologians for millennia. In his *Confessions*, for example, Augustine wrestled with this question within the framework of "memory." Reflecting on his life, Augustine realized he could not remember anything about what it was like to be an infant. He wondered how he, as an adult, could be the same person as the infant he once was if he had no memory at all of that prior phase of his life.[23] Augustine lived in a time before anything was known about cellular structure. He would have been equally perplexed by the fact that between infancy and adulthood a large portion of the body's cells have been entirely replaced.[24] Augustine, like most premodern Christian thinkers, dealt with the question of identity through the concept of the "soul." Today many philosophers reject any kind of dualism, including any concept of the "soul." Even with a notion of the "mind" or "soul" as an enduring component of human nature over time, we are left speaking of human beings as entities with "parts" or "attributes" that can change over time, sometimes dramatically so, and sometimes dramatically for the worse—indeed, ultimately, inevitably culminating in death and decay.

23. Augustine, *Confessions*, I.2-10 and X.
24. The common belief that all the cells in the human body are replaced every seven to ten years is not true. Certain tissues in the brain, the heart, and elsewhere are never replaced, and other tissues, such as certain kinds of fat cells, are replaced at such a slow rate that some remain throughout the body's lifespan. Nevertheless, the obvious phenomenon of the body's change over a lifespan reflects the death and replacement of billions upon billions of cells, certainly at least two-thirds of the body, over time. See Nicholas Wade, "Your Body Is Younger Than You Think," *New York Times*, August 2, 2005, http://tinyurl.com/y65lqdbv.

We cannot say such things about God, if God is really God. If goodness, beauty, love, and justice are just "attributes" of God, if God has "parts" that could be peeled off from his essential self, then God could cease to be good, beautiful, loving, or just but remain omnipotent and omniscient. What could be more horrifying than an omnipotent, omniscient, evil being? Such a being would not be, could not be, what Christian theology calls "God." For this reason, Christian theology traditionally has said God is "simple." God does not "have" parts. And since God does not have parts, He cannot and does not change. Unlike our hypothetical Bob the businessman, it is impossible that God might get fed up with things at some point in the future and decide to go back on his promises and defraud humanity. This is not only because God will continue to *will* the good, as though he were a stronger, better version of Bob. It is because God simply *is* good.

Further, unlike Bob, God's actions are not contingent in time. If Bob is good and just in the early part of his career, that does not mean he inevitably will be good and just in the later part of his career. For Bob, the future remains contingent. Circumstances might change. Bob might change. In traditional Christian thought, this is not the case for God. God is outside time and therefore does not change with or in time. This, again, is a question with which Augustine wrestled in his *Confessions*. Interestingly, Augustine connected this to his questions about "memory." If God is outside time, then God does not have "memory" because "the past" is not experienced by God as a flow of time like it is for us. For Augustine, this meant that God could see the unity of a human person, from birth through death, even though the human person, within time, could not fully understand his own unity. The answer to the human existential question, Augustine saw, was in the human relationship to God's transcendence.[25]

The classical notions of God's simplicity and aseity—unfortunately, in my view—are not widely accepted today even among Christian theologians. In fairness, these themes were developed in certain strands of the tradition in ways that made God seem uncaring or even irrelevant. This is particularly the case as we confront the problem of evil. If God is simple, outside of time, and unchanging, does that mean he is indifferent to the enormous suffering of history? Does it mean our prayers and laments are pointless? Or, if God's response to the problem of evil is the incarnation and the cross of Christ, doesn't that mean God really does exist within history and experience change? These are valid questions, of

25. Augustine, *Confessions*, X, XI; Rowan Williams, *On Augustine* (London: Bloomsbury, 2016), chap. 1.

course, but responding to them by limiting God's simplicity and aseity reflects a misunderstanding of those concepts as they were used by the best early Christian minds.[26]

I am emphasizing these theological themes here because I believe they connect directly to the question of natural law. The truth that God is good, just, and beautiful all at once, without change or remainder, means that there is a stable, universal source of the goodness, justice, and beauty in creation. The natural law does not change: it is the same everywhere, in every time, in all of creation because God himself does not change. Creation is a *gift*, a completely unnecessary act of God's grace, a product of the superabundance of God's love. Yet this donation of being, from God's being to the being of that which is not-God, is not constructed arbitrarily: it is good, indeed very good, because God, who gave it, is good. The "good" of creation cannot constrain God's freedom because God, who is other than creation, gave creation its being, constructed its goodness, and established its limits and purposes. Precisely because *this* God, the Triune God who *is* good, formed this creation, we know that the goodness of this creation has a reality beyond itself, and is not merely arbitrary.[27]

NATURAL LAW, VIOLENCE, AND EVIL

Christian theology says that within the persons of the Trinity, the Son proceeds from the Father, and the Spirit proceeds from the Father and the Son (or, in the Eastern tradition, the Spirit also proceeds from the Father). This notion of the "processions" of the Trinitarian persons is a way of speaking of God's active, dynamic presence. It is reflected in the *Logos*, the Son, who speaks creation into existence, and in the Spirit as the breath of the church beginning the new creation. At the same time, we speak of the "interpenetration" of the Triune persons: whatever is of the Father is of the Son and the Spirit, whatever is of the Son is of

26. For a good historical recover of patristic thought on this question, see Paul L. Gavrilyuk, *The Suffering of the Impassible God: The Dialectics of Patristic Thought* (Oxford: Oxford University Press, 2006). For a discussion of these issues in contemporary perspective, particularly as they relate to doctrines of Christology and creation, see Rowan Williams, *Christ the Heart of Creation* (London: Bloomsbury, 2018), particularly chap. 1.

27. For further discussion on these themes relating to natural law and a specific theological and narrative approach, see, e.g., Pamela M. Hall, *Narrative and the Natural Law: An Interpretation of Thomistic Ethics* (South Bend, IN: University of Notre Dame Press, 1984); Jean Porter, *Ministers of the Law: A Natural Law Theory of Legal Authority* (Grand Rapids: Eerdmans, 2010); Jean Porter, *Natural and Divine Law: Reclaiming the Tradition for Christian Ethics* (Grand Rapids: Eerdmans, 1999); Jean Porter, *Nature as Reason: A Thomistic Theory of the Natural Law* (Grand Rapids: Eerdmans, 2004).

the Father and the Spirit, whatever is of the Spirit is of the Father and Son—three persons (*prosopon*), one essence (*ousia*), one God.[28] The God who created the universe is a sending God, and creation itself is part of God's sending. The Trinitarian persons who are sent return and interpenetrate each other, and analogously the creation sent into existence by the divine Word returns to participate in God's own life.

Because creation is sent by God and participates in God's own life, everything in creation partakes in God's own goodness. Christian theology's way of stating this negatively is to say that God is not the author of evil. Another negative statement Christian theology has traditionally made here is that evil has no affirmative existence. Nothing exists other than God and God's creation. God does not create evil; therefore evil does not exist.

A statement like this should cause any reader to jump out of her chair as if stricken by an electric shock. Of course evil exists! Just look at history, turn on the news, look out the window, or look into your own heart! Examples of human suffering because of human pride, greed, lust, and hate stare us in the face continually. True. But we are using the word "exists" here in a somewhat technical fashion to refer to things that have their own being. God has his own being because he simply is. The things within creation—galaxies and stars, atomic elements, the manifold creatures of the Earth, humans—have their own being donated to them by God's gracious act of creation. The Christian doctrine of creation is clear that nothing else "exists." God is the only self-existing one; all else that exists is God's creation, within God's dominion.

This is why Christian theology traditionally spoke of evil as parasitic on the good, a deprivation or diminishment of the goodness of God's creation, not as a thing itself. We of course experience the painful effects of evil, including the terrible separation of death. But death itself is a deprivation, a cessation of life, the ending of an affirmative reality, not its own affirmative reality. And death cannot occur without life. The dissolution of death is entirely parasitic on the affirmative reality of life. God created life, not death. Life is creation; death is de-creation.[29]

---

28. This is the language of the Chalcedonian Definition.

29. This is not to suggest that no plants or animals died "before the fall" or that the human body was originally created immortal. "Death" should be understood in a final sense as the final termination of the ends for which something was created. A plant that is eaten by an animal and dies fulfills its purpose as a plant and is part of the broader purposes of a created ecology that produces life. Human beings, however, are created for beatitude, that is, for perfect rational fellowship with God. This purpose is unique to humans among the creatures of the earth, as the only creatures made in God's image. It transcends our physical experience and includes what the Christian tradition has referred to as the human "soul." In this sense, for human beings, the finality and deprivation of "death" can be synonymous with "hell" (cf. Rev 1:18).

The same is true of justice and injustice. The state of creation is a state of justice. "Justice" here is used in the fullness of its biblical sense, including the Hebrew concepts of *tsedeq*, *mishpat*, and *shalom*, and the Greek New Testament term *dikaiosunē*.[30] Injustice is the lack of justice, the failure to realize states of relationships embodying love, peace, beauty, and truth.

LAW AND THE DIVINE COMMAND

But what about God's commands? For example, what about the command from Deuteronomy 21 in chapter 1 to stone a rebellious son? The divine command involves another layer of contingency beyond the contingency of creation: the contingency of time. The divine command is given to particular people or forces acting within time, in history. The divine command therefore addresses circumstances defined by countless contingent variables, including the variables of human choice and evil. The same is not true for creation itself. Time is a feature of creation, so it is improper to suggest that any temporal variables defined the circumstances under which God chose to create.[31] God's decision to create was radically contingent, utterly free.

Yet, having established *this* creation, with the feature of time and creaturely freedom, God ordained a world in which his specific commands occupy locations in time. There seems to be some element of constraint over God's commands because he commands within time. Further, the time in which God commands is embedded in this created world, which embodies the natural law as appropriate to this creation. It does not seem to be the case, then, that God could command anything at all while upholding the consistency of his own character and the integrity of creation. To the extent this is a limitation on God's power, it is a *self*-limitation through which God, in love, allows creaturely freedom to supply at least some of the context for his commands. All of this dense

---

30. For a good discussion of this concept, see Nicholas Wolterstorff, *Justice in Love* (Grand Rapids: Eerdmans, 2011), chaps. 20–21.

31. Time is another big problem arising from the contingency of creation. Classical Christian theology asserts that God is timeless. Much of modern philosophical theology argues that this is incoherent and that God must in some way experience time. In my view, modern theology on this point makes a category mistake between God and creation. It is because God is utterly transcendent of creation that we *must* say God is timeless. It is also because God is utterly transcendent of creation that we can speak without contradiction of God's commands and actions *in* time, because such speech is analogical and not literal. We do not know, and cannot know, precisely what it means for the timeless God to act in time. Is it as though all moments in time are simultaneously present to God? However we try to think of it, this remains beyond our comprehension, precisely because we are not God.

theological discussion means that, unlike the natural law, God's commands are not necessarily binding everywhere and always. As we have seen, the first-century church made just such a judgment concerning whether the gentile followers of Jesus were required to obey the entire Torah.

Even the most fundamental divine commands recorded in Scripture seem to entail some element of contingency. Most Christians, for example, would agree that the Ten Commandments are a summary of moral law that is binding on all people everywhere, including on Christians today. But the fifth commandment, the hinge on which the others connect, is the command to "remember the Sabbath day by keeping it holy" (Exod 20:8 NIV). Neither the immediate hearers of this command "nor your son or daughter, nor your male or female servant, nor your animals, nor any foreigner residing in your towns" are permitted to work on the Sabbath (Exod 20:10 NIV). The traditional day of worship in most Christian churches, however, is not the Jewish Sabbath but Sunday, and most Christian churches today do not forbid all work on Sundays. We recognize that even if the principle of Sabbath-keeping—a regular cycle of work, rest, and worship—is basic and essential for everyone, the specific implementation of the principle is culturally and historically contingent. In the references to slaves ("servants"), animals, and resident aliens, we may see in this command even more directly anachronistic cultural references that do not apply today.

This brief discussion of divine commands shows that even God's commands as recorded in Scripture cannot always be directly applied in every time and place. God's commands *facilitate* his mission, but *the command is not the mission*. The divine command and its fulfilment are not the final goal of creation. Creation does not exist only to demonstrate the inexorable power of God's will. Rather, the divine command facilitates the mission by structuring relationships among people, between people and other parts of creation, and between people and God until all the purposes of creation are fulfilled and the union of these relationships is repaired. And, as we have seen, even in the garden the divine command marks the ground of union by establishing the difference between God and creation.

The New Testament draws out this theme in relation to the Torah in both the Gospels and in the letters of Paul. Both the Gospel writers and Paul understand the Torah in christological terms. In the New Testament, the purpose and fulfillment of the law is found in Christ, who is the fulfilment of true humanity. As noted in the discussion of biblical materials in chapter 1, the relationship between "law" and "grace" has always been a challenging theme in Christian thought, and the apparent tensions between these biblical themes were heightened by the Protestant Reformation. Christian theology asserts that all human beings break God's law and that we can be restored to a proper state with God only by God's grace. Historic Christian thought has always asserted, however, that grace does not *nullify* the law. Instead, grace frees us to live according to the law, not as a way of trying to win God's favor, but as the grateful reception of the kind of authentically human life God created us to enjoy.[32]

As discussed in chapter 1, recent scholarship on Jesus and Paul's Jewish context confirms that neither Jesus nor Paul were rejecting the Jewish emphasis on the law in favor of a new teaching on grace. Both Jesus and Paul were expressing the deeply Jewish theme that the deep purpose of the Torah was not rote external observance but the internal renovation of the heart. Grace was there all along, from creation, to the covenant with Adam, to the covenant with Noah, to the covenant with Abraham, to the covenant with Moses, to the covenant with David, to the new covenant in Jesus. The basis for relationship with God, the writer of the letter to the Hebrews (probably Paul) so passionately observed, had always been grace, received by a faith that can recognize and gladly receive the goodness of God's commands. The divine command, then, is a *means of grace*. As Paul also passionately argued, one of the essential operations of this means of grace is to show us that we do not live as the law demands, causing us to look outside of ourselves, to find there Christ, the true Adam who fulfilled the law, who unites us with himself so that we can become what we are meant to be. The purpose of the divine command is our union with Christ. The purpose of our union with Christ is the *missio Dei*: that the God who created everything will be "all in all" and the plenitude of God's Trinitarian love will thereby fill everything without remainder (1 Cor 15:28).

THE LIMITS OF POSITIVE LAW

So far we have covered some substantial ground: while natural law is universal, at least in this universe, the laws of God's divine commands might be relative, at least in part, to particular historical and cultural circumstances. What is true of God's divine commands is even more true

---

32. Even Martin Luther, the reformer who most clearly distinguished "law" and "grace," wrote a lengthy "Treatise on Good Works" in which he discusses the importance of good works resulting from faith. Martin Luther, *Treatise on Good Works*, in *The Annotated Luther: The Roots of Reform, Vol. 1*, ed. Timothy J. Wengert (Minneapolis: Fortress, 2015).

of human law. No two jural societies are organized in exactly the same way, under exactly the same principles, for exactly the same reasons, within exactly the same historical circumstances. This means *positive law is never absolute*. And it means that *no* dispute over a specific legal rule is *ever*, in itself, a dispute about "absolute truth."

It's important to notice the qualifier—"in itself"—in this statement. Disputes about specific legal rules often, perhaps always, *ultimately* implicate questions of absolute truth, including very important moral truths embedded in the natural law. But the specific legal rules themselves are not matters of absolute truth. Specific rules are always relative to a very particular context. If we fail to grasp this distinction, we will begin to think specific legal rules *are* the mission of God instead of realizing that specific legal rules, in particular context, may or may not help *serve* the mission of God. As a result we will misdirect and waste energy and resources, and perhaps even create bitter conflicts, instead of fostering the peace and reconciliation God desires.

Here we must remember the distinction between natural law and positive law: *natural law is not the same thing as "positive" law*. Natural law is part of creation. It is not written in a statute book or court decision, but it simply is part of the fabric of the universe we inhabit. "Positive" law, in contrast, is law that is incorporated into some authoritative text and promulgated by a properly constituted authority.

Notice that there is *no* positive law, as traditionally defined, in Genesis 1–2. There is no indication in these texts of any system of human government through which a code of law could be promulgated. Without a system of human government, by definition, positive law cannot exist. The narrative arc of Scripture does not seem to suggest anything directly about organized systems of human government until the story of the Tower of Babel in Genesis 11, and it does not really delve into what we today might call "political theology" until the stories of the captivity of Israel, the exodus, and the giving of the Decalogue to Moses—that is, until the formation of the Hebrews into a political entity.[33] At this point

33. I have tried to qualify this statement carefully because I think the biblical texts assume and describe other forms of political organization well before these events. Notably, after Cain murders Abel he is given a "mark" to protect him from unidentified people who might kill him, and Cain settles "in the land of Nod, east of Eden" (Gen 4:15). The biblical text here shows no concern about where all these other people came from or how the "land of Nod" came to be. This is a further clue that the text is not a "literal" history but assumes some kind of geographic and political background that would have been familiar to its original hearers. Similarly Genesis 4:20–22 describes elements of bronze-age culture in the characters of Jabal, Jubal, and Tubal-cain; there is the enigmatic reference to the "mighty men who were of old" as the fruit of human-Nephilim unions in Genesis 6:4; the Tower of Babel resided in a "city" in Genesis 11:1–9; and by the time of Terah's sojourn in Genesis 11:27–32 the text assumes a well-

the biblical narrative has moved well past the ideal state of creation and is describing God's missional prerogative to redeem a humanity that has terribly tarnished that ideal, beginning with the formation of Israel into a political entity as a light to all the nations.

Positive law, therefore, is always removed at some distance from natural law. Another way to say this is that natural law is *ideal*, while positive law is *a pragmatic approximation of the ideal oriented toward broader ends that exceed the positive law itself.* Not every principle derived from natural law can be, or should be, encoded into positive law.

LAW, WISDOM, AND CULTURAL LIMITS

These ideas about how positive law is always relative might sound like relativ*ism*, maybe as the result of some kind of mushy "postmodern" thinking. But, as we saw in chapter 2, this is how some of the greatest historical Christian thinkers about "law"—Augustine and Aquinas—dealt with the question. The great Reformers John Calvin and Martin Luther agreed. Indeed, even Jesus demonstrated that the law is contingent: he told the Pharisees that the Torah's relatively permissive divorce laws were a concession to human weakness and sin (Matt 19:8).

Positive law is a human cultural product. It is expressed in human language and addresses specific human circumstances involving competing ultimate values. As such, positive law is always provisional, never perfect. Positive law cannot achieve the fullness of what the Bible calls justice or peace. Our Christian hope is in the person of Christ, in the power of his crucifixion and resurrection, and in the promise of his return, not in any present political-legal system.

The preceding paragraph will produce agreement both from some ecclesial and Augustinian ethicists. What we too often miss today, however, is the important note of pragmatism that this more humble posture toward positive law must entail. In this sense, the philosophical pragmatists referenced in the introduction to this book are correct: the positive law can never achieve some sort of metaphysically "best" outcome in this world. But this does not mean metaphysics can be swept aside. When I refer to "pragmatism" here, what I mean is the classical virtue of practical reason or "wisdom." In the biblical and Christian intellectual traditions, wisdom is related to truth, indeed to the truth of creation itself, as suggested in Proverbs 8:22–23: "The Lord created me at the beginning of

established city-state known in the historical-archeological record, "Ur of the Chaldeans." And, of course, the narrative from Abraham through Moses is set against the backdrop of Egypt, a global superpower (Genesis 12).

his work, / the first of his acts of old. / Ages ago I was set up, / at the first, before the beginning of the earth" (RSV).

Practical reason tells us that some legal rules will work reasonably well in some circumstances, others will not, and this may change as circumstances change. Often—usually—a set of legal rules will relate to competing, seemingly contradictory higher principles (what I would call principles of the natural law), such that not all higher principles cannot be fully satisfied. Positive law is always a "second best," a kind of compromise, not only with other people who have differing ideas, but also with the reality of our circumstances.

The great Christian thinkers about law all recognized that positive law can never fully realize the natural law. In the *City of God*, for example, Augustine argued that whatever peace obtains in the earthly city is a limited good that serves the true good of the peace of the heavenly city. He did not mean by this that the spiritual power should dominate the temporal power in this life. Rather, he offered a theology of history in which the present imperfect time serves the future perfect time. This meant, for Augustine, that the church should support temporal laws that promote the present good of earthly peace, but that the church also should not concern itself too much with temporal law.

In his reflections on the difference between the present, imperfect time and the future, perfect time, Augustine wondered whether Rome was ever truly a commonwealth.[34] In the concept of a commonwealth (*res publica*), Augustine meant not only a government authorized by public consent but also a community bound by true justice in love. He adopted Scipio's definition of a commonwealth from Cicero's *Republic* as "a people's wealth" (*res populi*), that is, as a community that exists for the good of its people and of a "people" as "a gathered multitude united by common consent to right (*ius*) and common interest."[35] There is no "right" without "right-dealing," that is, justice, Augustine said, so under Scipio's definition there can be no commonwealth without justice. But since the Romans were pagans who directed people away from God, Augustine argued, their society cannot have been characterized by justice. "What human rightness," he asks, "can there be in taking man himself away from God and subjecting him to unclean demons?"[36]

It sounds like Augustine must say there is no justice in the earthly city at all. He does not stop here, however, and instead offers an alternative

---

34. Augustine, *City of God* 19.20, in O'Donovan and Lockwood O'Donovan, *From Irenaeus to Grotius*, 160.

35. Augustine, *City of God* 19.20.

36. Augustine, *City of God* 19.20.

definition of a "people": "A people, we may say, is a gathered multitude of rational beings united by agreeing to share the things they love."[37] This shifts the definition of a people, and a commonwealth, from the absolute requirements of justice to something more limited and contingent: "the better the things [the people love], the better the people; the worse the things, the worse their agreement to share them."[38] Even a people that loves wealth or other vices, Augustine suggested, "loves its own peace—something not to be despised, though it will not possess it at the end because it has not used it well before the end."[39] And this common love of peace, Augustine suggested, is what concerns the church: that the earthly city "should have this peace in this life in the meantime, is a matter that concerns us as well; for while the two cities are mingled together, we, too, make use of the peace of Babylon."[40] Still, this is not a final peace. "No peace here," Augustine said, "whether that shared peace or our own proper peace, can be more than a solace to unhappiness" until we know perfect justice and peace in the heavenly city.[41]

We might criticize some of the theology inherent in this brief section of the *City of God*. Augustine's eschatology can be viewed as overly dualistic, spiritualized, and futurist, perhaps not yet fully purged of his Manichean roots. Unlike some of the Greek Fathers, his Christology at times does not seem to credit the possibility that there were "seeds of the Word" already present in pagan cultures. He does not seem to possess a pneumatology that considers the possible activity of the Holy Spirit in the histories of the pagan nations. His theology of creation and fall, at least in this brief section, seems to elide the capacity for human reason to establish laws that would embody true justice. His definition of a "people" as a gathered multitude of *rational* beings that can love improper things seems to sever the connection between reason, the good, and love. Whether these various moves are matters of conviction, rhetoric, mere inconsistency, or all of these, is debatable.[42] Nevertheless, this famous section of the *City of God* at least reminds us that we can neither expect nor require perfection from any commonwealth in this life. Moreover, the various commonwealths the church will find itself embedded within throughout the sweep of history will vary in their loves, laws, and morals, and none will love God as they should. The best

37. Augustine, *City of God* 19.24.
38. Augustine, *City of God* 19.24.
39. Augustine, *City of God* 19.24.
40. Augustine, *City of God* 19.24.
41. Augustine, *City of God* 19.24.
42. For a good recent discussion on reading the *City of God*'s discussion of community and public life, see Williams, *On Augustine*, chap. 6.

the church can hope for and seek in the earthly city is some measure of peace, yet, as Rowan Williams has noted, an imperfect measure of peace that still shares in some limited way in God's perfect peace.[43]

Augustine made the connection between the changeability of the earthly commonwealth and the changeability of law even more explicit in his *The Free Choice of the Will*.[44] In the form of a dialogue, this text posed the question whether the temporal law can vary if it derives its legitimacy from the eternal law. Augustine said the temporal law can vary depending on the specific circumstances of the commonwealth. For example, he said, if the people of the commonwealth are moderate, prudent, and generous, the temporal law might allow them to elect their own magistrates, while if the people are greedy and selfish, an "honest man of great ability" might justly take over the government.[45] Augustine's specific example might not appeal to us today, but his point is that the form of a temporal government and the specifics of its laws must embody the broad principles of the eternal law in ways that are calibrated to the contingent circumstances of history.

In his treatise on law within the *Summa theologiae*, Aquinas agreed with Augustine that the temporal law is changeable.[46] He also addressed the specific question of whether the temporal law should repress all vices.[47] He said that the temporal law cannot suppress all vices because different people have very different capacities for avoiding vice. He compared this to the different capabilities of adults and children: "The same is not possible to a child as to a full-grown man: for which reason the law for children is not the same as for adults, since many things are permitted to children, which in an adult are punished by law or at any rate are open to blame. In like manner many things are permissible to men not perfect in virtue, which would be intolerable in a virtuous man."[48] The temporal law therefore generally prohibits "only the more grievous vices, from which it is possible for the majority to abstain; and chiefly those that are to the hurt of others, without the prohibition of which human society could not be maintained: thus human law prohibits murder, theft and such like."[49] Further, Aquinas said, "the purpose of human law is to lead men to virtue, not suddenly, but gradually."[50]

43. Williams, *On Augustine*, chap. 6.
44. Augustine, *On the Free Choice of the Will*, trans. Robert P. Russell, OSA (Washington, DC: Catholic University of America Press, 1968).
45. Augustine, *On the Free Choice of the Will*, 6.84.
46. *ST* I-II, 97.
47. *ST* I-II, 96.
48. *ST* I-II, 96.
49. *ST* I-II, 96.
50. *ST* I-II, 96.

In fact, he argued, imposing a higher legal burden on people who are not yet virtuous would cause them to fall into even greater evils without making any progress in virtue.[51]

Both Augustine and Aquinas were so pragmatic about the limits of the temporal law that they each suggested prostitution should be legal in some places because although consorting with a prostitute was sinful, it is better to confine and regulate this activity in certain parts of the city.[52] It is somewhat shocking to realize that these great Christian writers on law made pragmatic arguments in favor of legalizing prostitution. A constructive theology of law today, in a context that is at least as chaotic as Augustine's at the fall of the Roman Empire, must also recognize that the positive law cannot achieve all the goods of the natural law. That is, the positive law cannot restore creation to its divinely intended state of love.

LAW, LIBERATION, AND FREEDOM

So far, this chapter has reflected a kind of flowing and ebbing of concepts about the natural and the positive law. The natural law participates in the divine being as an element of creation, and legitimate positive law participates in the natural law and thereby also participates in the divine. At the same time, the positive law is rather limited in what it can achieve. How can we begin to identify vectors at which the church *should* press for greater congruence between the natural and the positive law? In this section, I suggest that the prophetic theme of "liberation" should be central to any such consideration.

In contemporary discussions, "natural law" is often raised as a way of restricting certain activities that someone considers immoral. The classical and biblical conceptions of natural law, however, are much broader than this. A Christian concept of natural law should connect law and justice to God's desire for all of creation, which is the *liberation* of creation from the powers of sin, injustice, and death. Natural law and justice therefore are intimately connected with *love*.

As Christian philosopher Nicholas Wolterstorff notes in his magnificent book *Justice in Love*, "Doing justice is an example of love. Moses does not pit love and justice against each other."[53] Wolterstorff cites the

---

51. For a good discussion of the pragmatism of Aquinas's legal theory, see David VanDrunen, "Aquinas and Hayek on the Limits of Law: A Convergence of Ethical Traditions," *Journal of Markets and Morality* 5, no. 2 (Fall 2002): 315–37.

52. *ST* II–II, 10.11; Vincent M. Dever, "Aquinas on the Practice of Prostitution," *Essays in Medieval Studies* 13 (1996).

53. Wolterstorff, *Justice in Love*, 84. Though I think Wolterstorff's book is a great achieve-

famous definition of "justice" from the Roman jurist Ulpian, found in Justinian's *Digest*. Ulpian said justice "is a stead and enduring will to render to each his or her due."[54] When we hear this definition, we usually think first of retribution: someone has done wrong, and what they are due is punishment. But as Wolterstorff notes, Ulpian's Latin speaks of rendering each person his or her *ius*—that is, his or her *right*. Even with this nuance of translation, our modern ears are prone to hear something about a legal right granted by a form of positive law, such as the Constitution, in a fundamentally agonistic context, in which competing rights must always be asserted negatively against each other. Rights are always with respect to another person, and therefore may be asserted against another person, Wolterstorff suggests, but the basis for rights is a deeper kind of sociality: "Rights are normative bond between oneself and the other. In good measure those normative bonds of oneself to the other are not generated by any exercise of will on the part of either party. The bond is there already, antecedent to will, binding oneself and the other together. The other comes into my presence already standing in this normative bond of her to me and me to her."[55]

This means that a concept of rights must include not only *negative* rights but also affirmative obligations. Justice requires not only freedom from certain kinds of interference to exercise individual rights, such as freedom from violence embodied in laws against murder and theft. Justice also requires that each person render to each other person the appropriate opportunity to function as a human being within a society. If resources and opportunities are distributed within a society in ways that fundamentally limit some people's ability to function as human beings, there might be a failure of justice the law can address. Law can help keep people free from infringements of right, and it also can help liberate people so that they are free to live in right relation with each other.

The *missio Dei* is a mission of liberation. Christopher J. H. Wright cites Latin American liberation theology, as well as Dalit, Minjung, black, and feminist theologies, as examples of "interested," contextual readings from which missional theology can and should learn.[56] Although Wright is not advocating liberation theology without reservation, he argues that "inasmuch as the Bible narrates the passion and action (the mission) of *this* God for the liberation not only of humanity

ment, I agree with Stephen Long that Woltersorff's position that human beings have "rights" against God is theologically problematic. See Long, *Augustinian and Ecclesial Ethics*, 53–64.

54. Wolterstorff, *Justice in Love*, 85.
55. Wolterstorff, *Justice in Love*, 87.
56. Christopher J. H. Wright, *The Mission of God* (Grand Rapids: Zondervan, 2013), 42–43.

but of the whole creation, a missional hermeneutic of Scripture must have a liberationist dimension."[57]

However, the connection between the church's mission and liberation does not always sit well with some kinds of ecclesial or Augustinian ethics. Ecclesial ethicists might worry that some kinds of liberation theology connect the church too closely with political violence, even if they might agree with some of the ends liberation theologians desire. Augustinians might worry that liberation theology is overly optimistic about the possibility of reforming human society in the near term. In both instances, ecclesial and Augustinian ethicists might argue that liberation theology's eschatology is too immediate and immanent.

These reservations are important. As Leonardo and Clodovis Boff note, "Liberation theology was born when faith confronted the injustice done to the poor."[58] Liberation theology tends toward a realized, politicized eschatology, which in some forms even advocates violence.

Consider, for example, James Cone's seminal text, *A Black Theology of Liberation*. This book was first written, as Cone notes in the postscript to the Fortieth Anniversary Edition, at the height of the civil rights and black power movements in 1969.[59] Cone says that "no one can understand this book apart from the social and political context in which it was written."[60] In particular, at the time he wrote this book, Cone had become frustrated with theology written by "white privileged intellectuals."[61] He wanted to write a specifically *black* theology within, to, and for the black experience.

57. Wright, *Mission of God*, 45.

58. Leonardo Boff and Clodovis Boff, *Introducing Liberation Theology* (Maryknoll, NY: Orbis, 1987), 3. Since publishing this book, the Boff brothers have been engaged in a personal and theological dispute with each other, with roots in the Roman Catholic Church's hesitancies about liberation theology. Leonardo has left the priesthood, while Clodovis now criticizes liberation theology, and the brothers openly criticize each other. See Sandro Magister, "Clodovis and Leonardo Boff, Separated Brethren," Chiesa, July 14, 2008, https://tinyurl.com /y3yt2nvo. For a discussion of the ongoing relationship between liberation theology and the Roman Catholic Church under Pope Francis, see Jeffrey Klaiber, SJ, "Pope Francis and Liberation Theology," *Political Theology Today*, December 6, 2013, https://tinyurl.com/y4va7smb; "Pope Francis and the Ongoing Dialogue of Liberation Theology," *Political Theology Today*, December 20, 2013, https://tinyurl.com/y3qtu4ky.

59. James H. Cone, *A Black Theology of Liberation*, 40th anniv. ed. (Maryknoll, NY: Orbis, 2010), 152. My discussion of this one text by Cone is meant primarily to raise questions, not as an effort at a full account of black theology, which would range far beyond the scope of this book and beyond my expertise. For a broader introduction to the relationship between black theology and other liberation theologies, see Dwight N. Hopkins, "General Introduction," Edward P. Antonio, "Black Theology and Liberation Theologies," and James H. Evans Jr., "The Future of Black Theology," all in *The Cambridge Companion to Black Theology* (Cambridge: Cambridge University Press, 2012).

60. Cone, *Black Theology of Liberation*, 152.

61. Cone, *Black Theology of Liberation*, pref. to 1986 ed.

The book begins with a description of Cone's theological method. For Cone, "Christian theology is a theology of liberation."[62] In particular, Christian theology "is a rational study of the being of God in the world in light of the existential situation of an oppressed community, relating the forces of liberation to the essence of the gospel, which is Jesus Christ."[63] This definition of theology seems consistent with other kinds of liberation theologies, and indeed seems somewhat conventional. Cone draws his existentialist approach from noted white theologians such as Barth and Tillich. However, Cone not only argues for "liberation" as a central motif in an existentialist theology but further states that "black theology affirms the black condition as the primary datum of reality."[64]

The centrality of blackness to existential reality and therefore to theology, for Cone, means that "whites are in no position whatever to question the legitimacy of black theology."[65] White theology, Cone argues throughout the book, is a theology of oppression, beginning with the extermination of Amerindians and running through the enslavement of blacks. Indeed, for Cone, "whites have only one purpose: the destruction of everything which is not white."[66] The rationality of black theology therefore need not, and should not, remain subject to the criterion for legitimacy drawn from white theology.

Notwithstanding this strong affirmation of the independence of black theology, Cone proceeds to describe the sources and methods of black theology in apparently conventional terms: they include Scripture, experience, and above all Jesus Christ.[67] The "experience" Cone thinks is relevant, however, is the black experience of oppression. The black experience is in fact the lens Cone uses to interpret Scripture and Christ: "The meaning of Scripture is not found in the words of Scripture as such but only in its power to point beyond itself to the reality of God's revelation—and in America, that means black liberation."[68] The meaning of "black liberation" is crucial to Cone's theology in this book. As noted above, Cone wrote the book in the midst of the black power movement. Cone's view of "black liberation," therefore, included potentially violent resistance to white America. For Cone, "the black experience is the feeling one has when attacking the enemy of black humanity by throwing

---

62. Cone, *Black Theology of Liberation*, 1.
63. Cone, *Black Theology of Liberation*, 1.
64. Cone, *Black Theology of Liberation*, 5.
65. Cone, *Black Theology of Liberation*, 8.
66. Cone, *Black Theology of Liberation*, 12.
67. Cone, *Black Theology of Liberation*, chap. 2.
68. Cone, *Black Theology of Liberation*, 34.

a Molotov cocktail into a white-owned building and watching it go up in flames."[69]

Cone then proceeds to a discussion of what "God" means in black theology. Consistent with his existentialist bent, he understands the term "God" to point to a transcendental reality that interprets history. For Cone, this means in particular the history of God's liberation of Israel as narrated in Scripture and the history of God's liberation of black people.[70] At this point in the text, an apparent contradiction arises in Cone's argument. While "the black theology view of God must be sharply distinguished from white distortions," Cone suggests that "this does not mean that black theology rejects white theology entirely."[71] Nevertheless, on the very next page after this statement, Cone says "the goal of black theology is the destruction of everything white, so that blacks can be liberated from alien gods."[72]

The final chapter of Cone's book discusses ecclesiology, culture, and eschatology. Cone's eschatology is strongly immanent. He criticizes futurist eschatologies as means by which whites have encouraged blacks to remain docile in their servitude in hope of a future reward.[73] His view of culture is similarly immediate to the lived experience of oppressed black people: "The world is not a metaphysical entity or an ontological problem. . . . It is very concrete. It is punching clocks, taking orders, fighting rats, and being kicked around by police officers."[74] Similarly, eschatology, for Cone, must be realized in the present struggle for black liberation. Nevertheless, he also recognizes the importance of "the future reality of life after death" as "grounded in Christ's resurrection" because this hope supplies the courage to face death in the struggle for liberation.[75]

What can any Christian theology of law say about Cone's perspective—particularly a theology of law, like the one offered in this book, written by a white person? We could suggest the contrast in Cone's work is intentionally dialectical, as begins to become clearer in Cone's discussion of theological anthropology and Jesus Christ.[76] While Cone does identify blackness with black bodies, he also notes that "in the literal sense a black person is anyone who has 'even one drop of black blood in

69. Cone, *Black Theology of Liberation*, 25.
70. Cone, *Black Theology of Liberation*, chap. 4.
71. Cone, *Black Theology of Liberation*, 64.
72. Cone, *Black Theology of Liberation*, 65.
73. Cone, *Black Theology of Liberation*, 145.
74. Cone, *Black Theology of Liberation*, 140.
75. Cone, *Black Theology of Liberation*, 150.
76. Cone, *Black Theology of Liberation*, chaps. 5–6.

his or her veins.'"[77] In Cone's chapters on anthropology and Christology, blackness begins to seem more like an existential condition summed up in the black American experience rather than merely a skin color.

So, if not by violence, how should the fight for liberation be waged? The Boff brothers suggest that liberation theology must reject traditional approaches based in external aid and reform. Instead, liberation requires political action led by the poor: "The poor can break out of their situation of oppression only by working out a strategy better able to change social conditions: the strategy of liberation. In liberation, the oppressed come together, come to understand their situation through the process of conscientization, discover the causes of their oppression, organize themselves into movements, and act in a coordinated fashion."[78] This coordinated action, for the Boff brothers, results in political change: "First, [the poor] claim everything that the existing system can give: better wages, working conditions, health care, education, housing, and so forth; then they work toward the transformation of present society in the direction of a new society characterized by widespread participation, a better and more just balance among social classes and more worthy way of life."[79]

As these quotations suggest, liberation theology is connected with Marxism. The Boff brothers suggest that "liberation theology uses Marxism purely as an instrument. It does not venerate it as it venerates the gospel.[80]" Like Marxism, liberation theology is deeply concerned with *history*, and it offers a philosophy or theology of history. The Boff brothers argue that "*the kingdom is God's project in history and eternity*. Jesus Christ, second person of the Blessed Trinity, incarnated in our misery, revealed the divine plan that is to be realized through the course of history and to constitute the definitive future in eternity; the kingdom of God."[81] Even more dramatically, they suggest, "The banner of liberation theology, firmly set in biblical ground, waves in the winds of history. Its message is that today the history of faith is embarking on its third great period, the period of construction."[82] The present period of "construction" is contrasted with the "contestatory" period of the first few centuries of church history and the Constantinian "conservatory" function during which the church improperly "consecrat[ed]" the powers of the world. The present "construction" period returns to a pre-Constantinian age of contestation, but with "a longer range view—that is, taking on its

77. Cone, *Black Theology of Liberation*, 69.
78. Boff and Boff, *Introducing Liberation Theology*, 5.
79. Boff and Boff, *Introducing Liberation Theology*, 5.
80. Boff and Boff, *Introducing Liberation Theology*, 28.
81. Boff and Boff, *Introducing Liberation Theology*, 52 (emphasis in original).
82. Boff and Boff, *Introducing Liberation Theology*, 92.

responsibility in history, which is to persuade society to conform to the utopia of the kingdom."[83] Liberation theology therefore agrees with the ecclesial critique of Constantiniansm but offers solutions that *require* the church to directly influence the state on behalf of the poor.

LIBERATION, SALVATION, AND AUGUSTINIAN VIOLENCE

Liberation theology, or at least some versions of it, acknowledges that a vision for a peaceful and just society under the rule of law sometimes requires force. Force might be necessary even when a person or group refuses to obey the law based on conscience. On this point, if on few others, liberationists agree with Augustinians. An example of this dilemma in the history of Christian thought about law stems from Augustine's arguments and activism against the Donatists.

Tertullian and Lactantius, who wrote to mitigate the persecution of Christians by the Roman state, advocated a broad concept of religious freedom of conscience based on a theological concept of human dignity (see chap. 2). Augustine, writing to Christian rulers facing the Donatist controversy, took a different approach.

The Donatists were a group of "purist" Christians who argued that leaders and parishioners who recanted their faith under persecution should not be readmitted into the church. The Donatists controversy caused significant unrest in the North African church during Augustine's time.

The exercise of violence in the service of the law, for Augustine, could represent an act of love, if such violence was necessary to secure the peace and foster the conditions under which people could move toward God. This included not only general breaches of the peace but also specifically religious concerns—particularly when, as is often the case, those religious concerns bled into general breaches of the peace. The persecuted church could become the persecutor.

This is illustrated starkly in Augustine's treatise *The Correction of the Donatists*. There, Augustine advised the emperor, "For both the physician is irksome to the raging madman, and a father to his undisciplined

---

83. Boff and Boff, *Introducing Liberation Theology*, 93. At the same time, the Boff brothers recognize that it is possible to overemphasize liberation theology's political dimension at the expense of its mystical and "other, more supple and more deeply human aspects: friendship, pardon, feeling for leisure and celebration, open dialogue with everyone, sensitivity to artistic and spiritual riches." They also warn against "subordinating considerations of faith to considerations of society in one sided constructs" and "absolutizing of liberation theology, downgrading the value of other theologies, and overemphasizing the socio-economic aspects of evangelical poverty."

son—the former because of the restraint, the latter because of the chastisement which he inflicts; yet both are acting in love. But if they were to neglect their charge, and allow them to perish, this mistaken kindness would more truly be accounted cruelty."[84] Augustine argued that the Donatists could not position themselves as martyrs, because true persecution occurs only when a person is unjustly punished for disobeying a law that contradicts truth. A person who disobeys a law that promotes truth, however, is justly punished and therefore not a martyr.[85] Since the laws against the Donatists were in the service of the true church, those who disobeyed them were justly punished and not martyrs. Moreover, since just laws can be enforced by violence, the punishment received is not a form of unjust persecution.[86] And, since the church seeks man's salvation, persecution inflicted on behalf of the church should be seen as an act of love: "Moreover, she persecutes in the spirit of love, they in the spirit of wrath; she that she may correct, they that they may overthrow: she that she may recall from error, they that they may drive headlong into error."[87]

Love, Augustine suggested, demands that Christian rulers not shrink from inflicting pain: "What then is the function of brotherly love? Does it, because it fears the short lived fires of the furnace for a few, therefore abandon all to the eternal fires of hell?"[88] Finally, Augustine argued, it is an act of faith in God's provision of civil authorities to invoke the force of law rather than merely enduring schism: "When the Church, therefore, was reduced to these straits in its affliction, anyone who thinks that anything was to be endured, rather than that the assistance of God, to be rendered through the agency of Christian emperors, should be sought, does not sufficiently observe that no good account could possibly be rendered for neglect of this precaution."[89]

This view was tied to Augustine's theology of history. He recognized that the apostles who were persecuted for Christ's sake did not invoke civil law on their own behalf, but he argued that this illustration fails to "consider the different character of that age, and that everything comes

---

84. Augustine, *Correction of the Donatists* 7, https://tinyurl.com/y4uu6g6l.
85. Augustine, *Correction of the Donatists* 8.
86. Augustine, *Correction of the Donatists* 10.
87. Augustine, *Correction of the Donatists* 11. Augustine states, "Finally, she persecutes her enemies and arrests them, until they become weary in their vain opinions, so that they should make advance in the truth; but they, returning evil for good, because we take measures for their good, to secure their eternal salvation, endeavor even to strip us of our temporal safety, being so in love with murder, that they commit it on their own persons, when they cannot find victims in any others."
88. Augustine, *Correction of the Donatists* 14.
89. Augustine, *Correction of the Donatists* 18.

in its own season. For what emperor had as yet believed in Christ, so as to serve Him in the cause of piety by enacting laws against impiety."[90] Christian kings should indeed view the persecution of schism as part of their sacred duty: "In this way, therefore, kings can serve the Lord, even in so far as they are kings, when they do in His service what they could not do were they not kings."[91]

Not surprisingly, how one interprets the political theology underlying Augustine's activity against the Donatists depends in large part on one's perception of the value of his goals. A sympathetic Catholic Augustinian may take Augustine's expressed motives at face value: he was deeply concerned with the unity of the body of Christ and encouraged strong but still moderated civil legal action to bring this schismatic group back into fellowship.[92] Anabaptist and other peace church writers may interpret Augustine's role in the Donatist controversy as the height of Constantinianism.

CONSCIENCE AND CONSENT

Augustine's actions against the Donatists seem authoritarian and extreme. Consistent with Augustine's views, our most direct example of positive law in the Bible, the legal materials in the Torah, reflect the ideal of a theocratic society. Other great thinkers about law in the patristic and medieval eras assumed that the rule of kings was ordained by God. In fact, Aquinas wrote an entire treatise titled "On Kingship," which argues that ordinary people are too sinful and stupid to rule themselves.

At the same time, there is abundant material in Scripture and in the tradition explaining that a wise and just ruler should not enact laws that lack public support. Even in times when most people believed in the divine mandate of kings, Jewish and Christian sources insisted that the king is accountable to God and to the people. There also has always been a theme, particularly in the first few centuries of church history before Constantine, in some strands of the Reformation, and in modern Western thought, that stresses the rights of conscience and civil disobedience.

The "consent of the governed" is a bedrock of modern liberal democratic theory. I am not, however, offering an apology for liberal demo-

90. Augustine, *Correction of the Donatists* 19.
91. Augustine, *Correction of the Donatists* 19.
92. See, e.g., Donald X. Burt, *Friendship and Society: An Introduction to Augustine's Practical Philosophy* (Grand Rapids: Eerdmans, 1999), 215–18. Burt notes that Augustine allowed, but did not favor, the use of the death penalty in cases of heresy, and that he was more tolerant of outsiders such as Jews and pagans than of the Donatists, whom he viewed as insiders under the church's direct jurisdiction (218–21).

cratic theory as an ideal form of governance. Compared to other modern political ideologies, such as fascism and totalitarian communism, liberal democracy undoubtedly has proven the better alternative. There are elements of modern liberalism that resonate deeply with some Christian theological themes, in particular the principles of human dignity and conscience.[93] But there is a dark side to modern liberalism as well, in its hyperindividualism and entirely market-driven ethic.[94] Even within the tradition of Christian kingship, however, a notion of consent was central to the legitimacy of positive law.

The roots of consent in Christian jurisprudence run back to Roman law. In his *Digest*, Justinian noted the third-century jurist Ulpian's comment that "a decision given by the emperor has the force of a statute . . . because the populace commits to him and into him its own entire authority and power, doing this by the *lex regia* which is passed anent [concerning] his authority."[95] The *lex regia* played a central part in Roman jurisprudence. It was supposed to have been an original legal instrument through which the Roman people transferred their public authority, embodied in the original Roman republic, to the emperor.[96] Historians today agree that the *lex regia* was a fiction or rationalization, constructed largely by Ulpian, to explain the failure of Republican government and the authority of Augustus Caesar.[97] Nevertheless, the idea that political sovereignty resided first with the people remained central to the Roman imagination and found its way into Christian jurisprudence.

Aquinas picks up this theme in his "Treatise on Law" within the *Summa theologiae*. Here Aquinas addresses the question whether the "old law"—that is, the law of the Old Testament, the Torah—failed to provide an adequate mechanism of governance.[98] Aquinas's typical method of discourse in the *Summa* was to state a question, followed by possible objections to the question's presumptive answer, followed by a common argument in support of the presumptive answer (*Sed contra*, "on the

---

93. See, e.g., Michael J. Perry, "Christianity and Human Rights," in *Christianity and Law: An Introduction*, ed. John Witte Jr. and Frank Alexander (Cambridge: Cambridge University Press, 2008). I use *liberalism* here not to refer to the differences between "liberals" and "conservatives" in American politics, but rather in the classical Enlightenment sense.

94. See, for example, William T. Cavanaugh, *Being Consumed: Economics and Christian Desire* (Grand Rapids: Eerdmans, 2008); James K. A. Smith, *Desiring the Kingdom: Worship, Worldview, and Cultural Formation* (Grand Rapids: Baker Academic, 2009).

95. *The Digest of Justinian* 1.4.1, trans. Alan Watson (Philadelphia: University of Pennsylvania Press, 2009).

96. Daniel Lee, *Popular Sovereignty in Early Modern Constitutional Thought* (Oxford: Oxford University Press, 2016), 27.

97. Lee, *Popular Sovereignty*, 28.

98. *ST* II-I, 105, art. 1.

contrary"), followed by Aquinas's own gloss on the common argument (*respondeo dicendum*, "I answer that"), followed by specific replies to the objections. In Article 1 of Question 105 within the "Treatise on Law," Aquinas asks "whether the Old Law enjoined fitting precepts concerning rulers."[99] The presumptive answer to the objections in the *sed contra* is that it did, because God's law is good. The biblical text Aquinas alluded to here, Numbers 24:5, seems a bit odd: "The people of Israel is commended for the beauty of its order: 'How beautiful are thy tabernacles, O Jacob, and thy tents.'" Aquinas said "the beautiful ordering of a people depends on the rights establishment of its rulers," and "therefore the Law made right provision for the people with regard to its rulers."[100] The objections Aquinas lists include the following: the Torah provides for inferior rulers but not for a king; the people were allowed to decide for themselves whether to have a king rather than God selecting the best king; and the form of kingship the law instituted was unjust and tyrannical.[101]

In the response, Aquinas dealt with these objections by arguing that the Torah provided for a king and for subsidiary rulers who properly derived their authority from the people. According to Aristotle, he noted, "all should take some share in the government: for this form of constitution ensures peace among the people, commends itself to all, and is most enduring."[102] He followed Aristotle in holding that the best form of government is a kingdom ruled by a single king, followed by an aristocracy governed by a few of the best citizens, but he tied this to the consent of the governed through their ability to choose their rulers. "A government of this kind," he said,

> is shared by all, both because all are eligible to govern, and because the rules are chosen by all. For this is the best form of polity, being partly kingdom, since there is one at the head of all; partly aristocracy, in so far as a number of persons are set in authority; partly democracy, i.e. government by the people, in so far as the rulers can be chosen from the people, and the people have the right to choose their rulers.[103]

This form of government, according to Aquinas, was in fact established originally in the Torah. Moses ruled as a kind of king; Moses chose seventy-two elders to help him govern, a kind of aristocracy; and

---

99. *ST* II-I, 105, art. 1.
100. *ST* II-I, 105, art. 1.
101. *ST* II-I, 105, art. 1, obj. 1, 2, 5.
102. *ST* II-I, 105, art. 1.
103. *ST* II-I, 105, art. 1.

there was a kind of democracy, because the elders Moses chose initially were recommended to him by the people.[104]

Aquinas also recognized in his reply to the first objection that Moses's office initially was directly established by God not through the people, but he brushed this aside because "this people was governed under the special care of God" and was God's chosen people.[105] In response to the second objection, Aquinas noted that a king's power "easily degenerates into tyranny, unless he to whom this power is given be a very virtuous man," and for this reason Israel's first rulers did not possess "kingly authority with full power" but instead functioned as "judges and governors."[106] Only when Israel demanded a king like the kings of other nations did the provisions for how the people should select their king come into effect as a way of mitigating the dangers of this process.[107] In response to the fifth objection, Aquinas argued that the law did not institute tyranny but that God warned Israel that their kings would abuse their authority "by framing unjust laws, and by degenerating into tyrants who preyed on their subjects."[108]

Aquinas provides an important source, then, for the claim that a Christian theology of law must connect legal legitimacy with the consent of the governed. Of course, even if we exchange Aquinas's role for the king with elected representatives, the ideal that the democratic/legislative process truly reflects the consent of the governed is questionable at best. If a given piece of legislation really reflected the wishes of a majority of the populace, up to 49 percent of the people may not have agreed to it. Where is their consent?

This alone would constitute an insuperable problem, but even this notion of an engaged and informed population voting up or down on discrete legislative proposals is wildly unrealistic. Most people do not vote in general elections, and even most people who vote have no idea what the vast bulk of legislation considered by their elected representatives says or potentially means. Indeed, the average legislator only pays careful personal attention to a handful of bills in which he or she is most invested. Most legislative proposals do not arise directly from "the people" as such but rather originate from lobbying groups supported by corporate money or by wealthy private foundations. The legislative process

104. *ST* II-I, 105, art. 1. Aquinas quotes here from Deuteronomy 1:13, 15 and Exodus 18:21.

105. *ST* II-I, 105, art. 1, ad 1.

106. *ST* II-I, 105, art. 1, ad 2. This reply includes a bit of anti-Jewish sentiment, unfortunately not uncommon for a Christian writer of this age: "especially were the Jews inclined to cruelty and avarice, which vices above all turn men into tyrants."

107. *ST* II-I, 105, art. 1, citing Deuteronomy 17:14.

108. *ST* II-I, 105, art. 1, ad 5.

involves tradeoffs and compromises that often have little to do with an elected representative's view of the merits of a proposal, and for the most part legislators follow the wishes of their party's majority leaders. Meanwhile, the lower chamber (the House) is apportioned within the states through Byzantine processes of gerrymandering designed to perpetuate the dominance of whichever party is in power when legislative districts are designed, with the help of highly paid consultants using GIS mapping technology and big-data analytics. The two-party system and the ubiquitous gerrymander were never contemplated by the Constitution's framers, but they have been upheld by the Supreme Court, so long as the motivation is not expressly racial.[109]

Further, the bicameral system in Congress and in most state legislatures ensures that the upper chamber (the Senate) includes a fixed number of representatives that does not reflect total population—at the federal level, every state, no matter how large or small, gets two senators. This is a feature of the constitutional design, not a bug, meant to limit the possibly radical effects of popular sentiment. Aside from the distortions of lobbying, corporate money, the two-party system, and the gerrymander, the United States is a republic, not an absolute democracy.

Even acknowledging all these complications, the point is that Aquinas emphasizes the political body *as a whole*. The virtuous king cannot act arbitrarily. The virtuous king must recognize that his authority comes to him by God through the people. A just political order requires some basic principle of consent.

109. Cf. *Shaw v. Reno*, 509 U.S. 630 (1993) (applying strict scrutiny to racial gerrymandering claim), *Miller v. Johnson*, 515 U.S. 900 (1995) (discussing standards for evaluation of racial gerrymandering claims); *Shaw v. Hunt*, 517 U.S. 899 (1996) (racial gerrymandering); *Bush v. Vera*, 517 U.S. 952 (1996) (racial gerrymandering); *Lawyer v. Department of Justice*, 521 U.S. 567 (1997) (racial gerrymandering); *Easley v. Cromartie*, 532 U.S. 234 (2001) (racial gerrymandering); *Gaffney v. Cummings*, 412 U.S. 735 (1973) (applying limited rational basis scrutiny to political gerrymander); *David v. Bandemer*, 478 U.S. 109 (1986) (same); *Vieth v. Jubelirer*, 541 U.S. 267 (2004) (dismissing political gerrymandering claim, with four justices suggesting the claim should not even be reviewable by a court); *League of United Latin American Citizens v. Perry*, 548 U.S. 399 (2006) (upholding partisan gerrymander); *Gill v. Whitford*, 585 US. ___, 137 S.Ct. 2268 (2018) (holding that voters lacked standing to bring partisan gerrymandering claim). The Court heard arguments in three important gerrymandering cases again in March, 2019. See Scotusblog, *Virginia House of Delegates v. Bethune-Hill*, http://tinyurl.com/y4fnvaka; Scotusblog, *Rucho v. Common Cause*, http://tinyurl.com/yy2bm247; Scotusblog, *Lamone v. Benisek*, http://tinyurl.com/y5b3pdx8.

LIBERATION, ECCLESIAL ETHICS,
AND CHRISTIAN PACIFISM

Liberationists and Augustinians, like Augustine himself, have at times been to ready to employ violence to impose a vision of the good. As the previous section discusses, one problem this raises is that of the consent of the governed. As our discussion of the Sermon on the Mount in chapter 1 and of the radical reformers in chapter 2 also suggests, some Christian thinkers have argued that the premise of state violence is fundamentally flawed and that all Christians should be pacifists.

This raises a major question in our development of a constructive theology of law. Christian pacifists generally have not offered a satisfying response to the dilemma of using force or allowing innocent people to suffer violence. There seem to be at least two broad streams of thought (with many subbranches) among pacifists. One is a quietist strand exemplified in Robert Brimlow's essay titled "What about Hitler?" in a recent collection of essays offering an apologetic for Christian pacifism.[110] Brimlow attempts in that essay to respond to the common belief that the violence of war was just and necessary to stop the Nazi machine—a belief finally held, famously, even by the great Christian pacifist Dietrich Bonhoeffer. The other focuses on "just policing."

Brimlow, representing the quietist stream, admirably does not shy away from the connection between the violence of large-scale war against Hitler and the violence of any state action against a dangerous person: "I think it is important," he says, "for us to bear in mind that when we think of just war and the just war tradition that we are also referring—at least implicitly—to the state's police power as well [as] to the war-making power of the state in international affairs. The justifications for each is the same, so much so that I have referred to police powers and war powers as flip sides of the same coin. And the ultimate source of those justifications is the same. It lies in the fundamental function of nation-states."[111] The justification for violence by nation-states against despots and criminals, Brimlow argues, is in turn rooted in the presumptive right of self-preservation. Indeed, he says, "to paraphrase Hobbes again, the threat of the sword underlies every statute, every treaty, as well as every interpersonal relationship."[112]

For Brimlow, then, all exercises of war and police power are founded

110. Robert Brimlow, "What about Hitler?" in *A Faith Not Worth Fighting For: Addressing Commonly Asked Questions about Christian Nonviolence*, ed. Tripp York and Justin Bronson Barringer (Eugene, OR: Wipf and Stock, 2012).

111. Brimlow, "What about Hitler?" 52.

112. Brimlow, "What about Hitler?" 55.

on a sinful desire to preserve the self at the expense of others. In contrast, he argues, "We are heirs to a new politics of faith and love that overturns the politics of the nations and rejects the violence of states. This new politics makes love of God and love of neighbor our sole virtues from which everything else flows, and thus replaces the primacy of the right of self-preservation."[113] There is little doubt, he concludes, that if we were to confront a new Hitler with such an ethic, "given that we are dealing with a powerful evildoer, the result is that we will fail."[114] Apparently, then, Christians would be obligated to leave the innocents consumed in this new Hitler's genocide to their fates or at best to suffer martyrdom with them. Brimlow does not quite draw out the consequences of his ethic for law in ordinary circumstances, but it seems hard to escape the conclusion that all state coercion, including all positive law of any kind, is sinful and invalid, and that all legal institutions represent only ungodly powers.

There is something that rings true in Brimlow's attempt to wrestle with the demonic ghost of Hitler. He is right to decry the "Hitlerization of politics," by which Christians and others justify fights to the death (often quite literally) over every threat or disagreement.[115] Brimlow's account fails, however, because of his cramped understanding of the virtues, which leads to a devolution of the self.

For Brimlow, apparently, *any* self-regard must comprise a form of violence against God and against neighbor. There doesn't seem to be any room in Brimlow's thought for a self-regard that *derives from* love, in which the self is known and received *as gift*. And this deprives Brimlow's ethic of a self that is even capable of loving God or neighbor, and therefore of love itself.

Other Christian pacifists, led by Gerald Schlabach, have argued for "just policing" ethic instead of "just *war*" theory.[116] Schlabach acknowledges that policing is a lacuna in Christian pacifist thought.[117] He also readily admits that "no community can do without some kind of police

113. Brimlow, "What about Hitler?"*Id.* at 56.
114. Brimlow, "What about Hitler?" 56.
115. Brimlow, "What about Hitler?" 52.
116. Gerald W. Schlabach, "Must Christian Pacifists Reject a Police Force?" in York and Barringer, eds., *Faith Not Worth Fighting For*; Schlabach, ed., *Just Policing, Not War: An Alternative Response to World Violence* (Collegeville, MN: Liturgical Press, 2007).
117. Schlabach, "Must Christian Pacifists Reject a Police Force?" 61. Schlabach acknowledges, "As we turn to ask whether Christian pacifism entails a rejection of police force, readers may quickly realize that this is where those practitioners of nonviolence are often ambivalent. Frankly, Christian pacifists have not had a consistent answer to this question. . . . Ethically, they have not always been sure how to square actual practices with their peace theology."

function. No Christian community. No human community."[118] Schlabach further notes that the peace churches have advocated for the rule of law, and particularly international law, as a hedge against war, which necessarily implies the police function.[119] Schlabach agrees that a rule of law backed by a "just" police force requires the potential exercise of force: if "terrorist crimes against humanity should be treated within the rubric of prosecuting criminals not waging war," he says, "we must assume that *as* criminals, the perpetrators would probably refuse to turn themselves in."[120] Therefore, "some kind of SWAT team with recourse to lethal violence still seems necessary," along with "prison guards to hold the criminal terrorists they apprehend."[121] Schlabach and his coauthors describe a number of practices that could distinguish "just policing" from war, including community policing models, strengthening international organizations such as the United Nations, and the networking of nongovernmental organizations through new technologies.[122]

Stanley Hauerwas's work reflects the tension between the nodes of Anabaptist thought represented by Brimlow and Schlabach. In one of his seminal works, *The Peaceable Kingdom*, Hauerwas starkly reverses Mao's pragmatic thesis: Christians, he says, "cannot seek justice from the barrel of a gun; and we must be suspicious of that justice that relies on manipulation of our less than worthy motives, for God does not rule creation through coercion, but through a cross."[123] In *The Peaceable Kingdom*, Hauerwas argues that this ethic of radical nonviolence extends even to efforts to promote justice for others:

> We must be a people who have learned to be patient in the face of injustice. But it may be objected: Surely that is too easily said if you are not the ones who are suffering from injustice. Precisely, but that does not mean that we ought to legitimize the use of force to overcome injustice. Such legitimation often comes from the attempt to have justice without risking the self, as when we ask the 'state' or the 'revolution' to see that justice is done, but in a manner that does not significantly affect our own material position. If we are to be a helpful and patient people in a world of injustice, however, we

118. Schlabach, "Must Christian Pacifists Reject a Police Force?" 66.
119. Schlabach, *Just Policing, Not War*, 99, noting that "Mennonites have faced this question with varying degrees of consistency when their own ministries have positioned Mennonites to take governmental roles in health systems, welfare programs, international development agencies, and so on. Yet these state functions already assume the rule of law, made possible through policing."
120. Schlabach, *Just Policing, Not War*, 80.
121. Schlabach, *Just Policing, Not War*, 80.
122. Schlabach, *Just Policing, Not War*, 153–67.
123. Stanley Hauerwas, *The Peaceable Kingdom* (South Bend, IN: University of Notre Dame Press, 1983), 104.

cannot just identify with the 'cause' of the poor, we must be like them poor and powerless.[124]

Nevertheless, Hauerwas insists that injustice must be resisted: "Those who are violent, who are also our neighbors, must be resisted, but resisted on our terms, because not to resist is to abandon them to sin and injustice."[125] Yet the primary form of this resistance, for Hauerwas, is not violent action but the power of the church's life in its witness to the story of the gospel, its sacraments, and its prayers.[126]

Is this an adequate response of love to the child who is being raped in snuff films distributed by a child pornographer? If a Christian knows where and when the rape is occurring, should she contact the police? Can a Christian serve as a lawmaker, lawyer, judge, police officer, investigator, or other government official whose job involves locating, arresting, and prosecuting child rapist pornographers?

Hauerwas is not deaf to these questions. He asks, "Can Christians ever be justified in resorting to arms to do 'some good'? Are Christians not unjust if they allow another person to be injured or even killed if they might prevent that by the use of violence?"[127] His response is that he has "some sympathy" for this view, and that "it certainly cannot be discounted as a possibility for Christians," but that the exercise of power is dangerous because it is intoxicating and corrupting.[128] Moreover, "true justice," he says, "never comes through violence, nor can it be based on violence."[129] He seems to view Christian participation in any sort of state violence as a rare and extreme possibility, at most.

At the same time, Hauerwas suggests that Christians might participate in a society's government depending on the nature of the society and the nature of the role to be performed.[130] "Most governmental functions, even within the military," he suggests, "do not depend on coercion and violence."[131] This might even mean that Christians could serve as police officers or prison wardens, so long as they also "work to help their societies develop the kind of people and institutions that make possible a government that can be just without resort to violence."[132]

The problem with Hauerwas's qualification here is that he is wrong

124. Hauerwas, *Peaceable Kingdom*, 105.
125. Hauerwas, *Peaceable Kingdom*, 106.
126. Hauerwas, *Peaceable Kingdom*, 106–11.
127. Hauerwas, *Peaceable Kingdom*, 114.
128. Hauerwas, *Peaceable Kingdom*, 114.
129. Hauerwas, *Peaceable Kingdom*, 114.
130. Hauerwas, *Peaceable Kingdom*, 169n19.
131. Hauerwas, *Peaceable Kingdom*, 169n19.
132. Hauerwas, *Peaceable Kingdom*, 169n19.

about the dependent relation between "most governmental functions" and "coercion and violence." All "governmental functions" are *governmental* only insofar as they are authorized by law. An act that purports to be "governmental" but is not authorized by law is not properly considered an act of "government"; such an act is simply an exercise of individual or group power. The rule of law is what defines something as properly "governmental." And in any earthly society, the rule of law, always, without exception, even in societies based on social contracts, is finally secured by power and violence. Anyone who participates in any function of government, including the arrest and detention of child rapists, is implicated in state violence.

This conundrum was recognized in a recent symposium on Hauerwas and the law at Duke Divinity School. Law professor and theologian Cathleen Kaveny stated the problem succinctly: "Unlike the 'peaceable kingdom' of Jesus, earthly kingdoms are inherently built on violence—not only the violence of warfare, but also the threats of coercive force that ultimately and undeniably back any system of positive law. The law, in other words, describes and implements the operating system of the strikingly unpeaceable secular world. Upon what basis could Hauerwas possibly engage it?"[133] Kaveny notes that she writes from the Roman Catholic tradition, "which tends to recognize more continuities between nature and grace, and therefore more possibilities for natural theology and natural ethics (sometimes called natural law) than Hauerwas ordinarily acknowledges."[134] As Kaveny notes, Hauerwas's theological project is a sharp critique of any "natural theology" that purportedly is "defensible and intelligible on grounds fully independent from the complete and vigorous account of reality offered by Christianity."[135] Kaveny notes two ways in which Hauerwas's broader theological project could interface with the law: through the casuistic tradition of the common law, and through Barth's covenantal framework for creation.[136] The common law, Kaveny notes, is a historically embodied narrative reflected in the practices of the community governed by the law—much as Hauerwas understands the relationship between the church, the church's practices, and Scripture.[137] Barth's understanding of creation and covenant—that God's purpose in creating was the establishment of covenant—Kaveny suggests, supplies the basis for *ad hoc* engagement

133. Cathleen Kaveny, "Hauerwas and the Law: Framing a Productive Conversation," *Law and Contemporary Problems* 75 (2012): 135.
134. Kaveny, "Hauerwas and the Law," 135.
135. Kaveny, "Hauerwas and the Law," 135.
136. Kaveny, "Hauerwas and the Law," 145–51.
137. Kaveny, "Hauerwas and the Law," 145–51.

between the church and the world on matters such as law.[138] This, again, corresponds to Hauerwas's account of theology, particularly his aversion to natural theology, and ethics.[139] Kaveny concludes that "although Hauerwas may be opposed to 'Christendom,' he ought not to dismiss the efforts of Christians to discern, over the centuries, the concrete requirements of morality in particular cases and controversies, in light of the demands of justice, demands that are themselves shaped by the biblical narrative."[140]

Hauerwas responded to some of these questions and suggestions at the symposium in his conversation with H. Jefferson Powell, a former student of Hauerwas's who is an attorney with the US Department of Justice.[141] Hauerwas noted that he identifies himself as a "theocrat" in the sense that he takes the claim "Jesus is Lord" as a statement of public truth.[142] However, he said, "That doesn't mean I want the rule of priests. Indeed, that would be the worst possible thing. What we have fundamentally in this country is a rule of lawyers. Now that is not all bad. I assume that elite law practice very much determines some of the limits on our political life that I think is very much to the good."[143] Those "limits," of course, imply the sorts of restraints that suggest state violence. Hauerwas attempted to negotiate this boundary by distinguishing certain legal processes from the sort of "violence" Christian faith forbids. "Violence," he suggested, "is an analogical description. It works pretty well as a description of killing someone, but there may be forms of force that those of us associated with nonviolence can understand as an alternative to more determinative forms of violence."[144] Consistent with his focus on casuistry, he suggested that Christians committed to nonviolence could work with other Christians "to see how we can make the law, as nearly as possible, a service into the community in which those called to the police function are more nearly able to fulfill that calling nonviolently. They are called *peace* officers."[145] Hauerwas also noted that John Howard Yoder, the thought leader of contemporary pacifist Anabaptism, never thought of "law" as univocally violent. Rather, Hauerwas noted, "Yoder observed that lawyers write wills and contracts, defend the poor against housing authority, defend people against capi-

138. Kaveny, "Hauerwas and the Law," 145–51.
139. Kaveny, "Hauerwas and the Law," 145–51.
140. Kaveny, "Hauerwas and the Law," 157.
141. John D. Inazu, ed., "A Dialogue between a Theologian and a Lawyer," *Law and Contemporary Problems* 75 (2012): 221.
142. Inazu, ed., "Dialogue," 223.
143. Inazu, ed., "Dialogue," 223.
144. Inazu, ed., "Dialogue," 229.
145. Inazu, ed., "Dialogue," 229.

tal punishment, prosecute, judge, postpone environmental rules, structure corporate mergers leveraged with junk bonds, and so on."[146] The "so on," Hauerwas suggested, "makes clear that the many things done in the name of 'the law' are not morally the same."[147] In short, Hauerwas agreed that Kaveny had read him well and that her constructive proposal for viewing the common law as a narrative that provides points of contact between creation, church, and culture was important.[148]

Hauerwas's conversation with these legal scholars, together with Schlabach's work on just policing, may help reconcile Christianity's nonviolent ethic with its emphasis on law. Schlabach's work on just policing suggests some potentially rich connections between Anabaptist and pietist peacemaking theologies and with the broader catholic-Augustinian tradition.[149]

SUMMARY

Our effort to develop a constructive Christian theology of positive law suggests the following themes:

1. Natural law is embedded in creation. Some things are inherently right and good, and some things are inherently wrong and harmful. This is part of creation's existence as divine gift. Creation is a gracious donation of being by God, who is the ground of being.

2. Legitimate positive law participates in the natural law, which participates in God as an aspect of creation. Legitimate positive law restrains evil, mirrors God's good purposes for creation, guides Christians and non-Christians alike (at least through "seeds of the Word"), *and* embodies the kingdom of God

146. Stanley Hauerwas, "Hauerwas on Hauerwas and the Law," *Law and Contemporary Problems* 75 (2012): 233, 237.

147. Hauerwas, "Hauerwas on Hauerwas," 233, 237.

148. Hauerwas, "Hauerwas on Hauerwas," 233, 237. In typical Hauerwasian fashion, however, he offered this qualification about the notion of covenant: "I have never trusted Calvinists, other than Barth, when they talk about contracts being a form of covenant. When Calvinists talk that way about contracts, it usually indicates they are representatives of a rapacious business practice and they would eat you alive if they were able."

149. Indeed, Schlabach, a Mennonite convert to Catholicism, describes himself as a Mennonite Catholic. See Prof. Schlabach's faculty page at the University of St. Thomas at https://tinyurl.com/yyovgo4d. For further discussion on how peace church traditions might develop a constructive account of positive law, see also Thomas L. Shaffer, in conversation with John Howard Yoder, "Anabaptist Law Schools," in Robert F. Cochran, ed., *Faith and Law: How Religious Traditions from Calvinism to Islam View American Law* (New York: New York University Press, 2008).

LAW AND THEOLOGY   141

through liberation from oppression.

3. Positive law is nevertheless contingent and limited. Not all the goods of the natural law can be embodied in the positive law in any given moment in history. The positive law refers to absolute truth but is never itself a question of absolute truth. Consideration of what can be achieved through the positive law requires the virtue of wisdom.

4. Legitimate positive law refers to the consent of the governed. Legal rules without some essential justification in the consent of the governed will lack force and legitimacy.

5. Positive law is backed by force. A theology of positive law must embrace a just peacemaking ethic that recognizes the legitimacy of some use of governmental force as constrained by the rule of law. Such an ethic could be "pacifist" in the sense of eschewing inter-state warfare as a political tool, but it must recognize the spiritual and moral legitimacy of the police power, or else there can be no rule of law.

PART II

Praxis

Part 1 of this book developed a biblical, historical, and theological approach to positive law. In part 2 of the book, I try to apply some of the principles in part 1 to some practical problems in the law. In the conclusion to this part, I try to draw some lessons in plea for a more patient, thoughtful Christian praxis in relation to the positive law.

My perspective here is in the contemporary American context, because that is where I live and where I practice and teach law. In some ways, the contemporary American context is unique because of our history, our legal system with its emphasis on constitutional values, and our current involvement with hot-button issues at the intersection of faith and law both at home and around the globe. In other ways, our current American story is just one more iteration of a long history of the church's engagement, struggles, triumphs, and failures in relation to the law.

4.

Praxis of Law in Ordinary Time

INTRODUCTION

A discussion of Christian thought and law usually defaults to the hot-button culture war issues and related questions of religious liberty. These are important subjects that I will address in chapter 6. I want to begin, however, with some seemingly more mundane topics. In many ways, these more mundane topics are more important than those that tend to make headlines.

The materials in part 1 suggest that the positive law, as it relates to the natural law woven into creation, has both a preservative and a liberative function. Both of these functions related to the call of Israel in the law and the prophets, and both relate to the mission of the church in the present time of history, after the resurrection of Christ and before the parousia. The church is not a temporal nation, and therefore the church's mission is not to establish temporal political power. However, the church *is* called to embody the new politics of Christ's kingdom as *part of* particular temporal political societies in history. This means that the church's *first* interest concerning the positive law in any historical context is simply to support the structures and institutions of a functioning legal system in which there is at least some restraint on grave violence, some principle of consent of the governed, some commitment to the flourishing of creation, including created humanity, and some space for the church's institutional life.

This sounds like a rather minimalistic set of concerns, but in much of the world throughout history and today, it is more than many people can imagine. As Christian lawyer and activist Gary Haugen has noted,

"Without the world noticing, the locusts of common, criminal violence are right now ravaging the lives and dreams of billions of poor neighborhoods."[1] While Christians in the United States become agitated over whether a transgender student can use one bathroom or another, poor people all over the world are dying in the streets from starvation, disease, and official violence, without any functional rule of law at all. From a global, historical perspective, our culture war problems are luxuries within an otherwise basically functional legal system.

I am not, of course, suggesting that the American legal system functions perfectly, or even that it always functions in a basic way for everyone. As discussed in chapter 5, the legacy of racism in America runs deep, and continues to cause structural injustices particularly in our criminal justice and immigration systems.[2] But it is also true that in the United States, most of the time, it is possible to buy and sell property and commodities, start a business, resolve a civil dispute, enter into a contract, obtain liability insurance, travel freely, write a book, go to church or not, pass on an estate, get married, get divorced, deposit funds in a bank, take out a loan—and engage in the myriad other transactions of daily life—without violence against the backdrop of an established rule of law.[3]

The first year of law school in the United States includes a set of courses in "private law" subjects that developed as part of the common law we inherited from England—property, contracts, and torts. It also includes a course in civil procedure, which concerns the jurisdiction and functioning of the courts. In the first or second year, students take a constitutional law course, which examines the structure and limitations of the federal government and individual guarantees of due process and equal protection. These and other courses introduce students to a flawed yet robust system through which daily life usually functions reasonably well without descending into chaos.

Law school and legal practice in the United States also introduces students and young lawyers to a set of cultural conventions that help make things work. Lawyers are often vilified in the popular culture, and movies and television shows make law practice seem like an exercise in flamboyant lying at best or intolerable nastiness at worst. Of course,

1. Gary Haugen and Victor Boutros, *The Locust Effect: Why the End of Poverty Requires the End of Violence* (Oxford: Oxford University Press, 2014), Kindle loc. 124.
2. For one bracing discussion of such problems, see Nell Bernstein, *Burning Down the House: The End of Juvenile Prison* (New York: The New Press, 2014).
3. I recognize that, too often, these basic goods are *not* readily accessible to people who do not have the money or means to understand their rights or obtain legal representation. This is a problem of *access* to justice, not necessarily a problem with the law as such. Nevertheless, it is a significant problem that any Christian social ethic must address.

there are lawyers who are flamboyant liars or nasty loudmouths, but most day-to-day law practice is not like a movie or television show.

When I used to appear on behalf of corporate clients in the Newark, New Jersey, federal courthouse, usually in intellectual property or other business cases, I always noticed a brass plaque just inside the door inscribed with the Bill of Rights. This kind of element, along with all the other mahogany, marble, and brass, reminded us that we were entering a kind of secular temple in which a certain kind of decorum and attention to facts and legal principles were required. The better lawyers knew that once we passed through those doors, we were required to represent our clients zealously and honorably and to work with the court to move cases toward some kind of reasonable conclusion. The less effective lawyers who thought their primary job was to fight at all costs or to showboat usually learned quickly from the court that this was not the way to help their clients. But whether in any given case the system worked as well or as efficiently or with as much collegiality as we or our clients might have liked or not, there was rarely, if ever, a question of resorting to blood feuds to settle business disputes.[4]

When I represented clients in transactional matters, the same kind of dynamic obtained. Each side tried to get the best terms possible; there might be some puffing, and some cards might be held close to the vest, but in the end, lawyers on opposite sides of the table, at least the good lawyers, knew that the goal was to come to terms that would allow the clients to do business without unnecessary future disputes. And again, even if things did not always go as smoothly as possible, there was rarely, if ever, a question of resort to violence.

This unglamorous material is the real stuff of the rule of law. *This* is what occupies most of the time of most lawyers and judges. Before diving into the heated domains of abortion, LGBTQ rights, and religious liberties, *this* is where we should focus to get our bearings on what the rule of law looks like in everyday life.

4. I say "rarely" because I did experience one civil corporate case in which there was an undercurrent of potential violence, though it was more in the form of hints and insinuations than action. Of course, there are certain kinds of businesses at certain times in history that have been rough-and-tumble to the point of violence, particularly if organized crime is involved. As a New Jersey lawyer, I could say that movies like *The Godfather* and shows like *The Sopranos* were not entirely fiction, particularly in industries like construction, retail, and waste disposal. But these dramas are dramatic precisely because they differ from the happily boring experience of, say, filing a car insurance claim.

A CONTEMPORARY EXAMPLE: USURY AND
BANKRUPTCY LAW

Consider an example from modern bankruptcy law. A young person graduates college with some significant student loan debt and gets his first job working in the tech industry. He buys a condominium, takes a very expensive vacation, and buys a new car and some high-end home electronics, all on credit. What he didn't know, however, was that the owners of his company were engaged in a massive fraud. The company collapses, he loses his job, and he can no longer manage his debts. This crisis causes him to return to church, where is faith is kindled, moving him toward a new career in ministry. A lawyer advises him that he can file for personal bankruptcy and discharge many of his consumer debts (although his student loans, by law, are nondischargeable). His pastor, however, counsels him that he should "keep his promises" to repay the consumer debts and not declare bankruptcy. Is the bankruptcy law immoral? What should the young man do?

It's easy to suggest that, indeed, it is immoral to declare bankruptcy if that process discharges debts one has contractually promised to pay. The young man's job situation is unfortunate, but his debt load is still his own responsibility. If his ministry career must be delayed, that will provide a valuable lesson for the future.

All of this is not bad advice, but it overlooks some important facts. Prior to the advent of personal bankruptcy laws, a person could be jailed for failure to pay a debt. In the American colonial era, "debtor's prisons" were filled with farmers, craftsmen, and other average people who had fallen behind on loans for farm equipment, seed, tools, and the like. This made what to us seems like a merely civil, commercial dispute into a crime. Further, interest continued to accrue while the debtor was in prison, and of course a debtor in prison cannot earn money to pay the debt. The result was that debtor's prison could spell permanent ruin for a worker and his family. Meanwhile, the creditor still did not recover his capital.

Some moralists at the time argued that this was all as it should be. The looming threat of debtor's prison, they argued, compelled debtors to be very careful about their borrowing and compelled creditors to be very careful about the extension of credit. If some people acted recklessly and suffered the consequences, they got what they deserved.

Reformers countered that debtor's prisons were overflowing because neither creditors nor debtors were really being deterred by this legal regime. The founding generation thought the problem significant enough to include a clause in the Constitution empowering Congress to enact uniform bankruptcy laws.[5] Congress passed only a limited involuntary bankruptcy statute relating to certain commercial transactions in 1800.[6]

Some idealistic reformers, such as Henry David Thoreau, thought this dynamic was an inevitable result of movement away from the wilderness. Others suggested that unscrupulous capitalist speculators were taking advantage of a system in which a small number of very rich lenders got richer at the expense of average people and local businesses. The reality is that both of these perspectives had some merit. More broadly speaking, rapid technological change in communication and transportation (telegraph and railroads), global economic and political instability (the Napoleonic Wars, the War of 1812), deep regional divisions (slavery and the Northern vs. Southern economies), religious ferment (the Second Great Awakening, Old Light vs. New Light Presbyterians), the decline of family farms, Western land speculation, industrialization—these and a host of other tensions destabilized old patterns of life. The economic dimensions of these crises led to the Panic of 1819, which crippled the US economy for several years. If all of this sounds familiar, it should! The same kinds of pressures gripping the nation in the nineteenth century are with us today. Nevertheless, voluntary bankruptcy statutes were first passed by Congress in 1841 and 1867, and they were expanded as part of the New Deal legislation after the Great Depression and again in 1978 after another period of financial instability.[7]

As this very brief history shows, bankruptcy law is a pragmatic response to problems that arise when banks and other lenders extend credit to businesses and consumers. Bankruptcy helps protect debtors from predatory lending practices and eliminates the injustice of debtor's prison. It also induces creditors to undertake more careful underwriting before extending credit. Every commercial transaction is undertaken against the backdrop of the bankruptcy laws. The credit a card-issuing bank makes available, and the interest rates and other contractual terms of the debt, all are prepared by sophisticated players and account for the reality that some percentage of borrowers will default and declare bankruptcy. This is one of the reasons the market interest rate for a consumer credit card will be something like 17–20 percent instead of 4–5 percent.

We might say to our budding young pastor, then, that he should have no moral qualms about using the bankruptcy laws if that seems to

5. U.S. Const., Art. I, Sec. 8, cl. 4.
6. Bankruptcy Act of 1800, available at https://www.loc.gov/item/rbpe.22500300/.
7. See David Haynes, "History of Bankruptcy in the United States," The Balance, April 29, 2018, https://tinyurl.com/y3qlkme7.

be the best option in his circumstances. But this would not mean we think the circumstances morally neutral. It was not good for him to have incurred all this consumer debt, and we might also say more broadly that the economic system under which such debt can be incurred is morally problematic. The are many ways in which a financial system can be structured and many ways in which creditors and debtors can be protected within a given financial system. The broader values at stake—things that get closer to basic natural law principles—include fairness, reciprocity, hospitality, and the like. The details of implementation can vary widely and will never produce a perfect system.

Bankruptcy law might seem like an odd, somewhat dull example here, but I chose it because it raises a hotly contested question in church history: the meaning of biblical prohibitions on usury. In numerous places the Bible condemns all lending at interest. In the patristic and medieval eras, theologians universally understood this to mean that usury—lending at interest—was sinful. Such a blanket prohibition might be workable in a rural, agrarian society dotted by cities where commodities were exchanged through barter or using hard currency based in precious metals such as gold and silver. It is not workable in larger economies where significant amounts of capital are required to finance agricultural production, construction, and trade.

This problem was evident in the medieval era, when Christian rulers relied on Jewish bankers to finance their large-scale building projects and military campaigns, including the crusades. Although usury was prohibited in the Hebrew Scriptures, Jewish interpreters believed this applied only within the Jewish community, so lending at interest to Christians was permitted.[8] Christian leaders hypocritically argued that the Jewish lenders, and not the Christian borrowers, were engaging in the sin of usury, reflecting and contributing to deep-seated anti-Semitism across Christendom.

The problem became even more acute during the Swiss Reformation, where city-states such as Geneva, for historical and geographical reasons, could not exist independently without trade fueled by banking capital. John Calvin therefore developed a theology of trade that allowed interest-taking for some business purposes. Calvin argued that "usury must be judged, not by any particular passage of Scripture, but simply by the rules of equity."[9] Martin Luther, in contrast, eschewed usury in

8. See Wayne A. M. Visser and Alastair McIntosh, "A Short Review of the Historical Critique of Usury," *Accounting, Business and Financial History* 8, no. 2 (1998): 175–89.

9. Letter quoted in David H. Eaton, "The Economists of the Reformation: An Overview of Reformation Teaching Concerning Work, Wealth, and Interest," *SAGE Open* (July–September 2013): 1–9, https://tinyurl.com/y2pgewbd.

favor of an agrarian vision for German society, and not all Calvinists subsequently followed Calvin's views on usury. In time, however, no mainstream Christian denomination condemned interest-taking outright. "Usury" came to mean the charging of excessive or unjust interest, not merely interest itself.

I offer this brief history of usury in Christianity because it shows that even a legal prohibition rooted in a specific biblical command might be modified for practical reasons. Perhaps we could still debate whether Calvin and other Christian leaders were right to change the rule, but there is simply no way the modern world could function without lending at interest. Nearly every element of your life at this very moment—your school, your town, your home or apartment, your car, your local hospital, the job that supplies your income, the farms that produced the food you ate today, the factories that made the clothes you're wearing, the chair you're sitting in, the phone, computer, and/or tablet you're using, the book in your hands—all of it depends on embedded webs of commercial finance. As a practical matter, we must allow lending at interest. The best we can do is regulate the conditions under which credit is extended and provide a safety net through bankruptcy law.

ANOTHER CONTEMPORARY EXAMPLE:
PHARMACEUTICAL PRODUCT REGULATION

Another contemporary example of law's contingency, which has been the focus of some of my legal practice and scholarship, relates to pharmaceutical product regulation. Like bankruptcy law, this example seems less missionally significant than hot-button culture war issues such as abortion and gay marriage. I say "seemingly" less missionally significant because, in fact, pharmaceutical product regulation matters a great deal, particularly to poor and vulnerable people.

When I was in full-time law practice, I worked on some large class-action cases involving pharmaceutical products. Plaintiffs claimed that these products, the first generation of SSRI antidepressants, caused severe side effects in some patients, leading some to commit suicide or to engage in violent acts against others. All of these cases were troubling, but some were particularly gruesome, including one in which a mother had killed her own young children.

My law firm represented the drug manufacturer, a large pharmaceutical company. The company acknowledged that depression is a complicated illness, that all drugs have side effects, and that the plaintiffs in these cases had indeed committed the suicidal or violent acts. The company argued, however, that its product did not cause any exceptional, undisclosed side effects leading to the suicide or violence of these patients. The company's products may have been ineffective for these patients, or may even have been somewhat helpful for a time, but in the end, tragically, these patients succumbed to a terrible illness. The analogy here could be to a cancer drug: sadly, even with the best available drugs, some patients still die of their cancer. Cancer drugs also cause side effects, which sometimes are severe, but we do not impose liability on the drug manufacturer so long as the drug was properly tested and approved by the FDA and the potential side effects were properly disclosed to the patient and her doctor.

A key question in these cases, as in many product liability or negligence cases, involved "causation." Did the medication actually cause the side effect of suicidal actions or outbursts of violence against others?

"Actual causation" is sometimes easy to establish using what American tort law calls a "but for" test: but for the negligent action, would the harm have occurred?[10] Say Able runs a red light and slams into Baker, who was walking across the street under a green light. There were no other cars on the road at the time, and there was no impediment to Baker otherwise crossing the intersection. But for Able's negligent act of running the red light, would Baker have suffered these injuries? The answer, obviously, is "no," so actual causation is established. This is an easy case for actual causation, and it likely is also an easy case for other elements of a negligence claim: that it was a breach of a duty of care (that is, that it was "negligent") for Able to run the red light; that there was both an actual and "proximate" cause; and that Baker suffered compensable damages.[11]

In a case like our pharmaceutical example, it is not nearly so simple. There are complicated questions about what an SSRI drug is doing in the human body as well as about the nature of mental illness generally, and those questions become even more difficult as applied to a specific case with its own detailed history. So how should the law handle this problem?

We could start with very broad principles of truth and justice. These, we might say, are part of the natural law. Legal tribunals should be estab-

10. See Restatement (Third) of Torts: Liability for Physical Harm, § 3.
11. We could imagine a case in which running a red light is not a breach of a duty of care. For example, assume Able is an ambulance driver and that he observes all the standard precautions for ambulance drivers when they cross an intersection against a signal, such as engaging the lights and sirens. These kinds of details are what make law an endlessly interesting profession!

lished to resolve disputes peacefully and truthfully. What form should the proceeding take? Should it be inquisitorial (as is usually the case today in continental Europe) or adversarial (as is usually the case today in the US and the UK)? Should the court itself conduct the evidentiary investigation (as in inquisitorial systems), or should the litigating parties do the investigation (as in an adversarial system)? Should the court appoint a neutral scientific expert, should the parties hire experts who might provide differing perspectives, or both? Should the court hold a hearing to determine whether the purported "scientific" expert reached his or her conclusions based on accepted scientific methodology, or should the weight of the evidence be a matter for a jury alone?

These latter two questions were the subject of debate and litigation when I worked on the SSRI cases. Mainstream medical opinion supported the company's position that the SSRI medications did not cause suicidal or violent actions. But the plaintiffs' lawyers found doctors who dissented from the majority opinion and who had their own theories about why SSRIs might cause sudden spikes in suicidality or violence in some people. The mainstream experts thought these dissenters were purveying "junk science" rather than informed scientific opinion.

In 1993, the US Supreme Court decided *Daubert v. Merrill Dow Pharmaceuticals*, which established standards for the admission of scientific expert testimony under the Federal Rules of Evidence.[12] The *Daubert* court held that the trial judge must act as a "gatekeeper" to determine what scientific testimony is given to a jury, that the evidence must be relevant and rest "on a reliable foundation," and that scientific evidence must rely on "scientific methodology."[13] The court offered a number of indicia of whether a methodology is "scientific," including whether the theory or technique is generally accepted in the scientific community, whether it is testable, and whether it was subject to peer review.[14]

These all sound like sensible criteria, but it's easy to see that they are subject to challenge and could be stated differently. The result of these criteria, after all, is that views outside the "mainstream" of scientific opinion will be far less likely to be admissible in court, regardless of whether the mainstream view is correct. Sometimes today's dissenting voice becomes tomorrow's mainstream opinion. Science is supposed to follow the evidence and be particularly resistant to the lure of groupthink. Shouldn't a jury be allowed to hear all the testimony and make its own determinations about merit?

12. 509 U.S. 579 (1993).
13. 509 U.S. 579 (1993).
14. 509 U.S. 579 (1993).

On the other hand, the average juror is not well qualified to discern when a dissenting voice makes a valid point or when it really is far off base or even based in quackery or fraud. Although courts are charged with discerning the truth in a dispute, the judicial system is not institutionally suited to determine the progress of science. With a very limited amount of time and resources and a specific charge to resolve particular cases and controversies, the judicial system must make pragmatic choices based on a trust that, in the long term, the institutions and methods of mainstream science will roughly sort out legitimate ambiguities, upon which reasonable practitioners might disagree, from opinions that fall outside the boundaries of the enterprise of science itself.

This perspective also highlights the role of *courts* in the social problems presented by potentially dangerous prescription medications. Why should a court get involved in the safety of prescription medications at all? In the United States, certain kinds of drugs can only be sold to the public if a government agency, the Federal Food and Drug Administration, first determines that the drug is safe and effective for its intended use. This approval process involves many years of tests in the lab, on animals, and in human subjects, and it can costs billions of dollars in research and development expenses. Why not adopt a rule that says no civil lawsuits can proceed against a drug that has been cleared by the FDA?

The issue of whether FDA approval "preempts" state product liability lawsuits was decided by the Supreme Court in *Wyeth v. Levine*, which held that FDA approval does not preempt state tort litigation.[15] The heart of the question was whether Congress, acting under the Constitution's commerce clause, intended to preclude the states, under the Constitution's supremacy clause, from regulating liability for defective prescription drugs under state tort law. The question entails concerns about federalism, methods of constitutional interpretation, regulatory economics—things constitutional law professors love but many steps removed from the basic principles of the natural law.

Whether with or without preemption, why should the *federal government* get involved at all in regulating the medical profession through drug approvals? Is the government a better arbiter of drug safety than the medical profession? Should free markets have a role to play here? If a drug is not safe and effective, after all, presumably it will not gain or keep market share. We do not require most other products to go through an expensive government preapproval process. If a laptop manufacturer's products constantly lose data or spontaneously combust, people will buy laptops from a better manufacturer. Although a variety of government

15. 555 U.S. 555 (2009).

agencies play some role in the safety and marketing of consumer products like laptops, there is no specific "Federal Laptop Agency." Why not do the same with medicinal drugs?

The standard answers to these questions relate to the economics of health care, the potential population-level effects of large numbers of people ingesting chemical compounds, the history of unregulated quack medicine, the specialized knowledge required to understand how medicines work, and the like. To be clear, I think these are good answers, at least in their broad outlines, and that the sale of prescription drugs should be regulated by the government. But again, as we move from general principles—protecting public health and safety—to the details of any legal-regulatory system, we quickly run into a thicket of highly contextual, undetermined choices.

In fact, in the pharmaceutical context, the legal and moral questions become even more complicated if we step away from the assumption that prescription medicines should be developed and supplied primarily by for-profit companies. The reason there are questions about evidence in private tort litigation for allegedly defective pharmaceuticals is that our health care system depends on for-profit corporations to bring most drugs to market.

In the US, our system of drug discovery and development involves a government agency that funds basic research (the National Institutes of Health [NIH]), universities and other research centers that receive NIH funding to carry out basic research, and for-profit corporations that conduct applied research and bring drugs to market, as well as another government agency (the FDA) that regulates the marketing and sale of finished products. The for-profit corporations may be privately held, meaning that their stock is not traded on public markets, or they might be publicly traded companies. Privately held companies in this space often receive financing from venture capitalists, whose ultimate goal usually is to sell the company or its technology to a publicly traded multinational or to take the company public. There are then two primary sources of funding for drug discovery and development: government funding—that is, tax revenue—for basic research and private capital, raised through private equity markets or public stock markets, for applied research and marketing of finished products.[16]

16. This is a bit of an oversimplification for purposes of our discussion. For-profit companies often enter into joint venture or other business arrangements with universities and thereby participate in basic research. Large research universities have technology transfer offices and thereby seek to monetize some of their research. And there are some private foundations and other nonprofits, such as the Gates Foundation and the Medicines Patent Pool, that engage in applied research and marketing efforts. These kinds of activities, however, occur against the backdrop of the basic model described in the text.

This entire system is undergirded by patents. A patent is a unique kind of property or property-like right: an exclusive right to make, use, sell, or offer for sale an invention. Patent law involves specific rules for what qualifies as a patentable invention and somewhat complicated procedures for obtaining a patent grant from the government. In general, newly created chemical compounds or biological products, or existing products with newly discovered uses, can qualify for a patent. Patents usually last for twenty years, with some slight adjustments upward in some cases, including for some pharmaceutical products. A drug company needs to patent promising compounds early in the development process, and most drug candidates do not survive the rigorous and lengthy safety and efficacy testing process required by the FDA. Smaller companies supported by venture capital also obtain patents early in the development cycle, usually in the hope of selling the patent to a larger company after passing initial phases of testing. As a result, when a typical pharmaceutical compound comes to market, it usually will have three to five years of remaining patent life.

Estimates of development costs for drugs that make it to this stage range from hundreds of millions to several billions of dollars. This makes those three to five golden patent years a high-stakes game. Drug companies historically have relied on "blockbuster" drugs, protected by patents that supply billions of dollars in profits per year, to sustain this business model. This dynamic, in turn, focuses the companies' research and development efforts on drugs for which there is a large, wealthy market, which may not coincide with what could be considered more significant areas of need from a national or global public health perspective.

Many public-health advocates have argued that this system is fundamentally flawed.[17] For example, the Health Impact Fund, supported by luminaries such as Nobel Prize–winning economist Kenneth Arrow and global health advocate Paul Farmer, advocates a global fund supported by governments and private foundations to kick start a competition for drugs and treatments for diseases that impact developing countries. I think the Health Impact Fund (HealthImpactFund.org) is a promising approach, but it also raises difficult legal, ethical, and moral questions. Is it right for the law to require workers in the wealthy developed world to bear an increased tax burden in order to help the developing world, or is this sort of appeal better suited to private charity? What will happen if a drug developed through this kind of mechanism allegedly produces unacceptable side effects? Will injured victims have a remedy in court,

17. For my contribution to this discussion, see David W. Opderbeck, "Patents, Essential Medicines, and the Innovation Game," *Vanderbilt Law Review* 58 (2005): 501.

as they would against a private company? Who will insure against the inevitable risks?

All of these questions arise in only one very specific area of the law relating to only one aspect of the economy, and the brief summary of one small set of issues above only scratches the surface of all that a large-scale pharmaceutical product regulation entails. Very few Christians would argue that a particular resolution of all these questions is central to the mission of the church. Most would probably say the church should be concerned about public health; some people in the church with particular interest and expertise might become engaged in policy debates about the safety and efficacy of prescription drugs or the best way to fund new drug discovery; religiously affiliated nongovernmental organizations, such as World Vision, might participate in large-scale public health projects; churches might sponsor information or charitable programs to help underprivileged people understand their medical treatment options and obtain treatment; and individual people facing health challenges might receive prayer and care from their church family members. Those of us with some specialized knowledge of the issues might work to educate others, often with great passion. But all of this can, and usually does, happen without any sense that any single policy outcome *defines* the *missio Dei*.

5.

The First Big Question: Slavery and Race

INTRODUCTION

Chapter 4 suggested some ways in which we could think about and debate the specific provisions of law relating to bankruptcy and pharmaceutical regulation without imagining that one specific legal rule or another is the only correct alternative. In this chapter, we introduce a more fractious problem: legalized slavery and racism.

THE DARK WOUND OF RACE IN AMERICAN LAW

The body of the US Constitution was drafted by the Constitutional Convention in 1787, ratified by the states in 1788, and made effective on March 4, 1789. The states that made up the United States at that time originally were colonies of England. The colonies had joined together in rebellion against England, for the reasons stated in the Declaration of Independence, as well as for other political and sociological reasons debated by historians. The Revolutionary War was effectively concluded with the Battle of Yorktown in 1781. The Treaty of Paris formally granting the American Colonies their independence was signed on September 3, 1783.

During the Revolutionary War, the Continental Congress adopted the Articles of Confederation, which were not formally ratified until 1781. The Articles of Confederation provided for only a limited central government, which often reads more like a treaty than a constitution. Article II, for example, states that "each state retains its sovereignty, freedom, and independence, and every power, jurisdiction, and right, which is not by this Confederation expressly delegated to the United States, in Congress assembled," and Article III states that "the said States hereby severally enter into a firm league of friendship with each other, for their common defense, the security of their liberties, and their mutual and general welfare, binding themselves to assist each other, against all force offered to, or attacks made upon them, or any of them, on account of religion, sovereignty, trade, or any other pretense whatever." The Articles did, however, leave foreign relations powers such as treaty making and war to the central Congress. Congress could request money from the states to help fund the Continental Army and other central functions, but it lacked a power of taxation or any ability to regulate foreign trade or interstate commerce as against the states.

The weaknesses of the central government in the Articles of Confederation left the United States vulnerable to internal trade wars and rebellions (such as Shays' Rebellion in Massachusetts in 1786 to 1787) and external threats such as piracy on the high seas. These tensions led to the movement that produced the new Constitution establishing a stronger central government. Advocates of the new Constitution were called "Federalists." Three of them, Alexander Hamilton, James Madison, and John Jay, left behind a collection of articles and essays published in newspapers called *The Federalist Papers*, which are sometimes cited in Supreme Court opinions as evidence of the purpose of the new Constitution. The Federalists were opposed by critics of a strong central government, generally called Anti-Federalists.

Federalist arguments ultimately carried the day, but not without compromise. One of the most significant compromises was that promises were made to Anti-Federalists in some states that the Constitution would be amended with a Bill of Rights shortly after ratification. The first ten amendments to the Constitution, written by James Madison, comprise this Bill of Rights. It contains familiar substantive guarantees such as the freedom of speech, the right to bear arms, and freedom from unreasonable searches and seizures.[1]

The first three Articles of the 1789 Constitution establish the three branches of our federal government. Article I establishes the legislative power, Article II the executive power, and Article III the judicial power. We could say that these three Articles establish a "horizontal" relationship among the three branches of government. Article I established a

---

1. Madison initially proposed changes to the Constitution's text. These changes were placed into a list of seventeen amendments, all of which were approved by the House of Representatives. The Senate approved only twelve of these, and only the ten that now comprise the first ten amendments of the Constitution were ratified by the States. See Erwin Chemerinsky, *Constitutional Law: Principles and Policies*, 5th ed. (New York: Wolters Kluwer, 2015), 12.

bicameral legislature with enumerated powers comprised of a Senate and a House of Representatives; Article II vests the executive power in a president; and Article III vests the judicial power in "one supreme Court and such inferior Courts as the Congress may from time to time ordain and establish." Article IV is a federalism article that addresses what we could call a vertical axis—between the federal government and the various state governments—as well as a horizontal axis among the various state governments. Article V establishes the procedure for constitutional amendments, which is intentionally cumbersome. Article VI includes provisions on prior debts incurred under the Articles of Confederation, the supremacy of national law, and oaths of office. Article VII supplies the procedures for ratification of the Constitution. All of these provisions are often lauded, and rightly so, as examples of prudent checks and balances on individual and institutional power, grounded in a notion of consent, and rooted at least in part on Christian ideas about the strengths and weakness of human nature.

But the 1789 Constitution also encoded America's national original sin: black slavery. Many of the founding fathers, including Thomas Jefferson (who drafted the Declaration of Independence), James Madison (who drafted the Bill of Rights), and George Washington owned black slaves. Jefferson, Madison, Washington, and others sometimes expressed sentiments against slavery, but nevertheless they continued to own slaves. At the time of the Constitutional Convention, slavery existed in Northern states but had become particularly entrenched in the Southern states. Delegates to the Constitutional Convention disagreed about how slaves should be counted for the purposes of taxation and congressional representation, the legality of the ongoing transatlantic slave trade (that is, the importation of new slaves into North America, not the status of existing slaves), and the return of runaway slaves to their owners from Northern territories.

The three-fifths clause in Article I, section 2, clause 3 was a compromise on how slaves were counted. It gave Southern states disproportionate representation in relation to their potential tax obligations. The three-fifths clause also implied that slaves were not fully persons. Defending this clause against critics who thought it would give Southern states too much power, James Madison said in *The Federalist Papers*, no. 54 that "the federal Constitution . . . decides with great propriety on the case of our slaves, when it views them in the mixed character of persons and of property. This is in fact their true character."

Article I, section 9, clause 1 prohibited Congress from enacting any legislation banning the transatlantic slave trade until 1808. That clause is

worded in terms of the states' power to permit the "migration or importation" of persons the states "shall think proper to admit," sidestepping
or ignoring the personhood of the slave. Article IV, section 2, clause 3,
the "fugitive slave clause," required free states to return runaway slaves to
their owners. These compromises ultimately contributed to the instability that led to the Civil War.[2]

Historian Mark Noll aptly describes the American Civil War as a
"theological crisis."[3] On one side were Christians who believed black
slavery violated basic biblical principles of love and justice, and who supported the abolitionist movement. On the other side were Christians
who believed slavery was supported by the Bible and that African slavery
was part of God's providential plan for Christianizing blacks.[4] As we look
back on this cancerous period in American history, it is hard to imagine
that any mainstream Christian thinker would have supported slavery, but
in fact, the supporters of slavery argued that they were the more "orthodox" Christians and that the abolitionists were the "radicals."

AN EXAMPLE: JAMES HENLEY THORNWELL

Consider the example of James Henley Thornwell, a leading figure
among antebellum Southern Presbyterians, called by some of his contemporaries "Our Southern Giant" and "the Calhoun of the church."[5] He
served as Professor of Sacred Literature and the Evidences of Christianity
at South Carolina College starting in 1840 and became a strong advocate of "Old School" Presbyterianism.[6] He was a founder of the *Southern
Presbyterian Review*, a prominent orthodox Presbyterian publication, and
later became president of the South Carolina College, a highly prestigious position in South Carolina life at that time.[7]

Like other conservative Southern Presbyterians, Thornwell offered a

2. We should also note that neither the 1789 Constitution nor the Bill of Rights granted
political representation to women. A Constitutional guarantee of women's suffrage was only
conferred under the Nineteenth Amendment, ratified in 1920.

3. Mark A. Noll, *The Civil War as a Theological Crisis* (Durham: University of North Carolina
Press, 2006).

4. Although there were groups on either side of the debate who were not traditional Christians, including Unitarians and some rationalist skeptics—perhaps even including Abraham
Lincoln, whose personal theology seems to have been something like a form of Deism—the
mainstream intellectual currents at that time were framed in terms of Christian belief. See Noll,
Civil War.

5. James O. Farmer Jr., *The Metaphysical Confederacy: James Henley Thornwell and the Synthesis
of Southern Values* (Macon, GA: Mercer University Press, 1986), 41.

6. Farmer, *Metaphysical Confederacy*, 57–58.

7. Farmer, *Metaphysical Confederacy*, 58.

vigorous theological defense of African slavery.[8] This defense is set out most directly in his sermon "The Rights and Duties of Masters."[9] Thornwell preached the sermon on May 26, 1850, in Charleston, South Carolina, at the dedication of a church "erected for the religious instruction of the Negroes."[10] In many ways Thornwell's arguments are typical of other proslavery preachers and theologians, but in some respects, particularly relating to his political theology, his arguments are more subtle than those of other apologists.

Proslavery apologists argued that both the Old Testament and New Testament sanctioned slavery and that the abolitionists therefore were distorting the plain sense of Scripture.[11] These arguments usually were offered in what today seem like naively biblicist terms. In his book *A Defence of Virginia*, for example, Southern theologian Robert Louis Dabney thundered that "our best hope is in the fact that the cause of our defence is the cause of God's Word, and of its supreme authority over the human conscience. For, as we shall evince, that Word is on our side, and the teachings of Abolitionism are clearly of rationalistic origin, of infidel tendency, and only sustained by reckless and licentious perversions of the meaning of the Sacred text."[12] Dabney argued that the Old Testament explicitly recognized and sanctioned slavery (in the examples of the Curse on Canaan, Abraham, Hagar, the Mosaic law, and the Decalogue), and that in the New Testament, slavery was never condemned by Christ and was approved by Paul.[13] This was a typical laundry list of proslavery Bible passages. In the literate, polemical context of the Bible wars over slavery, however, "southern preachers had to be careful with biblical citations" because "a mere grumble from a few congregants would send others scurrying to check their Bibles."[14] Thornwell knew this and tied his biblical arguments to a broader political philosophy.

In the sermon, Thornwell focused his biblical arguments primarily on

8. See generally Noll, *Civil War*.

9. James Henley Thornwell, *The Rights and Duties of Masters: A Sermon Preached at the Dedication of a Church Erected in Charleston, S.C. for the Benefit of the Coloured Population* (Charleston: Steam Power Press of Walker & James, 1850) (hereinafter "Sermon").

10. Thornwell, introduction to *Rights and Duties*.

11. Noll, *Civil War*, chap. 3.

12. Robert L. Dabney, *A Defence of Virginia (and through Her, of the South) in Recent and Pending Contests against the Sectional Party* (New York: E. J. Hale & Son, 1867), 21. This book was published two years after the conclusion of the Civil War. Dabney had staunchly supported the Southern cause before and during the war, and hoped and believed that God would raise the South again in providential judgment against the North.

13. Dabney, *Defence of Virginia*, 94–198.

14. See Elizabeth Fox-Genovese and Eugene D. Genovese, *The Mind of the Master Class: History and Faith in the Southern Slaveholder's Worldview* (Cambridge: Cambridge University Press 2005), Kindle loc. 14819.

one passage from Colossians 3:22–4:1.[15] As Thornwell summarized this text, "The Apostle briefly sums up all that is incumbent, at the present crisis, upon the slaveholders of the South, in the words of the text—Masters, give unto your servants that which is just and equal, knowing that ye also have a Master in heaven."[16]

Thornwell believed this command was not merely arbitrary because although all persons, white and African alike, were equally human, God had ordained people to different stations and responsibilities. In response to the abolitionist argument that the relationship of master and slave violates a fundamental human right of the slave, Thornwell argued that there is a distinction between basic human rights of all persons and the rights and duties of persons within specific relationships.[17] Paul's injunctions to masters and slaves, Thornwell claimed, embedded a moral principle of duty particular to the roles God had providentially assigned: "Let masters and servants, each in their respective spheres, be impregnated with the principle of duty."[18] Thornwell saw this kind of difference in right and duty based on contingent relationships throughout society, such as between parent and child or husband and wife. The slave is just another "actor on the broad theatre of life" whose reward depends on playing his role appropriately.[19]

Thornwell conceded, however, that slavery was not an intrinsic good. "Slavery," Thornwell argued in the sermon, "is a part of the curse which sin has introduced into the world, and stands in the same general relations to Christianity as poverty, sickness, disease or death."[20] Colossians 3:22–4:1 encoded a form of positive law relating to a set of relationships—master and slave—that was contingent on the present fallen state of the world and that would be erased in the eschaton. Slavery, like other differences in social condition, was "founded in a curse, from which the Providence of God extracts a blessing."[21]

Even more directly, Thornwell conceded that the initial enslavement of Africans, like the beginnings of any enslavement, was violent and morally wrong. But, he insisted, "the relations to which that act gave rise, may, themselves, be consistent with the will of God and the foun-

15. Thornwell, "Sermon," 15. In the modern NIV translation, Col. 3:22 and 4:1 read as follows: "Slaves, obey your earthly masters in everything; and do it, not only when their eye is on you and to curry their favor, but with sincerity of heart and reverence for the Lord. . . . Masters, provide your slaves with what is right and fair, because you know that you also have a Master in heaven."

16. Thornwell, "Sermon," 15.
17. Thornwell, "Sermon," 40.
18. Thornwell, "Sermon," 41.
19. Thornwell, "Sermon," 44.
20. Thornwell, "Sermon," 31.
21. Thornwell, "Sermon," 33.

dation of new and important duties."[22] In fact, Thornwell claimed, in the present fallen state of the world, "an absolute equality would be an absolute stagnation of all enterprise and industry."[23]

Thornwell equated the demand for "absolute equality" with "the agitations which are convulsing the kingdoms of Europe," a reference to the Revolutions of 1848.[24] For Thornwell, the parties in the conflict over slavery "are not merely abolitionists and slaveholders—they are atheists, socialists, communists, red republicans, jacobins, on the one side, and the friends of order and regulated freedom on the other."[25] This appeal to established order was a "central theme" in Old School Presbyterianism, and Thornwell certainly echoed this theme.[26]

Thornwell's focus on this principle of duty appealed to the Southern honor culture and removed his biblical reference from the category of mere biblical proof texting. It tied together a kind of natural law argument with Calvinist theology in a systematic defense of slavery as at least a contingent feature of some social structures. It also allowed Thornwell to sidestep some of the roiling "scientific" arguments over the origins of Africans and to claim that in the end his intent was to defend blacks as fully human along with whites.

Scholarly Old School Presbyterians such as Thornwell were deeply interested in the emerging natural sciences and believed proper scientific methods would verify their beliefs about social order.[27] Thornwell departed from proslavery scientists and clergy who argued that black Africans were cursed or subhuman, either because of the "curse of Canaan" or through some theory of biological polygenesis.

There was an interesting tension in Thornwell's day between apologetics for African slavery based on polygenetic theories and "biblical" defenses of African slavery based on the "curse of Canaan."[28] Polygenetic

22. Thornwell, "Sermon," 45.

23. Thornwell, "Sermon," 32.

24. Thornwell, "Sermon," 12. For background on the revolutions in Europe during this period, see generally R. J. W. Evans and Hartmut Pogge von Strandmann, eds., *The Revolutions in Europe 1848–1849: From Reform to Reaction* (Oxford: Oxford University Press, 2000). For a discussion of how these revolutions affected the views of Southern slaveholders in the US, see Fox-Genovese and Genovese, *Mind of the Master Class*, chap. 2.

25. Fox-Genovese and Genovese, *Mind of the Master Class*, 14.

26. See Theodore Dwight Bozeman, "Inductive and Deductive Politics: Science and Society in Antebellum Persbyterian Thought," *The Journal of American History* 64, no. 3 (1977): 704–22; Marilyn J. Westerkamp, "James Henry Thornwell, Pro-Slavery Spokesman within a Calvinist Faith," *The South Carolina Historical Magazine* 87, no. 1 (1986): 49–64.

27. See Farmer, *Metaphysical Conspiracy*, chap. 3; Fox-Genovese and Genovese, *Mind of the Master Class*, chap. 18.

28. See David N. Livingstone, *Adam's Ancestors: Race, Religion and the Politics of Human Origins* (Baltimore: Johns Hopkins University Press, 2008), 182–90.

theories developed by figures such as Samuel George Morton in the "American School of Ethnology" drew on the emerging evolutionary science of the day to argue that the present races had different biological origins—not a monogentic origin in a literal "Adam and Eve"—and that these differences in origin accounted for presumed differences in mental and cultural capacity.[29] Some Southerners were happy to use these theories in their defense of African slavery, but conservative theologians and churchmen thought these theories contradicted the biblical account of humanity's origin in a single couple.[30] Many of these Southern religious conservatives argued that black Africans did descend from Adam and Eve but that the Africans were a degenerate race because of the "Curse on Canaan" narrated in Genesis 9.

Genesis 9 describes events shortly after the great flood of Noah. The hero of flood story, Noah, plants a vineyard, gets drunk on the resulting wine, and passes out naked outside his tent (Gen 9:20). Noah's son Ham sees Noah's nakedness and tells his brothers, Shem and Japeth—perhaps meaning to make a scene or mock his father. Shem and Japeth cover Noah, taking care to cover their eyes in the process. When Noah awakes, he curses Ham's son, Canaan: "Cursed be Canaan! / The lowest of slaves / will he be to his brothers" (Gen 9:22–25).

The honor culture reflected in this narrative resonated with antebellum Southern readers, who were quick to identify black Africans as Ham and Canaan's descendants.[31] Many Southerners adapted the New American School of Ethnology's "scientific" views about racial differences to a genealogy that preserved Adamic monogenism with a divergence via the curse on Canaan.[32] Some of the leading Southern theologians were reticent to make this connection but still used this narrative as a key illustration. Robert Louis Dabney, for example, agreed that "it may be that we should find little difficulty in tracing the lineage of the present Africans to Ham," but thought the actual scientific evidence lacking.[33] For Dabney, the overall shape of the narrative was more important than the scientific details: this was one example among many of the Bible's moral sanction of slavery in general.

Thornwell was even more reluctant than Dabney to connect African slavery with any sort of genealogical or biological curse. In his sermon,

29. Livingstone, *Adam's Ancestors*, 173–80.

30. Livingstone, *Adam's Ancestors*, 180–82.

31. See Stephen R. Haynes, *Noah's Curse: The Biblical Justifications of American Slavery* (Oxford: Oxford University Press, 2002), chap. 4 (noting connection between Southern honor culture and the Genesis 9 narrative).

32. Haynes, *Noah's Curse*, chap. 4.

33. Dabney, *Defence of Virginia*, 101–4.

Thornwell never mentioned the curse on Canaan and directly rejected polygenetic views. Instead, Thornwell argued that "the Negro is of one blood with ourselves" and stated that "we are not ashamed to call him our brother."[34] This reflects not only a tactical decision to "soften" Southern rhetoric but also a commitment to integrate the Old Presbyterian theology with a form of contemporary science—that is, to reject the polygenetic theories on biblical *and* scientific grounds while upholding African slavery.

Thornwell stated in his inaugural lecture as professor of theology at South Carolina College that the "true method" of theology

> is to accept the facts of revelation as we accept the facts of nature. We are by enlightened interpretation to ascertain the dicta; these are to be received without suspicion and without doubt. They are the principles of faith. Then from these principles proceed to the laws, the philosophy if you please, which underlies them, and in which they find their explanation and their unity. In this way we shall reach truth, and shall be partially able to harmonize it with all other truth.[35]

Here, Thornwell reflects a relatively strong but not absolute view of the "integration" of faith and reason, including the findings of the natural sciences. Like most of his Old Presbyterian contemporaries, Thornwell cautiously accepted the findings of the new Lyellian geology, which showed the Earth was far older than a simple reading of the biblical records seemed to suggest. In this sense, Thornwell's views were consistent with his contemporary at Princeton Seminary, B. B. Warfield.[36] Thornwell departed somewhat, however, from the synthesis of Baconian science and common sense realism characteristic of Warfield by prioritizing "faith" in his epistemology.[37] Thornwell was careful to note that "all knowledge begins in faith; principles must be accepted, not proved, and it matters not whether you call them principles of faith or reason."[38]

Thornwell applied his subtle understanding of faith and reason not only to the natural sciences but also to the newly developing social sciences.[39] The notion that society could be studied according to princi-

34. Thornwell, "Sermon," 11.

35. John B. Adger, *The Collected Writings of James Henley Thornwell, Vol. 1* (Richmond, VA: Presbyterian Committee of Publication, 1871), 582.

36. See Mark A. Noll and David A. Livingstone, eds., *B. B. Warfield, Evolution, Science and Scripture: Selected Writings* (Grand Rapids: Baker, 2000).

37. Farmer, *Metaphysical Conspiracy*, 141–51.

38. Adger, *Collected Writings*, 579.

39. See Bozeman, "Inductive and Deductive Politics," 704–22; Bozeman, "Joseph LeConte: Organic Science and a 'Sociology for the South,'" *The Journal of Southern History* 39, no. 4 (1973): 565–82.

ples of reason rooted in faith, particularly a Calvinistic faith in the slow, inexorable, often hidden workings of providence, underpinned Thornwell's belief that established social institutions such as slavery should not be upset by radical change.[40] The same belief affected Thornwell's treatment of the role of the law in relation to slavery in the sermon. In his assessment of the law of slavery, the limits of Thornwell's method are evident. He could not countenance rapid legal change, and as a result—somewhat ironically in light of his views of Scripture—he had to dance around the law's plain meaning.

For Thornwell the Bible did not sanction the ownership of one person by another person as "property." Rather, the Bible, and the natural law, gave the master a kind of contractual right "not to the *man*, but to his *labor*."[41] This right came with corresponding duties, also reflected in Ephesians 4:5–9, upon the master to treat the slave properly.[42] This relationship was not literally contractual because it was grounded in biblical and positive law, and the slave's obedience, rendered in response to the moral obligation of the natural and biblical law, could properly be considered "voluntary."[43] The motion of the slave's "limbs or organs of the body" are voluntary in the literal sense, Thornwell argued, and the slave's internal "moral character" determined whether his or her actions were "voluntary" in an ethical sense—an ethical obligation that rested entirely on the slave.[44]

Thornwell's argument was ingenious, but it was belied by the actual law of slavery. In the sermon, he offered only a passing glance at "the technical language of the law, in relation to certain aspects in which slavery is contemplated" before claiming that "the ideas of personal rights and personal responsibility pervade the whole system."[45] The law in South Carolina and across the slave states, however, in fact held that "slaves are chattels personal," that is, a form of personal property.[46]

The slave codes did provide some limitations on how slaves should be treated. The slave codes also gave slaves some ability to form enforceable contracts and legitimated other aspects of commerce engaged in by slaves, but these provisions were designed to facilitate the use of slaves as business agents by the master, not to enable slaves to work for their own

40. Bozeman, "Joseph LeConte," 707.
41. Thornwell, "Sermon," 24.
42. Thornwell, "Sermon," 40–41.
43. Thornwell, "Sermon," 27.
44. Thornwell, "Sermon," 27.
45. Thornwell, "Sermon," 27.
46. John Belton O'Neall, *The Negro Law of South Carolina* (Columbia, SC: John G. Bowman, 1848), 5.

benefit.[47] While the slave was in one sense a legal "person," the ascription of personhood was not in recognition of any basic human rights, but only for the benefit of the master. As one modern commentator has suggested, under South Carolina law and the Southern slave codes more broadly, "slavery marked an ownership so utter that the status of property was insufficient to describe it."[48] To the extent Thornwell actually was concerned about describing the social and legal structure of slavery in the sermon, his description was wildly inaccurate.

So how could a well-educated intellectual leader such as Thornwell have been so wrong about slavery? Was he driven to self-delusion, or merely disingenuous because of a cultural need to defend this Southern institution?[49] In the intense hothouse of the slavery debate, some degree of delusion or dissembling cannot be discounted. Thornwell, however, was a rigorous and meticulous person who was well read in historical theology and classical literature and who did not shy away from controversy. His arguments about the personhood of slaves, notwithstanding the "technical language of the law," were rooted in deeper beliefs about the priority of the Bible, or more directly, the priority of his theological system, in relation to what he considered the "scientific" understanding of society. Careful study of Thornwell's sermon and its context might help us avoid overly simplistic, anachronistic judgments of Thornwell and his motives. Perhaps also it can serve as a cautionary tale about how social, political, theological, and biblical views can converge into a system that justifies oppression.

SLAVERY, LAW, AND CULTURE WAR

As suggested by the reference to Thornwell's understanding of the slave codes, slavery was a legal as well as theological crisis. The Southern states each had enacted versions of slave codes stating that slaves were the personal property of their owners. Prior to the Civil War, the Supreme Court held that the Bill of Rights applied only to claims against the federal government, not to claims against state governments.[50] Although the case that established this principle, *Barron v. Mayor and City of Baltimore*, related to the Fifth Amendment's takings clause in an economic dispute over a harbor, it foreclosed any claim that the slave codes in

47. O'Neall, *Negro Law*, 5.
48. John Samuel Harpham, "Two Concepts of a Slave in the South Carolina Law of Slavery," *Slavery and Abolition*, May 25, 2017, https://tinyurl.com/y5c9grqz.
49. Cf. Farmer, *Metaphysical Confederacy*, 196 (noting that some modern historians "have seen the proslavery argument as a clear case of self-serving rhetoric").
50. Barron v. Mayor and City of Baltimore, 7 Pet. (32 U.S.) 243 (1833).

Southern states violated the Bill of Rights.[51] Slavery was illegal in the Northern states, but many Northern states had fugitive slave laws that required runaway slaves to be returned to their Southern masters.

As new territories were being added to the Union, there were disputes about whether the new states should become slave or free states. Under John C. Calhoun, Congress agreed to the "Missouri Compromise," under which Missouri was admitted as a slave state and Maine was admitted as a free state. The Missouri Compromise also drew an imaginary line through the Louisiana Territory, a large swathe of land previously acquired by the United States by Thomas Jefferson in the Louisiana Purchase. New states above the line would be free, and new states below the line would be slave. The political debate leading up to the Missouri Compromise was exceedingly bitter.

Many Southerners believed even this compromise embodied an overly expansive notion of the federal government's ability to dictate basic policies to sovereign states. By 1837, there were thirteen slave states and thirteen free states, meaning that every change could significantly affect the balance of power in Congress. Abolitionists, on the other hand, saw the instability of the Compromise and the injustice of the fugitive slave laws as an opportunity for legal activism. Although under *Barron v. Baltimore* they could not sue to invalidate the Southern slave codes under the Bill of Rights, they pursued litigation to establish a legal right to citizenship for runaway slaves or other blacks who had been slaves but who since had found their way to the North.[52]

One such litigation led to the infamous Supreme Court case of *Dred Scott v. Sandford*.[53] Dred Scott had been born a slave in Virginia in 1799. His owner, Peter Blow, brought him to Alabama and then to Missouri during Blow's unsuccessful efforts at farming and the hotel business.[54] Blow died in Missouri in 1832, and Scott was purchased by Dr. John Emerson, a US Army physician, either shortly before or shortly after Blow's death. At this time, Scott attempted to run away, but he was cap-

---

51. See David J. Bodenhamer, *The Revolutionary Constitution* (Oxford: Oxford University Press 2012), 168.

52. An extensive collection of documents on these and related cases can be found in a Library of Congress collection titled "Slaves and the Courts: 1740–1860," available at https://tinyurl.com/pnrjsqo.

53. 60 U.S. 393 (1857).

54. For the background to the Dred Scott case, see Don E. Fehrenbacher, *The Dred Scott Case: Its Significance in American Law and Politics* (New York: Oxford University Press, 1978), esp. chap. 9; Paul Finkelman, *Dred Scott v. Sandford: A Brief History with Documents* (Boston: Bedford, 1997); Christopher L. Eisgruber, "The Story of Dred Scott: Originalism's Forgotten Past," in *Constitutional Law Stories*, ed. Michael C. Dorf (New York: Foundation, 2009); Missouri State Archives, "Missouri's Dred Scott Case, 1846–1857," available at https://tinyurl.com/gtgkwos.

tured in the Missouri swamps and delivered to Emerson. Scott became a valued servant to Emerson and accompanied Emerson to a posting in Illinois, a free state, in 1833, where he lived until 1836. Emerson brought Scott with him to a posting at Fort Snelling in the Wisconsin Territory, a free territory in an area that is now part of Minnesota. While there, Scott married Harriet Robinson, a slave owned by Lawrence Talieferro, another army officer. Talieferro, who was also a justice of the peace, presided over a civil wedding ceremony for Scott and Robinson.

In 1837, Emerson was transferred to the Jefferson Barracks, a military base along the Mississippi River south of St. Louis. Emerson left Scott behind and leased him out as a servant to other military officers, a common practice with household slaves. Emerson was then transferred to Fort Jesup in Louisiana, where he married Eliza Irene Sandford in 1838. Emerson and his new wife summoned Scott to Louisiana. Dred and Harriet Scott made the journey to Louisiana on the Mississippi River. Along the way, on a steamboat in free territory, Harriet gave birth to a daughter, Lizzie. Lizzie's birth in free territory meant that she legally was free.

In 1840, Dr. Emerson was reassigned to Fort Snelling, and the Scotts moved with the Emersons to St. Louis. While Dr. Emerson was away on military duties in the Seminole War, his wife, Irene, hired the Scotts out. In 1843, Dr. Emerson died while away on duty in the Iowa Territory, leaving his estate, including the Scotts, to Irene. Irene continued to hire the Scotts out over the next three years. In 1836, Scott attempted to purchase his family's freedom from Irene, but she refused. With the help and advice of some abolitionist activists and—remarkably—financial support from the daughter of his previous owner, Charlotte Blow, who was married to an officer of the Bank of Missouri, Scott sued for his freedom.[55]

There was significant legal precedent in Missouri holding that slaves who were brought into free territory could successfully sue for their freedom. In supporting cases like Scott's, abolitionists hoped to chip away at slavery's legal substructure, both by establishing that slaves become legally emancipated while residing in free territory and by establishing that slavery was not a common law property right but only an artificial creation of statutory law. Scott lost at trial because of a technicality concerning some of the trial testimony but was granted a new trial.

55. Charlotte was an extraordinary woman who later founded the "Home of the Friendless," a refuge for elderly indigent women in St. Louis, which remained an independent entity until 2006, when it was purchased by Bethesda Health Group and converted to an assisted living facility. Her second husband, Charles Charless, was murdered, and Charlotte wrote his biography. See John Y. Le Bourgeois and Ashton H. Le Bourgeois, *The Blows of Yesteryear: An American Saga* (2012), a self-published but well-researched biographical sketch of Charlotte Blow and three other descendants of Henry Taylor Blow, written by two present-day Blow descendants.

Irene Emerson appealed the grant of the new trial all the way to the Missouri Supreme Court, which affirmed that a new trial should be granted. The new trial was delayed for three years by a major fire in St. Louis, a cholera outbreak, and two continuances. During this time, the Scotts were remanded to the custody of the St. Louis County Sheriff, who leased them out, with the proceeds held in an escrow account that would belong to Emerson or the Scotts, depending on the final judgment.

In 1850, Scott prevailed in a jury trial and was awarded his freedom. Emerson appealed, and in 1852 the Missouri Supreme Court reversed and held that Scott and his family remained legally enslaved. In light of growing animosity between the free and slave states, the Missouri Supreme Court wrote, the trend of granting legal freedom to slaves who had resided in free states violated the sovereignty of slave states such as Missouri.

By this time, Scott had been sold by Irene Emerson to her brother, John Sandford. Or at least that is what was asserted in court. The record about Scott's transfer to Sandford is murky, and some historians have suggested that Emerson, Sandford, and Scott may have colluded to produce a test case in the federal courts.

The Blow family was no longer able to support Scott financially, but he obtained pro bono legal services from a prominent local real estate attorney, Roswell Field. Scott then sued for his freedom against Sandford in federal court in New York, where Sandford lived. Scott lost at trial and appealed to the US Supreme Court. Irene Emerson had moved to Massachusetts in 1850 and married Calvin Chaffee, an abolitionist who was elected to Congress on the Know-Nothing and Republican ticket. The Republicans were the antislavery Northern party. The Know-Nothings, oddly, began as a secret society that believed Roman Catholics—then an often-persecuted minority in the United States—were conspiring to take over the world. Sandford mounted a vigorous defense supported by proslavery advocates, however, so the collusion theory is doubtful.

President-elect James Buchanan believed the case could resolve tensions over slavery if the court would rule that slaves who had resided in the North have no right to sue for their freedom. He exerted improper personal influence on some of the justices and proclaimed in his inaugural address, before the case was decided, that the slavery question would be "speedily and finally settled" by the court.

The court ruled 7-2 in favor of Sandford. In a now-infamous opinion for the majority, Chief Justice Roger B. Taney wrote that enslaved blacks were not "citizens" under the US Constitution, that the Declaration of Independence's statement that "all men are created equal" did not apply to African blacks. Taney stated that black Africans

> had for more than a century before been regarded as beings of an inferior order, and altogether unfit to associate with the white race, either in social or political relations; and so far inferior, that they had no rights which the white man was bound to respect; and that the negro might justly and lawfully be reduced to slavery for his benefit. He was bought and sold, and treated as an ordinary article of merchandise and traffic, whenever a profit could be made by it. This opinion was at that time fixed and universal in the civilized portion of the white race. It was regarded as an axiom in morals as well as in politics, which no one thought of disputing, or supposed to be open to dispute; and men in every grade and position in society daily and habitually acted upon it in their private pursuits, as well as in matters of public concern, without doubting for a moment the correctness of this opinion.[56]

Taney also stated that the Missouri Compromise was unconstitutional when passed, throwing the already fragile political settlement into disarray. The Missouri Compromise had since been superseded by the 1854 Kansas-Nebraska Act, which drew a demarcation line that allowed more new territories to decide whether to become free or slave states, resulting in violence over slavery in Kansas (dubbed "bloody Kansas" or "bleeding Kansas" in the press). Taney's dicta about the Missouri Compromise raised questions about whether the Kansas-Nebraska Act was constitutional.

The court had reached the result desired by President Buchanan, but the opinion's effect was to deepen the political and legal divide over slavery. It also contributed to the economic panic of 1857 because of the fear that, absent a stable political compromise, violence would break out in Western territories over whether to become free or slave states.

Meanwhile, Irene Emerson's husband, Calvin Chaffee, was under increasing political pressure to free the Scotts. Although Chaffee protested that he had no legal title, the Chaffees signed a legal document transferring the Scotts to Taylor Blow—brother of Charlotte Blow Charless and son of Scott's deceased first owner, Peter Blow. Taylor Blow legally granted Scott his freedom on May 26, 1857. Scott enjoyed brief fame as a porter in a St. Louis hotel but died of tuberculosis on November 7, 1858. Harriet Scott lived until 1876.

The instability and violence preceding and following the *Dred Scott* decision, of course, did not abate. The Civil War began in 1861 and ended in 1865, resulting in at least one million casualties—the most

56. 60 U.S. at 407.

American casualties in any war in our history. Only after the North won the Civil War, and even then only over the opposition of President Andrew Johnson (successor to the assassinated Abraham Lincoln), did the Thirteenth Amendment finally outlaw slavery in the United States. And as discussed further below, from the Reconstruction era through Jim Crow and the civil rights movement and still today—indeed, even within the structure of the Thirteenth Amendment itself—the legacy of slavery and racism never fully went away.

When we look back at the antebellum era, we naturally sympathize with the abolitionists and with heroic figures such as Dred Scott. We can easily see that Justice Taney's opinion in *Dred Scott v. Sandford* is abominable, and we grieve that it took Dred Scott so many years to obtain his freedom, only to succumb not too long afterward to tuberculosis. We admire evangelical women such as Charlotte Blow Charless, who not only supported her father's former slave, but who later in life founded the "Home of the Friendless," a refuge for elderly indigent women in St. Louis. We marvel at the resilience these people showed in the face of adversity and tragedy.

Yet it was not at all obvious to many Christians at the time that the abolitionists were right. Southern Christian intellectuals praised Justice Taney's opinion for upholding the rule of law and the principle of state sovereignty against federal incursion. They aligned squarely on the other side of the legal fight. It is very likely that if you or I were alive at that time, our views would have aligned with whether we were Southerners or Northerners, not with what we might think as we look back on the issue now 150 years later. Indeed, the question was not even obvious to Charlotte Charless. She helped Dred Scott with his lawsuit, but when the Civil War began, she sympathized with the Confederacy.

There were some people at the time who recognized that the dispute over slavery was tearing apart both the nation and the churches. Like today's ecclesial ethicists, some of them argued that the churches should stay out of the political question entirely. Some of these people were, in fact, from the historic Anabaptist churches, such as the Mennonites. Others were from the mainline denominations, including even some Southern proslavery Presbyterians such as James Henley Thornwell, at least until it became impossible to remain neutral in the face of denominational splits.

Looking back on this period today, it is hard to suggest that it would have been better for abolitionist Christians to withdraw from the secular political culture and instead to embody an antislavery norm within the church community. Faced with public legal statements such as Justice

Taney's, we are glad there were some brave Christians who were willing to speak prophetically about the evils of slavery and to support legal advocacy on behalf of freeing slaves. Perhaps a more demure posture would have avoided, or deferred, the Civil War, though in the long run that seems doubtful.

FROM CIVIL WAR TO CIVIL RIGHTS

Even the Civil War, of course, did not end the struggle for racial equality in America. On April 14, 1865, President Lincoln was assassinated. Meanwhile, Northern leaders in Congress drafted a series of constitutional amendments relating to the end of African slavery, which became the Thirteenth, Fourteenth, and Fifteenth Amendments. The Thirteenth Amendment, proposed by Congress and ratified by the states in 1865, abolished slavery and involuntary servitude—"except as a punishment for crime whereof the party shall have been duly convicted." The Fourteenth Amendment overturned the *Dred Scott* decision by stating that "all persons born or naturalized in the United States and subject to the jurisdiction thereof, are citizens of the United States and of the State wherein they reside." The Fourteenth Amendment also included "privileges and immunities," "equal protection," and "due process" clauses that applied directly to the states: "No State shall make or enforce any law which shall abridge the privileges or immunities of citizens of the United States; nor shall any State deprive any person of life, liberty, or property, without due process of law; nor deny to any person within its jurisdiction the equal protection of the laws."[57] The Fifteenth Amendment guaranteed all citizens, regardless of race or previous condition of servitude, the right to vote.

The Southern states were brought back into the Union upon accepting these constitutional amendments, but they found ways to limit the effect of the amendments. Under the Thirteenth Amendment's "punishment" exception, they passed harsh laws through which many former slaves became contractually indentured servants, subject to cycles of indebtedness and abuse.[58] Under the Fourteenth Amendment, based on the pre–Civil War precedent of *Barron v. Baltimore*, they argued against any substantive "incorporation" of the Bill of Rights as applied to the

---

57. This provision was meant to overturn the Supreme Court's decision in *Barron v. Baltimore*, 32 U.S. (7 Pet.) 243 (1833),which held that the due process clause of the Fourth Amendment applied only to the federal government and not to the States.

58. In the modern context of mass incarceration and the "war on drugs," this is the subject of the fascinating documentary *13th*. See https://tinyurl.com/h46x7be.

States and continued to censor black people and their allies. Under the Fifteenth Amendment, they adopted literacy, financial, property ownership, and other onerous requirements for the right to vote and also engaged in intimidation and violence at polling places. The "slave codes" of the antebellum South became "black codes" that perpetuated a form of slavery under a different legal regime. They also adopted "Jim Crow" laws, which required black people to use different services than whites in public facilities, such as education and transportation facilities—services that were, inevitably, underfunded and of inferior quality to those available to whites.

Over time, the Supreme Court concluded that nearly all of the substantive guarantees of the Bill of Rights, such as the freedoms of speech and religion, apply directly to the states through "incorporation" under the Fourteenth Amendment, effectively overturning *Barron v. Baltimore*.[59] But the South's resistance to reconstruction after the Civil War led to another of the Supreme Court's most atrocious decisions: *Plessy v. Ferguson*, which established the "separate but equal" doctrine under the Fourteenth Amendment's equal protection clause.[60] The fallacious "separate but equal" doctrine became a legal pillar of American racism.

The "separate but equal" doctrine was challenged, along with other elements of legalized structural racism, by the civil rights movement of the 1950s and 1960s, led by Martin Luther King Jr. and other brave men and women. A crucial part of the movement's strategy was to combine nonviolent direct action, such as marches and sit-ins, with lawsuits aimed at overturning the remnants of Jim Crow and ultimately reversing *Plessy*. Much of the legal strategy was led by the NAACP Legal Defense and Education Fund, which was founded and directed by Thurgood Marshall, who later would serve as a justice on the Supreme Court. The marches and sit-ins often were held in defiance of statutes, ordinances, or court orders restricting when and how protests could be held. These actions are important for our discussion of "consent" because they relate to the tension between Acts 5 and Romans 13 highlighted in chapter 1.

In 1954, these efforts led to the Supreme Court's landmark opinion in *Brown v. Board of Education*.[61] In *Brown*, by a unanimous decision, the Supreme Court held that "separate but equal" public educational facilities for racial minorities violate the equal protection clause of the Fourteenth Amendment, overruling *Plessy*. Although the *Brown* opinion held that segregation of public schools was unconstitutional, the court did

---

59. For a general description of this doctrine, see Chemerinsky, *Constitutional Law*, 6.3.
60. 163 U.S. 537 (1896).
61. 347 U.S. 483 (1954).

not order immediate desegregation but requested additional argument on the issue of remedies. In 1955, in case referred to as *Brown II*, the court held that local school districts, overseen if necessary by local federal courts, should fashion remedies suited to local conditions, including "problems related to administration, arising from the physical condition of the school plant, the school transportation system, personnel, revision of school districts and attendance areas into compact units to achieve a system of determining admission to the public schools."[62] This process, the court said, must occur "with all deliberate speed."[63] This resulted in decades of additional legal battles over how desegregation should be accomplished—battles that, in some areas, still arise today.

One of the most dramatic of these battles occurred in Little Rock, Arkansas, in 1957. Asserting federalism arguments about states' rights, Arkansas governor Orval Faubus directed the Arkansas National Guard to prevent African American students from entering an all-white high school in Little Rock. When nine African American students entered the school to enroll, a riot erupted. The mayor of Little Rock sought President Eisenhower's help, and Eisenhower nationalized the Arkansas National Guard and deployed an additional one thousand Army paratroopers to Little Rock, restoring order.

Meanwhile, in addition to continued tensions over desegregation, the civil rights movement lobbied for legislative protections against racial discrimination in restaurants, movie theaters, and other businesses open to the public, as well as for protections against racial discrimination in employment. After *Brown v. Board of Education* in 1954, "separate but equal" was no longer the law, but this affected only *government* facilities such as public schools.[64] In general, the constitutional protections of the Bill of Rights apply only between individuals and the state, not between private persons—a principle called the "state action" doctrine.[65]

There are good reasons for the state action doctrine. At the broadest theoretical and historical level, the framers of the original Constitution were concerned about the basic structure and function of government, and the Bill of Rights was designed to define fundamental relationships between the government and the governed. Relationships between individual people were left to more ordinary level of social interaction—families, friendships, religious organizations, businesses, trades, and the like—governed at the local level by the criminal law and by the common

---

62. *Brown v. Board of Education of Topeka* (Brown II), 349 U.S. 284, 300–301 (1955).
63. *Brown v. Board of Education of Topeka* (Brown II), 349 U.S. 284, 301 (1955).
64. *Brown v. Board of Education*, 347 U.S. 483 (1954).
65. See Chemerinsky, *Constitutional Law*, 6.4.

law of torts, property, and contract. The state action doctrine embodies principles of federalism—the relationship between the federal and state governments, as well as principles of subsidiarity—the notion that it is best for local matters to be handled locally. But what if local values violate a more basic norm?

Local businesses in the South often maintained segregated spaces or refused to serve black people. They argued, correctly, that the Bill of Rights did not apply to them because they were private businesses operating on private property.[66] Moreover, local authorities had not adopted antidiscrimination laws in their municipal or state law codes. The local norm was that a businessowner should be free to serve or not serve whomever he wanted and that it was better for blacks and whites to be separated as much as possible.

KING'S "LETTER FROM A BIRMINGHAM JAIL"

It was in this fraught context of the ongoing battle to implement *Brown* and the effort to get a civil rights statute through Congress that the Southern Christian Leadership Conference, led by King, James Bevel, Fred Shuttlesworth, and others, organized a series of demonstrations in Birmingham, Alabama, in 1963. Birmingham was a deeply racially divided city. The demonstrations led to the infamous scenes of Birmingham police deploying high-pressure fire hoses and attack dogs on protesters, including children and other bystanders. They also led to King's arrest and to his "Letter from a Birmingham Jail," a justly famous document in the history of political theology. In his "Letter from a Birmingham Jail," King laid out a theological case for civil disobedience grounded in consent and the natural law.

King was arrested because Birmingham's commissioner of public safety, Eugene "Bull" Connor, a passionate segregationist, had obtained a legal injunction barring the protests, which King and the other protest organizers ignored. The protesters knew they would be arrested for disobeying the injunction and hoped the arrests would bring attention to their cause.

King wrote the letter on April 16, 1963, in response to an open letter titled "A Call for Unity" directed to King and signed by eight white religious leaders in Alabama.[67] Those same leaders had issued a letter

66. There were some cases of business operated on public or publicly financed property in which courts found that there was sufficient state action for the Bill of Rights to apply directly. See Chemerinsky, *Constitutional Law*, 6.4. But these cases represented narrow expansions of the state action doctrine.

67. It is not difficult to find a copy of "A Call to Unity" online, but most of the sites hosting

titled "An Appeal for Law and Order and Common Sense" on January 16, 1965, directed to segregationists who opposed pending court orders to desegregate Alabama schools. They pleaded with "those who strongly oppose desegregation to pursue their convictions in the courts, and in the meantime peacefully to abide by the decisions of those same courts."[68] In a similar vein, in their "Call for Unity" these clergy stated that the protests were "unwise and untimely" and argued that "when rights are consistently denied, a cause should be pressed in the courts and in negotiations among local leaders, and not in the streets."[69] The protests went forward, and King was arrested along with fifty other protesters on Good Friday, April 12, 1963.

In the "Letter from a Birmingham Jail," King responded as follows: "I have earnestly opposed violent tension, but there is a type of constructive, nonviolent tension which is necessary for growth. . . . The purpose of our direct action program is to create a situation so crisis packed that it will inevitably open the door to negotiation."[70] King noted that long experience in the quest for civil rights bore out his claim: "I must say to you that we have not made a single gain in civil rights without determined legal and nonviolent pressure." Nonviolent pressure, including litigation and other efforts to change the law, King said, was necessary because "lamentably, it is an historical fact that privileged groups seldom give up their privileges voluntarily."[71] One of the most stirring passages in the letter is King's response to the tension between patience and action:

> Perhaps it is easy for those who have never felt the stinging darts of segregation to say, "Wait." But when you have seen vicious mobs lynch your mothers and fathers at will and drown your sisters and brothers at whim; when you have seen hate filled policemen curse, kick and even kill your black brothers and sisters; . . .when your first name becomes "nigger," your middle name becomes "boy" (however old you are) and your last name becomes "John," and your wife and mother are never given the respected title "Mrs."; . . . then you will understand why we find it difficult to wait.

copies are run by white supremacist organizations. King began to compose his letter in the jail but may have finished it after release. See S. Jonathan Bass, *Blessed Are the Peacemakers: Martin Luther King, Jr., Eight White Religious Leaders, and the "Letter from Birmingham Jail"* (Baton Rouge: Lousiana State University Press, 2001), 136. For a review of Bass's views on the letter, see Randal Maurice Jelks, "Jelks on Bass," H-South, January 2004, https://tinyurl.com/yxhz2a8q.

68. Bass, *Blessed Are the Peacemakers.*
69. Bass, *Blessed Are the Peacemakers.*
70. Martin Luther King Jr., "Letter from a Birmingham Jail," April 16, 1963, https://tinyurl.com/ovcktqb.
71. King, "Letter from a Birmingham Jail."

There comes a time when the cup of endurance runs over, and men are no longer willing to be plunged into the abyss of despair.[72]

King was particularly concerned in the letter to rebut calls for patience from whites who were not overtly racist but who could not understand the black person's longing for liberation. "I have almost reached the regrettable conclusion," King said, "that the Negro's great stumbling block in his stride toward freedom is not the White Citizen's Counciler or the Ku Klux Klanner, but the white moderate, who is more devoted to 'order' than to justice."[73]

King's interlocutors criticized him for breaking the law in order to uphold the law. King wanted Alabama to implement desegregation as required by the Supreme Court and the lower courts, but the injunction procured by Bull Connor prohibited King from public protest over Alabama's failure to comply with the law. King's response was that civil disobedience is appropriate when the law is unjust: "One may well ask: 'How can you advocate breaking some laws and obeying others?' The answer lies in the fact that there are two types of laws: just and unjust. I would be the first to advocate obeying just laws. One has not only a legal but a moral responsibility to obey just laws. Conversely, one has a moral responsibility to disobey unjust laws. I would agree with St. Augustine that 'an unjust law is no law at all.'"[74]

But how can anyone tell the difference between a just and an unjust law? King referred the question to the natural law: "A just law is a man made code that squares with the moral law or the law of God. An unjust law is a code that is out of harmony with the moral law. To put it in the terms of St. Thomas Aquinas: An unjust law is a human law that is not rooted in eternal law and natural law."[75] For King, this led to a basic principle: "Any law that uplifts human personality is just. Any law that degrades human personality is unjust."[76] This principle led King to conclude that "an unjust law is a code that a numerical or power majority group compels a minority group to obey but does not make binding on itself," while "a just law is a code that a majority compels a minority to follow and that it is willing to follow itself."[77] The unjust law is "difference made legal" while the just law is "sameness made legal."[78]

72. King, "Letter from a Birmingham Jail."
73. King, "Letter from a Birmingham Jail."
74. King, "Letter from a Birmingham Jail."
75. King, "Letter from a Birmingham Jail."
76. King, "Letter from a Birmingham Jail."
77. King, "Letter from a Birmingham Jail."
78. King, "Letter from a Birmingham Jail."

King weaved a prophetic theology of history throughout the letter. There is a time to wait quietly, but there also is a time to engage in peaceful resistance, including through efforts at legal change. In the middle part of the letter King responded to a letter he received "from a white brother in Texas" who suggested that the kingdom of God eventually would arrive and produce change. King thought "such an attitude stems from a tragic misconception of time, from the strangely irrational notion that there is something in the very flow of time that will inevitably cure all ills. . . . We will have to repent in this generation not merely for the hateful words and actions of the bad people but for the appalling silence of the good people."[79]

King's letter highlights several themes that are central to this chapter. First, the struggle for liberation can only be understood through the experience of the oppressed. A call for patient endurance to the oppressed made from within the privileged elite is meaningless. Anyone who calls for patient endurance must be willing to endure oppression in solidarity with the oppressed. Second, law is the difference between the violent and nonviolent struggle for liberation. The nonviolent struggle for liberation is in significant part a struggle for legal change. As we noted in chapter 3, there is a kind of violence inherent in the law, because the law's prohibitions ultimately are enforced through force. But within a movement for nonviolent change, law backed by force differs from the direct application of force. Third, the rule of law is not absolute because only just laws are legitimately enforceable. A central function of nonviolent advocacy for legal change is to highlight where the positive law is illegitimate because of its injustice, perhaps even through civil disobedience. Finally, the church cannot sit on the sidelines of legal change if it truly loves the oppressed. Supporting legal change on behalf of the oppressed is a core part of how the church must live out the *missio Dei* in the difficult crucible of history.

THE ONGOING DEBATE ABOUT CONSENT AND CIVIL RIGHTS

As historian Mark Noll notes, "Civil rights legislation became the law of the land when self-sacrificing civil rights proponents compelled the federal government to act."[80] After much bitter debate, Congress passed the Civil Rights Act of 1964, which banned racial discrimination in places of

79. King, "Letter from a Birmingham Jail."
80. Mark Noll, *God and Race in American Politics: A Short History* (Princeton: Princeton University Press, 2010), 142.

public accommodation (such as restaurants) and prohibited employment discrimination based on race.[81] Many Southerners and other political and religious conservatives continued to insist that the Civil Rights Act of 1964 and other related civil rights laws represented improper assertions of federal power into state and local affairs. Some of these objections were taken up by other conservatives and remain a staple in debates about "big government" today. One of these key objections relates to religious liberty and conscience. Another relates to federalism.

Predictably, some conservative Christian groups were among those who resisted the civil rights laws as potential infringements of local sovereignty and religious liberty. This included Bob Jones University, which had a policy against "miscegenation," the mixing of the races in marriage. The university policy stated as follows:

There is to be no interracial dating.

1. Students who are partners in an interracial marriage will be expelled.

2. Students who are members of or affiliated with any group or organization which holds as one of its goals or advocates interracial marriage will be expelled.

3. Students who date outside of their own race will be expelled.

4. Students who espouse, promote, or encourage others to violate the University's dating rules and regulations will be expelled.[82]

Today this policy seems like part of a crazy law school exam question invented by a bored law professor. But for Bob Jones University, this policy reflected a long and deeply held religious belief that God intended for the races to remain separate and that racial interbreeding was sinful. It is correct to see the continuity here with the views of Southern Christians such as Robert Dabney and James Henley Thornwell prior to the Civil War.[83]

81. Pub.L. 88–352, 78 Stat. 241 (July 2, 1964).

82. Bob Jones University v. United States, 471 U.S. 574 (1983).

83. As John Fea notes, "Most white evangelicals were not particularly interested in the civil rights movement; they were far more concerned about—and opposed to—the way the federal government used its power to enforce desegregation and oppose Jim Crow laws in their local communities." John Fea, *Believe Me: The Evangelical Road to Donald Trump* (Grand Rapids: Eerdmans, 2018), 54; see also Noll, *God and Race in American Politics*, chap. 4.

Bob Jones University, like most private universities, was designated under US tax law as a not-for-profit charitable corporation. Among other things, this designation allows those who donate to the organization to deduct those donations from the gross income when they file their annual income taxes—an incentive for charitable giving. The IRS had changed its interpretation of the tax exemption rules so that institutions such as Bob Jones University with racially discriminatory policies would no longer be eligible for "charitable" status.

Bob Jones University fought the case all the way to the Supreme Court, arguing both that the IRS lacked authority to interpret the charitable deduction rule in this way and that the interpretation violated the university's rights to freedom of religion and speech under the First Amendment. The court ruled 8-1 against the university, with only then–Associate Justice Rehnquist dissenting.[84] For a period after this decision, the university chose to eschew not-for-profit status. In 2000, Bob Jones III, the grandson of the university's founder, reversed the miscegenation policy. We will return to the *Bob Jones* case when we discuss today's fights over LGBTQ rights and religious liberty in chapter 6.

CONSENT AND THE NEW FEDERALISM

Another objection to statutes like the Civil Rights Act of 1964 was rooted in federalism. Remember that the due process and equal protection guarantees of the Fourteenth Amendment apply directly only against the government (or, in very limited circumstances, against private entities that can be considered state actors). So how can Congress at the federal level enact legislation that extends equal protection–like rules to private entities such as restaurants and movie theaters?

The answer is the power to regulate "interstate commerce" granted to Congress under Article I, section 8, clause 3 of the Constitution (the "commerce clause"). Congress's power to regulate interstate commerce was interpreted relatively narrowly by the Supreme Court until the New Deal era. The New Deal was an effort under the Franklin D. Roosevelt administration to mitigate and reverse the effects of the Great Depression through federal economic and labor regulation. At first the Court rejected New Deal legislation as federal overreach under the commerce clause, prompting Roosevelt to devise a plan to "pack" the Supreme Court with additional justices presumably favorable to his views.[85]

---

84. Fea, *Believe Me*, 54.

85. For a discussion of the history of commerce clause interpretation, see Chemerinsky, *Constitutional Law*, 3.4.

The court packing plan was rejected by Congress, but within a few years the makeup of the existing Court changed, and the Court began upholding New Deal legislation under the commerce clause, usually by a 5–4 margin. A group of dissenters dubbed the "Four Horsemen," Justices McReynolds, Van Devanter, Sutherland, and Butler—argued that under the majority's now more extensive view of the commerce clause, "almost anything—marriage, birth, death—may in some fashion affect [commerce]."[86]

After the New Deal era, the commerce clause was broadly interpreted to allow the federal government to regulate many kinds of activities that were within the traditional state police power, so long as some connection with interstate commerce could be shown. This is how Congress in the Civil Rights Act of 1964 was able to require a business like a small lunch counter in a place like Birmingham to serve customers of all races equally.

Starting in the 1990s with *United States v. Lopez*, a conservative bloc on the Court led by Justice Rehnquist, with Justice Kennedy serving as a swing vote, seemed to breathe new life into the commerce clause when they struck down the Gun Free School Zones Act of 1990 as beyond the federal commerce power.[87] Some constitutional law scholars suggested a "new federalism" was emerging, although that characterization was and is debated. A conservative majority of the Court later agreed that the Obamacare individual mandate for health insurance was not authorized by the commerce clause, although Justice Roberts ultimately defected to the liberal bloc to uphold the individual mandate under the taxing power.[88]

All of this quickly gets deep into the weeds of constitutional doctrine. My point here is that even though today conservatives and liberals alike generally agree, or at least say they agree, with the goals of the Civil Rights Act of 1964 and of related federal civil rights legislation, deep doctrinal and ideological divisions remain about the legitimacy of the Congress's ability to reach into areas of state and local governance in order to impose national values. The history of slavery and the civil rights movement in America shows that positive law was, and remains, an important tool in the struggle for liberation against the American original sin of racism. It also shows that objections to Supreme Court precedents and federal legislation regarding civil rights on the basis of religious liberty and limited government are deeply connected to racism,

---

86. *NLRB v. Jones & Laughlin Steel Corp.*, 301 U.S. 1, 99 (McReynolds, J., dissenting).
87. *United States v. Lopez*, 514 U.S. 549 (1995).
88. *National Federation of Independent Business v. Sebelius*, 567 U.S. 519 (2012).

including racism in the church. While these ongoing debates about religious liberty and federalism today are legitimately contested and even interesting from a theoretical perspective, we should always keep in mind that they remain embedded in a painful and sinful national history of racism.

6.

The Second and Third Big Questions: Abortion and LGBTQ Rights

INTRODUCTION

As the discussion in chapter 5 suggests, the civil rights movement could not have made progress without both the Supreme Court's application of the Fourteenth Amendment's equal protection clause against the "separate but equal" doctrine and Congress's willingness to pass civil rights legislation. Some earlier generations of Christians opposed "judicial activism" and "big government" because they believed in the righteousness of black slavery or in divinely ordained racial separation—even opposed, as they were, by other Christians who thought differently.

Few Christians today outside the extremist fringe of identified white nationalist groups would hold to an overtly racist theology. But many conservative Christians today continue to believe fighting "judicial activism" and "big government" is an important priority for the church. Why? Some of the opposition could represent a reflex honed during the civil rights era, even if the racist ideology is in the past. No doubt there are also vestiges of racism among white conservative Christians. Much of the fight over federalism, however, has moved on to new fronts in the culture wars: abortion and gay marriage.

188 THE SECOND AND THIRD BIG QUESTIONS

ABORTION, GAY MARRIAGE, EQUAL PROTECTION, AND SUBSTANTIVE DUE PROCESS

The roots of the Supreme Court's substantive due process jurisprudence relating to sex, abortion, and sexuality lie in the 1965 case of *Griswold v. Connecticut*, which struck down a Connecticut statute banning the use of contraceptives and a related accessory statute.[1] The defendants in that case, the executive director and medical director of the Planned Parenthood League of Connecticut, were convicted as accessories under the Connecticut statute for providing counseling and prescriptions for contraception to married women.[2]

Unlike *Brown* and other civil rights cases, *Griswold* was not an equal protection case. The reason is that the Connecticut statute applied equally to everyone: neither men nor women could lawfully use contraceptives. But in addition to the equal protection clause, the Fourteenth Amendment also contains a "due process" clause, which prohibits a state from "depriv[ing] any person of life, liberty, or property, without due process of law."[3] Writing for the court, Justice Douglas stated that "specific guarantees in the Bill of Rights have penumbras, formed by emanations from those guarantees that help give them life and substance" and that "various guarantees create zones of privacy."[4] Justice Douglas thought these zones of privacy were particularly salient concerning intimate family relationships.

Eight years later, this idea underpinned Justice Blackmun's majority opinion in the case that established a constitutional right to an abortion, *Roe v. Wade*.[5] Justice Blackmun's majority opinion in *Roe* held that the right of privacy recognized in *Griswold* was "broad enough to encompass a woman's decision whether or not to terminate her pregnancy."[6] However, the court held that the state may have an interest in "safeguarding health, in maintaining medical standards, and in protecting potential life."[7] The balance of these interests, the majority held, varied depending on fetal "viability," which the court presumed began at about the third trimester of pregnancy.

The court's decision in *Roe* sparked conservative evangelicals to join forces with conservative Catholics in antiabortion activism. This

1. 381 U.S. 479 (1965).
2. 381 U.S. 480 (1965).
3. U.S. Const., Amendment XIV, Section 1.
4. 381 U.S. 484 (1965).
5. *Roe v. Wade*, 410 U.S. 113 (1973).
6. *Roe v. Wade*, 410 U.S. 153 (1973).
7. *Roe v. Wade*, 410 U.S. 154 (1973).

activism included state legislation designed to test the limits of the states' interests under *Roe* and also challenge the "viability" framework as medical advances pushed the date of survivability of early-term births earlier and earlier into the term of pregnancy.

As Republicans under presidents Ronald Reagan and George H. W. Bush had an opportunity to appoint more conservative justices to the Supreme Court, many pro-life activists hoped that the court would use one of these state experiments as a reason to overrule *Roe*. Those hopes were dashed when Justice O'Connor did not vote with the conservatives in *Planned Parenthood of Southeastern Pa. v. Casey* in 1992.[8] In a plurality opinion in *Casey*, Justice O'Connor stated an "undue burden" test, which asks whether a "state regulation has the purpose or effect of placing a substantial obstacle in the path of a woman seeking an abortion of a nonviable fetus."[9] Under this test, "the means chosen by the State to further the interest in potential life must be calculated to inform the woman's free choice, not hinder it."[10] Critics of Justice O'Connor's opinion in *Casey*, including Justices Rehnquist, White, Thomas, and Scalia, argued that this "undue burden" test was not tied to any constitutional framework. In a good example of his pithy and even acerbic style, Justice Scalia suggested that the "best the Court can do to explain how it is that the word 'liberty' must be thought to include the right to destroy human fetuses is to rattle off a collection of adjectives that simply decorate a value judgment and conceal a political choice."[11]

The next major test in the Supreme Court was *Gonzales v. Carhart* in 2007.[12] *Carhart* involved a ban on intact dilation and evacuation procedures—what pro-life advocates called "partial birth" abortions. The conservative bloc of Justices Roberts, Scalia, Thomas, and Alito, joined by Justice Kennedy, upheld the state law at issue in that case as at least not facially unconstitutional. The majority noted that procedures other than intact dilation and evacuation are usually available for late-term abortions, so that limits on this one procedure would not impact women's health.

The majority opinion drew a vigorous dissent from the court's liberal bloc, written by Justice Ginsburg. According to Justice Ginsburg, the "Court has consistently required that laws regulating abortion, at any stage of pregnancy and in all cases, safeguard a woman's health."[13]

8. 505 U.S. 833 (1992).
9. 505 U.S. 872–73 (1992).
10. 505 U.S. 877 (1992).
11. 505 U.S. 983 (1992).
12. 550 U.S. 124.
13. 550 U.S. 172.

The most recent major abortion case at the Supreme Court was *Whole Woman's Health v. Hellerstedt* in 2016.[14] That case involved a Texas law that required abortion clinics to meet the regulatory requirements of a surgical center and only to employ doctors with hospital admitting privileges. This time Justice Kennedy joined the liberal bloc of Justices Breyer, Ginsburg, Kagan, and Sotomayor. In his majority opinion, Justice Breyer argued that neither of these restrictions "confers medical benefits sufficient to justify the burdens that each imposes."[15] In a concurrence, Justice Ginsburg argued that laws that "do little or nothing for health, but rather strew impediments to abortion, cannot survive judicial inspection."[16]

LGBTQ CIVIL RIGHTS AND GAY MARRIAGE

Cases at the Supreme Court concerning LGBTQ rights and gay marriage at first met with less success than abortion cases. In the first major test, *Bowers v. Hardwick*, decided in 1986, a 5–4 majority of the court upheld a Texas criminal antisodomy statute as applied to homosexual sodomy. The majority held that homosexual sodomy is not a fundamental right under the equal protection clause of the Fourteenth Amendment.[17]

When *Bowers* was decided, many states had antisodomy laws on the books. Such statutes were almost never enforced against heterosexual couples. In some places with active gay populations, these statutes were sometimes enforced against LGBTQ people through raids on gay bars, surveillance of suspected gay people, efforts to deprive gay people of employment, and other forms of harassment by law enforcement.[18] By the time *Bowers* was decided in 1986, the AIDS crisis was in full swing, and public attitudes toward homosexuality were beginning to change. LGBTQ activists and other civil liberties groups began advocating for the recognition of sexual orientation as a protected class in state and federal civil rights statutes.

As discussed in chapter 5, the first civil rights statutes concerning racial discrimination were passed after the Civil War. The "separate but equal"

---

14. 136 S. Ct. 2292 (2016).
15. 136 S. Ct. 2299 (2016).
16. 136 S. Ct. 2321 (2016).
17. 487 US. 186 (1986).
18. See, e.g., Matt Apuzzo, "Uncovered Papers Show Past Government Efforts to Drive Gays from Jobs," May 20, 2014, https://tinyurl.com/y2e3eylq; Douglas M. Charles, *Hoover's War on Gays: Exposing the FBI "Sex Deviates" Program* (Lawrence: University of Kansas Press, 2015).

doctrine of *Plessy v. Ferguson*, decided in 1896, undermined the effect of these laws until *Brown v. Board of Education* was decided in 1954.[19]

Even after *Brown*, however, under the "state action" doctrine, the guarantees of the Bill of Rights and of the Fourteenth Amendment apply only against the federal and state governments, not to actions by individuals against other individuals. Civil rights claims by individuals against other individuals (including against corporations) usually can only arise under statutes that establish such claims. Federal civil rights statutes passed in the 1960s protect against racial discrimination in places of public accommodation, education, employment, voting, and housing, and federal statutes passed in 1980 and 1990 provide protections for institutionalized persons and persons with disabilities. Title II of the Civil Rights Act of 1964 prohibits discrimination in places of public accommodation based on "race, color, religion, or national origin."[20] Places of public accommodation include, for example, hotels, restaurants, lunch counters, and movie theaters.[21]

These statutes enjoy a justifiably iconic status in our culture. They result from the courage of Rosa Parks refusing to take a back seat on a public bus, "whites only" signs in restaurants throughout the South, the "colored bathroom" ensuring that a white person doesn't have to pee in the same place as a black person, and countless other indignities of the Jim Crow era. They were the direct fruit of the peaceful heroism of Martin Luther King Jr. and other leaders of the civil rights movement discussed in chapter 5.

But Title II does not mention sexual orientation as a protected category. Title VII, which protects against discrimination in employment, covers "race, color, religion, sex or national origin." It is unclear whether "sex" would include sexual orientation.[22] The addition of sexual orientation as a protected class in state and federal civil rights law has been a key battleground for the religious right, which wants to distinguish race from sexual orientation in the popular imagination. Religious conservatives have successfully fought efforts to amend federal civil rights statutes to cover sexual orientation since the first such proposed amendment was introduced in Congress in 1975.[23]

In addition to the federal statutes, every state except for Alabama,

19. Plessy v. Ferguson, 163 U.S. 537 (1896); Brown v. Board of Education of Topeka, 347 U.S. 483 (1954).
20. 42 U.S.C. § 2000a(a).
21. 42 U.S.C. § 2000a(b).
22. 42 U.S.C. § 2000e-2.
23. See Courtney Joslin, "Protection for Lesbian, Gay, Bisexual, and Transgender Employees under Title VII of the 1964 Civil Rights Act," *American Bar Association Human Rights Magazine* 31, no. 3 (Summer 2004).

Georgia, Mississippi, North Carolina, and Texas has its own civil rights statute relating to access to places of public accommodation for nondisabled people, most of which were modeled on Title II.[24] LGBTQ advocates and their supporters sought to add sexual orientation as a protected class under some of these state statutes. By 1992, they were successful in twenty-two states.[25]

One of the battles over this issue occurred in Colorado, a historically libertarian state that nevertheless was home to some prominent conservative evangelical parachurch ministries located in Colorado Springs, including Focus on the Family, led by Dr. James Dobson. In 1992, Colorado voters approved an amendment (Amendment 2) to their state Constitution that stated as follows:

> Neither the State of Colorado, through any of its branches or departments, nor any of its agencies, political subdivisions, municipalities or school districts, shall enact, adopt or enforce any statute, regulation, ordinance or policy whereby homosexual, lesbian or bisexual orientation, conduct, practices or relationships shall constitute or otherwise be the basis of or entitle any person or class of persons to have or claim any minority status, quota preferences, protected status or claim of discrimination.[26]

A constitutional amendment to *prevent* legislative bodies from adopting laws to protect certain classes of citizens is a strange animal, to say the least. Usually, the decision whether to extend some specific legal protection to some class of persons is part of the ordinary exercise of a legislature's authority under a constitution's general structural provisions. If Colorado citizens did not want to extend civil rights protection to LGBTQ people, they could have asked their legislators to follow the lead of the majority of states that also had not yet done so. If at some point voters' sentiments changed, they could lobby for a change. So why enshrine a strange legislative prohibition such as this in a constitutional amendment?

The reasons are nakedly political. Like many states, Colorado has an initiative process through which voters can approve constitutional amendments at the ballot box by an up or down vote. Such amendments

---

24. See National Conference of State Legislatures, "State Public Accommodation Laws," https://tinyurl.com/ycy9eugt.

25. These are California, Colorado, Connecticut, Delaware, Hawaii, Illinois, Iowa, Maine, Maryland, Massachusetts, Minnesota, Nevada, New Hampshire, New Jersey, New Mexico, New York, Oregon, Rhode Island, Vermont, Washington, and Wisconsin, as well as the District of Columbia. National Conference of State Legislatures, "State Public Accommodation Laws."

26. National Conference of State Legislatures, "State Public Accommodation Laws," 624.

are placed on the ballot through a petition process.[27] The petition requires signatures from only a small percentage of eligible voters: in Colorado, a number equal to "at least five percent of the total number of votes cast for all candidates for the office of secretary of state at the previous general election."[28] As legal scholars Richard Collins and Dale Oesterle suggest,

> The state-wide, constitutional initiative works a significant change in the traditional American concept of governmental structure. Differences between constitution and legislation are much reduced. The notion of a constitution as fundamental law that is seldom changed, and only with substantial consensus, is gone. Constitutions are amended often and by voting majorities that are typically a minority of a state's adult population. The role of the state's judiciary is reduced, and the executive is bypassed.[29]

As Collins and Oeseterle suggest, these features of ballot initiatives might prove beneficial if there are other sources of governmental stability, but they are not entirely consistent with how the American constitutional framers thought about the republican form of government.[30]

The ballot initiative process in Colorado meant that a small number of highly motivated voters were able to bring an anti–LGBTQ measure up for a statewide vote when they might not have possessed the political clout to influence the ordinary legislative process through their elected representatives. It also meant that, once on the ballot, the measure would stand a good chance of passing, since those same highly motivated voters also would show up at the polls on election day. And it meant that the state judiciary could not review the constitutionality of the measure after passage under state principles of equal protection, because the measure would become part of the state constitution itself.

That small number of highly motivated voters in Colorado was spearheaded by a nonprofit group called "Colorado for Family Values" (CFV), which included Focus on the Family founder James Dobson on its advisory and executive boards.[31] CFV had stated that is mission was to "stop gay activists before they trample on your freedoms."[32] Just before moving Focus on the Family's headquarters to Colorado Springs in 1990,

---

27. Colorado Constitution, Art. V., Sec. 1(2). For a discussion of this process, see Ballotpedia, "Laws Governing the Initiative Process in Colorado," https://tinyurl.com/y5zhnodd.

28. Colorado Constitution, Art. V., Sec. (2).

29. Richard B. Collins and Dale Oesterle, "Structuring the Ballot Initiative: Procedures That Do and Don't Work," *University of Colorado Law Review* 66 (1994–1995): 47, 52.

30. Collins and Oesterle, "Structuring the Ballot Initiative," 53–55.

31. Chet Hardin, "The Twisted Road from Amendment 2 to 'I Do,'" *Colorado Springs Independent*, May 1, 2013, https://tinyurl.com/yyb7rdqs.

32. Hardin, "Twisted Road."

Dobson wrote in a newsletter that "I am familiar with the widespread effort to redefine the family. It is motivated by homosexual activists and others who see the traditional family as a barrier to the social engineering they hope to accomplish."[33]

In a November 1993 PBS special, host Bill Moyers called Colorado Springs "ground zero in the new holy war."[34] Moyers's special includes a clip from a Focus on the Family video, which states, "Our nation is engaged in a civil war of values, and to the victor goes the prize: our children."[35] The video also includes a clip from a James Dobson sermon in which Dobson states, "We firmly believe that we're involved now in one of the most incredible cultural wars that has ever occurred in western civilization."[36] In another clip of an interview between Dobson and televangelist Pat Robertson about Amendment 2, Dobson says, "Colorado Springs has kind of been ground zero as they call it, a focal point for this struggle against homosexual activists, but it's coming to every city, every little town, every city council, every school. This is something that's going to be fought out all across the nation and people are just going to have to decide what they think about it."[37]

This sort of rhetoric was typical of Focus on the Family and other religious right groups. Moyers also interviewed Dan Griswold, editorial page editor of the *Colorado Springs Gazette Telegraph*, who frequently wrote in favor of Amendment 2. Griswold said Amendment 2

> is not a question of evangelical Christians trying to grab control of the levers of government here and impose some conservative Christian agenda on the community. It's basically Christian people, conservative Christian people in particular in the case of Amendment 2, trying to prevent the government from interfering in their lives. What they oppose is the force of government being brought on them, to force them to accept and condone this lifestyle that violates their most basic beliefs.[38]

Again, this was a typical kind of claim people like Griswold made in favor of anti–LGBTQ laws.

Amendment 2 passed by a 53 percent to 47 percent margin in the November 1992 Colorado elections.[39] The US Supreme Court, however, struck it down in the 1996 case of *Romer v. Evans*.[40] Justice Kennedy

33. Hardin, "Twisted Road."
34. See Bill Moyers Journal, "The New Holy War," https://tinyurl.com/y5997mfe.
35. Bill Moyers Journal, "The New Holy War," 4:42.
36. Bill Moyers Journal, "The New Holy War," 5:00.
37. Bill Moyers Journal, "The New Holy War," 5:26.
38. Bill Moyers Journal, "The New Holy War," 9:47.
39. Bill Moyers Journal, "The New Holy War," 9:47.
40. Romer v. Evans, 517 U.S. 620 (1996).

voted with the liberals and wrote the majority opinion. According to Justice Kennedy, "A law declaring that in general it shall be more difficult for one group of citizens than for all others to seek aid from the government is itself a denial of equal protection of the laws in the most literal sense."[41]

The *Romer* decision sent many conservative Christians into shock. In November 1996, religious right leader Charles Colson used the phrase "the end of democracy" to describe *Romer* and other Supreme Court decisions in a much-debated article in the journal *First Things*.[42] Colson, of course, ignored the fact that *Romer* had overturned a ballot initiative that itself undermined the ordinary democratic process.

In the first line of his article, Colson said that "in America today, we have very nearly reached the completion of a long process I can only describe as the systematic usurpation of ultimate political power by the American judiciary—a usurpation that compels evangelical Christians and, indeed, all believers to ask sobering questions about the moral legitimacy of the current political order and our allegiance to it."[43] Colson cited some of the same sources I have cited in this book concerning the relationship between the temporal and spiritual powers and the possibility of civil disobedience, such as Luther, Calvin, and Martin Luther King Jr.'s "Letter from a Birmingham Jail." But Colson went on to suggest that an armed rebellion might soon become necessary if the Supreme Court continued to protect abortion rights and if the court, as Colson foresaw in 1996, eventually should find a constitutional right to same-sex marriage: "Unfortunately for us, however, events in America may have reached the point where the only political action believers can take is some kind of direct, extra-political confrontation of the judicially controlled regime. . . . When peaceable means and limited civil disobedience fail . . . revolution can be justified from a Christian viewpoint."[44]

Colson acknowledged that the time for armed revolution had not yet come. Nevertheless, he concluded his essay with the suggestion that the time for revolution was not far off: "We dare not at present despair of America and advocate open rebellion. But we must 'slowly, prayerfully, and with great deliberation and serious debate' prepare ourselves for what the future seems likely to bring under a regime in which the

41. Romer v. Evans, 517 U.S. 633 (1996).

42. Charles W. Colson, "The End of Democracy? Kingdoms in Conflict," *First Things*, November 1996, https://tinyurl.com/y3xr2hp7.

43. Colson, "End of Democracy?"

44. Colson, "End of Democracy?"

courts have usurped the democratic process by reckless exercise of naked power."[45]

As the rhetoric around Colorado's Proposition 2 and Colson's nearly literal call to arms suggested, by the time *Romer* was decided, religious conservatives were at least as apoplectic about LGBTQ rights as they were about abortion. They would continue to find no succor from the Supreme Court. In 2003, in *Lawrence v. Texas*, the court struck down under the due process clause a Texas law that banned same-sex conduct, overruling *Bowers v. Hardwick*.[46] Again joining the liberal bloc and writing the majority opinion, Justice Kennedy stated that "liberty presumes an autonomy of self that includes freedom of thought, belief, expression, and certain intimate conduct. The instant case involves liberty of the person in both its spatial and more transcendent dimensions."[47] In a dissent, Justice Scalia made an argument that was becoming increasingly common among conservatives: "There is no right to 'liberty' under the Due Process Clause," but rather, the government may deprive a citizen of "liberty" so long as there is an adequate procedure through which the government acts.[48]

After *Romer* and *Lawrence*, activists on both sides of the debate began to focus on the issue of gay marriage. Much of the battle occurred in state legislatures over measures that would either prohibit or permit gay marriage. Before any state had adopted a law approving same-sex marriage, at the federal level, the "Defense of Marriage Act" (DOMA) passed with substantial bipartisan support and was signed into law by President Bill Clinton.[49] DOMA contained two key provisions. First, it stated that no state was required to give legal effect to any same-sex marriage approved by another state. Second, it stated that under federal law, "the word 'marriage' means only a legal union between one man and one woman as husband and wife, and the word 'spouse' refers only to a person of the opposite sex who is a husband or a wife." This meant, among other things, that same-sex couples legally married in a state that approved such marriages would not be entitled to federal spousal benefits under Social Security, housing, food stamp, veterans, and other social safety-net programs, or for federal spousal tax benefits.[50]

---

45. Colson, "End of Democracy?"
46. 539 U.S. 558 (2003).
47. 539 U.S. 562 (2003).
48. 539 U.S. 592 (2003).
49. 110 Stat. 2419.
50. See January 31, 1997 letter from Barry R. Berdick, Associate General Counsel, U.S. General Accounting Office, to Hon. Henry J. Hyde, Chairman, U.S. House of Representatives Committee on the Judiciary, https://tinyurl.com/y29wqrwh.

In 2013, in *United States v. Windsor*, the Supreme Court struck down DOMA.[51] By the time *Windsor* was decided, twelve states, including New York, had enacted laws approving same-sex marriage. Plaintiff Edith Windsor had married her spouse Thea Spyer (both women) in Canada, and the marriage was legally recognized in New York, where the couple resided. When Spyer died, Windsor sought spousal estate tax benefits under federal law. The IRS denied those benefits because of DOMA. In his majority opinion, Justice Kennedy stated that DOMA "seeks to injure the very class New York seeks to protect" and thereby "violates basic due process and equal protection principles applicable to the Federal Government."[52] He also found that the stated purpose of the law was discriminatory, and its effects were negative for same-sex couples and their children.[53]

While *Windsor* addressed a federal statute limiting marital benefits for same-sex couples even if state law recognizes the marriage, *Obergefell v. Hodges*, decided in 2015, addressed state laws *banning* recognition of same-sex marriage.[54] Again writing the majority opinion, Justice Kennedy found that the case arose under both the Due Process and Equal Protection Clauses of the Fourteenth Amendment:

> The Due Process Clause and the Equal Protection Clause are connected in a profound way, though they set forth independent principles. Rights implicit in liberty and rights secured by equal protection may rest on different precepts and are not always co-extensive, yet in some instances each may be instructive as to the meaning and reach of the other. In any particular case one Clause may be thought to capture the essence of the right in a more accurate and comprehensive way, even as the two Clauses may converge in the identification and definition of the right.[55]

According to Justice Kennedy, "The Constitution promises liberty to all within its reach, a liberty that includes certain specific rights that allow persons, within a lawful realm, to define and express their identity."[56] Marriage, Justice Kennedy stated, is a key aspect of personal identity: "the annals of human history reveal the transcendent importance of marriage."[57] Therefore, he held, "the right to marry is a fundamental right inherent in the liberty of the person, and under the Due Process and

51. 570 U.S. 744 (2013).
52. 570 U.S. 769 (2013).
53. 570 U.S. 773–74 (2013).
54. *Obergefell v. Hodges*, 570 U.S. ___, 135 S. Ct. 2584 (2015).
55. *Obergefell v. Hodges*, 570 U.S. ___, 135 S. Ct. 2603 (2015).
56. *Obergefell v. Hodges*, 570 U.S. ___, 135 S. Ct. 2593 (2015).
57. *Obergefell v. Hodges*, 570 U.S. ___, 135 S. Ct. 2593–94 (2015).

Equal Protection Clauses of the Fourteenth Amendment couples of the same-sex may not be deprived of that right and that liberty."[58]

In his dissent, Justice Scalia expressed the sentiments of many conservatives: "Today's decree says that my Ruler, and the Ruler of 320 million Americans coast-to-coast, is a majority of the nine lawyers on the Supreme Court."[59] In another dissent, Justice Roberts echoed that sentiment: "The majority's decision is an act of will, not legal judgment."[60]

ABORTION, LGBTQ CIVIL RIGHTS, AND SAME-SEX MARRIAGE IN PERSPECTIVE

As the dissents referenced above suggest, critics of the court's abortion, LGBTQ rights, and same-sex marriage decisions argue that the supposed "penumbras" and "emanations" of the Bill of Rights should not blot out legislation enacted by the people through their elected representatives. They also argue that blurring the equal protection and due process clauses creates a general, amorphous standard not specified in the Constitution, which allows unelected judges to make broad policy decisions and undermines the rule of law. In the cases that produced these constitutional interpretations, the people consented to legislation banning contraception and abortion and limiting "marriage" to one man and one woman. The people did not elect the members of the Supreme Court, and the supposed "penumbras" and "emanations" of the Bill of Rights are so diffuse that they serve as little more than fancy terms for whatever political preferences a majority of the Supreme Court—five of nine individuals—happens to hold at the moment of decision. These critiques are not just right-wing rantings. Even some thoughtful commentators who favor the policy choices made in these cases candidly acknowledge that the Supreme Court's substantive due process jurisprudence is doctrinally shaky.

Much of this debate turns on how the Constitution should be interpreted. The Constitution does not include any explicit rules for its interpretation. Indeed, the Constitution does not even explicitly say that the judicial branch has the last word in interpretation. The principle of "judicial review" was developed in the germinal case of *Marbury v. Madi-*

---

58. Obergefell v. Hodges, 570 U.S. ___, 135 S. Ct. 2604 (2015).
59. Obergefell v. Hodges, 570 U.S. ___, 135 S. Ct. 2627 (2015).
60. Obergefell v. Hodges, 570 U.S. ___, 135 S. Ct. 2612 (2015). Justice Roberts here echoed a statement by Alexander Hamilton in the federalist papers that the judiciary under the proposed 1789 Constitution would exercise "neither force nor will but merely judgment." *The Federalist*, no. 78, p. 465 (C. Rossiter ed. 1961) (A. Hamilton) (capitalization altered).

LAW AND THEOLOGY 199

son in 1803, though it had a basis in earlier jurisprudence.[61] Opinions about how to interpret the Constitution range from the view that it is a flexible, "living" document that must adapted to current circumstances to the "originalist" view that the text has a fixed meaning based on what the framers, or at least the founding generation, thought it meant. These interpretive theories, which involve many shades and variants, raise enormous questions about the nature of law, the use of language, the "intent" of a deliberative body as a whole, historiography and the availability and nature of historical evidence, and so on.

Are these arcane questions about the right way to interpret a post–Civil War amendment to the US Constitution central to the mission of the church in relation to a theology of positive law? Is a commitment to constitutional originalism, which presumably would result in peeling back the court's substantive due process and equal protection jurisprudence in the areas of abortion and gay marriage, a core part of God's work in history at this moment? In some circles, that would seem to be the case.

At the same time, social conservatives have engaged in their own versions of political manipulation and opportunism. As the Colorado Proposition 2 story illustrates, using the ballot initiative to enshrine a constitutional prohibition on future legislative protections for a disfavored group is a brilliant, if ruthless, piece of political gamesmanship. That story also shows that, to a significant extent, the religious right's fights over LGBTQ issues were and are driven by homophobia—that is, by an irrational fear of people with different sexual identities. The notion that large numbers of gay people are actively conspiring to overthrow the church, and would accomplish that goal if allowed, is the stuff of rabid conspiracy theories. To be sure, there were and are a handful of LGBTQ activists who might like to dismantle Catholic and conservative evangelical churches, but there are extremists at the fringes of every movement, including in the churches.

Yet the conservative Christians were, and are, right to notice a larger cultural movement that conflicts with traditional Christian teaching about sex and marriage. Dobson was not wrong when he observed in 1992 that the question of LGBTQ rights would become an issue throughout the country. In recent years, some Christians have argued that it is time to reconsider those traditional teachings, with proper consideration for the cultural contexts of the biblical texts that disfavor homosexual conduct, a better understanding of sexual orientation, and a social context that allows same-sex couples and their families to flourish

61. *Marbury v. Madison*, 5 U.S. 137 (1803).

in stable unions.[62] These are at best very difficult hermeneutical and ethical questions for any serious Christian (or Jewish or Muslim) believer,
however, so the concerns of more traditional believers are not motivated
only by irrational homophobia.[63]

The same is true for Christians who are concerned about abortion.
Reasonable people, including reasonable and faithful Christians, can disagree on whether or at what point a very early stage pregnancy involves
a "person" or at least a "potential person." Reasonable people, including reasonable and faithful Christians, also ought to hear the concerns
of feminist scholars and activists and other women about the historically
enormously disproportionate burdens women have borne in pregnancy
and child rearing. But it remains the case that human flourishing is a central concern for any serious Christian (or Jewish or Muslim) social ethic
and that pro-life Christians reasonably believe most abortions involve the
grave moral consequence of terminating innocent human life.

These valid concerns about marriage and abortion suggest that advocating for laws embodying their concerns can be part of a faithful Christian praxis relating to the positive law. The way in which this advocacy
has played out in recent history, however, raises serious concerns about
practical wisdom, intellectual consistency, and missional focus.

62. See, e.g., David P. Gushee, *Changing Our Mind*, 3rd ed. (Canton, MI: Read the Spirit,
2017); Matthew Vines, *God and the Gay Christian: The Biblical Case in Support of Same-Sex
Relationships* (New York: Convergent, 2015); James V. Brownson, *Bible, Gender, Sexuality:
Reframing the Church's Debate on Same-Sex Relationships* (Grand Rapids: Eerdmans, 2013); Justin
Lee, *Torn: Rescuing the Gospel from the Gays-vs-Christians Debate* (Nashville: Jericho, 2013); Ken
Wilson, *A Letter to My Congregation*, 2nd ed. (Canton, MI: Read the Spirit, 2016); Richard
Burridge, *Imitating Jesus: An Inclusive Approach to New Testament Ethics* (Grand Rapids: Eerd-
mans, 2007). For natural law arguments suggesting the possibility of same-sex relationships, see
Jean Porter, *Nature as Reason: A Thomistic Theory of the Natural Law* (Grand Rapids: Eerdmans,
2004), and Stephen J. Pope, "Scientific and Natural Law Analysis of Homosexuality: A Methodological Study," *Journal of Religious Ethics* 25, no. 1 (1997): 89–126.
63. Oliver O'Donovan addresses these difficult hermeneutical, ethical, and ecclesiological
questions effectively in *Church in Crisis: The Gay Controversy and the Anglican Communion*
(Eugene, OR: Wipf and Stock, 2008). The best case for a traditional reading of the biblical texts
without animosity toward LGBTQ people is in Richard Hays, *The Moral Vision of the New Testament: A Contemporary Introduction to New Testament Ethics* (New York: HarperCollins, 1996).
Wesley Hill argues for homosexual celibacy in *Washed and Waiting: Reflections on Faithfulness
& Homosexuality* (Grand Rapids: Zondervan, 2016). Robert Song offers an interesting proposal
that seeks to bridge some of the divides between progressive and traditional views in *Covenant
and Calling: Towards a Theology of Same-Sex Relationships* (London: SCM, 2014).

THE TRUMP FACTOR AND ORIGINALISM

We have already suggested that past fearmongering rhetoric on issues such as gay marriage has been missionally unfaithful. At this point we must address the elephant in the room: the presidency of Donald Trump. There were several reasons why, despite the concerns of prominent leaders such as Al Mohler, conservative evangelicals supported, and still largely support, Trump for president.[64] One central reason was his pledge to appoint originalist judges who presumably would have decided the abortion and gay marriage cases discussed above differently—a pledge on which he has, in fact, delivered.[65] But the movement to trust in Donald Trump as a kind of political messiah—or, as some conservatives have suggested, as a kind of modern King Cyrus who will deliver us from exile—is a grave mistake.

As the theology of positive law also suggests, the law is not the mission itself, and sometimes—often—it is impossible to encode our best ideals into the positive law. Concerning abortion, there are many ways in which the church can engage with young men and women, care for young mothers, receive unwanted babies, work to ameliorate the economic and other inequalities that lead some women to see abortion as their only option, and strengthen the bonds of mutual respect and community that support a Christian ethic of marriage, family, and sex. The church is already doing these things, and perhaps with less focus on the culture wars, it could do them even better.[66]

Most conservatives will agree with these comments, but some will also suggest that there are moments in history when the church must advocate for direct political change—moments such as those we have discussed in this book, such as the end of slavery and the civil rights

64. See, e.g., John Fea, *Believe Me: The Evangelical Road to Donald Trump* (Grand Rapids: Eerdmans, 2018); Frances FitzGerald, *The Evangelicals: The Struggle to Shape America* (New York: Simon & Schuster, 2017), 627–36.

65. See Fea, *Believe Me*, 138–40.

66. My comments here echo those of Stanley Hauerwas and Johnathan Tran, "A Sanctuary Politics: Being the Church in the Time of Trump," ABC Religion & Ethics, March 31, 2017, https://tinyurl.com/y3lwwywo. As Hauerwas and Tran note, "When Christians think that the struggle against abortion can only be pursued through voting for candidates with certain judicial philosophies, then serving at domestic abuse shelters or teaching students at local high schools or sharing wealth with expectant but under-resourced families or speaking of God's grace in terms of 'adoption' or politically organizing for improved education or rezoning municipalities for childcare or creating 'Parent's Night Out' programs at local churches or mentoring young mothers or teaching youth about chastity and dating or mobilizing religious pressure on medical service providers or apprenticing men into fatherhood or thinking of singleness as a vocation or feasting on something called 'communion' or rendering to God what is God's or participating with the saints through Marian icons or baptizing new members or tithing money, will not count as political."

movement. Freedom suits such as Dred Scott's were attempts to expose the injustice of slavery, and Martin Luther King Jr.'s "Letter from a Birmingham Jail" was written to respond to other Christian leaders who advocated patience instead of direct action. Many conservatives today also point to the efforts of the Confessing Church in Germany during the Nazi era and have adopted the German pastor and martyr Dietrich Bonhoeffer as an icon. Leaders of the religious right adopted the phrase "Bonhoeffer moment" in response to the fight over gay marriage at the Supreme Court.[67] One such leader, Eric Metaxas, a vigorous Trump supporter, wrote the bestselling book *Bonhoeffer: Pastor, Martyr, Prophet, Spy*, in which he depicted Bonhoeffer as essentially a conservative evangelical politically and theologically.[68]

Serious Bonhoeffer scholars have debunked these claims about who Bonhoeffer was as a pastor and theologian.[69] English readers can study recently released readers editions of Bonhoeffer's works, particularly his *Ethics, Discipleship,* and *Letters and Papers from Prison*—the latter so filled with faith, doubt, hope, and pathos—and readily observe from these writings that Bonhoeffer was not the man the religious right imagines.[70] But beyond scholarly debates about Bonhoeffer's biography and legacy, when conservatives invoke a "Bonhoeffer moment," they are suggesting images of Nazi Germany and a plot in which Bonhoeffer was involved to assassinate Hitler.

Neither abortion nor gay marriage rise to this level. Abortion arguably is a closer case. Abortion, after all, involves millions of terminated pregnancies each year around the world, including more than five hundred

---

67. See Stephen R. Haynes, *The Battle for Bonhoeffer: Debating Discipleship in the Age of Trump* (Grand Rapids: Eerdmans, 2018), chap. 7.

68. See Eric Metaxas, *Bonhoeffer: Pastor, Martyr, Prophet, Spy* (Nashville: Thomas Nelson, 2011). Metaxas's book was a *New York Times* bestseller.

69. See Haynes, *Battle for Bonhoeffer*; Charles Marsh, *Strange Glory: A Life of Dietrich Bonhoeffer* (New York: Vintage, 2015); Christiane Tietz, *Theologian of Resistance: The Life and Thought of Dietrich Bonhoeffer*, trans. Victoria J. Barnett (Minneapolis: Fortress, 2016). Marsh's biography has attracted its own critics among Bonhoeffer scholars, particularly for its depiction of Bonhoeffer as a closeted homosexual who harbored romantic feelings for his student and friend Eberhard Bethge. See, e.g., Ferdinand Schlingensiepen, "Essay Review: Making Assumptions about Dietrich: How Bonhoeffer Was Made Fit for America," The International Bonhoeffer Society, https://tinyurl.com/y4llsdqw. Schlingensiepen is also the author of a biography, *Dietrich Bonhoeffer 1906–1945: Martyr, Thinker, Man of Resistance* (London: T&T Clark, 2012). Bethge's biography is also a standard. See Eberhard Bethge, *Dietrich Bonhoeffer: A Biography* (Minneapolis: Fortress, 2000).

70. Dietrich Bonhoeffer, *Ethics*, Dietrich Bonhoeffer Works, Reader's Edition (Minneapolis: Fortress, 2015); *Discipleship*, Dietrich Bonhoeffer Works, Reader's Edition (Minneapolis: Fortress, 2015); *Letters and Papers from Prison*, Dietrich Bonhoeffer Works, Reader's Edition (Minneapolis: Fortress, 2015).

thousand each year in the United States.[71] Some pro-life advocates consider this a new Holocaust.

The murder of Jews and others during the Holocaust, however, involved no moral or theological ambiguity. There was no conceivable moral justification for the Holocaust and no question that it was anything less than demonically evil. The moral and theological questions around the status of human development at every stage from fertilization through birth, in relation to the burdens and risks borne by the mother, in contrast, at least involve some ambiguities.

The later stages of pregnancy, in my view, present a clear case for strong governmental regulation. An intact dilation and evacuation of a near-term baby is a grave action, with abortion potentially justified only in the most extreme circumstances. And in the middle stages of pregnancy, there is at least a very strong argument that an abortion involves terminating a distinct human life, again justifiable only in extreme circumstances.[72]

The earliest stages of pregnancy are more complicated. For example, it takes about five to six days after fertilization for an embryo to begin the biological process of implantation in the uterus.[73] At this point, the developing embryo is only a microscopic cluster of cells, invisible to the naked eye. About 40–60 percent of fertilized eggs are lost due to natural causes at this very early stage of pregnancy.[74]

From a theological perspective, this presents vexing questions. Are all of these naturally miscarried early-stage pregnancies human beings with an eschatological future? If so, what is their fate in the final

71. See CNN, "Abortion Fast Facts," November 23, 2018, https://tinyurl.com/ycle82nj.

72. These claims are about what I believe is the moral gravity of the circumstance and the corresponding arguments for legal regulation. They are not meant to minimize the suffering and distress of women who face the kind of extreme circumstances that might justifiably raise the question of abortion. I am, however, intentionally pushing back on the argument that abortion, particularly in the middle and later stages of pregnancy, does not entail any significant interests beyond a woman's health. This kind of argument is made by many pro-abortion advocates today, and is reflected in Justice Ginsburg's concurrence in *Whole Women's Health v. Hellerstedt*, 579 U.S. ___, 136 S.Ct. 2292 (2016) (Ginsburg, J., Concurring). In my view this kind of argument is mistaken because the fetus is a human life or at least a potential human life, which the state can and should have an interest in protecting, and that interest as well as the state's interest in the woman's health and autonomy should matter. Indeed, even *Roe v. Wade* recognized that the state has an interest in protecting potential life. *Roe v. Wade*, 410 U.S. at 154 (stating that "a State may properly assert important interests in safeguarding health, in maintaining medical standards, and in protecting potential life"). Of course, the Roe court went on to define at which points these interests might become "compelling" for purposes of substantive due process analysis.

73. See UCSF Health, "Conception: How It Works," https://tinyurl.com/hra3tg5.

74. Gavin E. Jarvis, "Early Embryo Mortality in Natural Human Reproduction: What the Data Say," PubMed Central, June 7, 2017, https://tinyurl.com/yag5ky6y.

judgment? Whether they are lost or saved in the final judgment, some combination of both, or granted a place in a sort of "limbo," what does the fact that half the human population throughout history never lived beyond the stage of a microscopic group of cells say about the doctrine of creation, the incarnation of Christ, and the atonement and resurrection? The central hinge of the Christian faith is our belief that Jesus affirms and redeems the goodness of our created humanity by living a fully human life, voluntarily taking up the cross, and rising again as a grown, thinking, speaking human being, still bearing the marks of his crucifixion. What does God's providence over the actual experience of human history mean if half of the human persons in the eschatological future, in the present experience of history, were never more than uncomprehending souls mystically connected to a clump of cells flushed out with the mother's menses without notice? What does all this say about God's goodness, the goodness of creation, and the problem of evil?

No one can answer such questions. There remain compelling reasons to oppose even very early term elective abortions on ethical grounds, including at least the potential for human life, the precautionary principle, and the historic Christian practice of welcoming children, particularly unwanted children.[75] These are good reasons to advocate for legal policies that restrict even early term abortions. At the very least, however, such questions suggest that not all the issues surrounding abortion are as clear as the Holocaust.

Further, and more significant for the purpose of this discussion, the Holocaust involved violence imposed and carried out by the *state*, without any ordinary process of the rule of law. Abortion in the United States remains voluntary. In the United States, abortions are not forced mass executions. They are voluntary choices by private citizens that the law *allows* but does not *impose*.[76] Indeed, even if *Roe v. Wade* and its progeny were reversed tomorrow, abortion would not automatically become *illegal* but would become a matter for legislative judgment absent a substantive due process right of the woman, likely resulting in wildly inconsistent laws throughout the country. As our discussion of the theology of positive law demonstrates, at any moment in history, many things that would be consistent with the natural law cannot be imposed by the positive law. This does not usually mean there is no rule of law or that the state is fundamentally illegitimate. It may be that other significant

75. See, e.g., Gilbert Meilaender, *Bioethics: A Primer for Christians* (Grand Rapids: Eerdmans, 2013), chap. 3; Stassen and Gushee, *Kingdom Ethics*, chap. 10.

76. Government *funding* of abortion services through Medicare, Medicaid, and other spending decisions, of course, also raises important ethical and legal questions. Nevertheless, no one is being forced to undergo an abortion in the United States.

changes—spiritual changes—must occur before there is ever a possibility of a change in the positive law concerning some issue of fundamental morality. The church need not withdraw from public advocacy when this is the case, or even from acts of civil disobedience, but neither need or should the church ordinarily invoke the rhetoric of armed rebellion or assassination. Under these circumstances, the calls by ecclesial ethicists for "the church to be the church" have great purchase.

Gay marriage, in my judgment, is a far easier case than abortion. No Christian heterosexuals are being forced into gay marriages. If gay marriage undermines a traditional concept of Christian marriage, it is only by a broader process of cultural acceptance. For Christians who are concerned with this bigger cultural issue, there is obviously nothing to gain by manipulating political power in an effort to impose temporal laws that most of society rejects. The most winsome witness to the goodness of traditional Christian marriage is evidence of joyful, thriving, flourishing marriages—something the divorce rate among professing Christians suggests is hard enough to sustain.

Christian conservatives will respond that they *are* already being forced to compromise their understanding of marriage through restrictions on their educational institutions, requirements that service providers such as bakers cater to gay weddings, and the threat of government intrusion into church polities and ministerial functions. There are legitimate concerns here about religious freedom, which I will address in the final section of this chapter. The most severe of these concerns, however, have not materialized and are unlikely to materialize any time in the near future. To the extent Christian institutions are business have faced challenges because of the legalization of gay marriage, these have mostly involved access to the government's money, a governmental seal of approval, or financial burdens imposed by generally applicable civil rights laws. Access to government money and approval, or uncomplicated success in the business world, are hardly things the church or individual Christians should usually expect. The heated rhetoric about a so-called "Bonhoeffer moment" is just hot air.

Moreover, if conservatives are concerned about erosion of the rule of law, the support of Donald Trump because of his affinity for originalist judges is ultimately counterproductive. First, if you want to advocate for originalist judges, you should do so not only for the opportunistic reason that such judges will produce a result you want regarding abortion or gay marriage. You should thoroughly understand the arguments for and against originalism and hold a consistent view. It is not at all clear that constitutional originalism is a coherent theory.[77] Justices Scalia and Thomas, the court's most consistent originalists prior to the additions of Justices Gorsuch and Kavanaugh, often disagreed with each other sharply about original meaning.[78] It is also not clear that "originalism" was the original intent of the framers, if the original intent of the framers could be discerned.

Second, and particularly significant to our inclusion of "liberation" as a theological basis for positive law, originalism calls into question the legal gains of the civil rights movement, including the equal protection basis for *Brown* and the commerce clause basis for the Civil Rights Act of 1964 and other civil rights legislation.[79] This does not mean an originalist must reject *Brown* or federal civil rights law, but it is fair to suggest that the constitutional basis for those rules is much more difficult for originalists.[80]

Third, and perhaps most important, the enormous effort and acrimony that has gone into efforts to ensure that "originalist" judges are appointed has damaged the church's witness and integrity in ways that seem almost impossible to repair. When I was young in the 1970s and early 1980s, my family attended an evangelical megachurch committed to most of the religious right's agenda. The church held a regular "Bible conference" with speakers who combined Cold War politics with dispensational eschatology. A vital religious right theme at that time was that *a leader's character matters*. These preachers mined the Old Testament to show that when the king was morally upright, good decisions followed and Israel prospered, while when the king was morally bankrupt, the nation turned to idolatry and was judged by God.

77. See, e.g., Jack Balkin, "Arguing about the Constitution: The Topics in Constitutional Interpretation," *Constitutional Commentary* 33 (2018): 145; Cass R. Sunstein, "Originalism," *Notre Dame Law Review* 99 (2018): 1671.

78. Consider, for example, Justice Scalia's dissent in *Zivotofsky v. Kerry*, 135 S. Ct. 2076, 2126 (2015), in which Justice Scalia said Justice Thomas's understanding of executive power "produces . . . a presidency more reminiscent of George III than George Washington." For an interesting discussion by originalist scholars discussing different schools of originalism and arguing for an originalism that takes into account both the "letter" and the "spirit" of the Constitution, see Randy E. Barnett and Evan D. Bernick, "The Letter and the Spirit: A Unified Theory of Originalism," *Georgetown Law Journal* 107 (2018): 1. Theories like Barnett and Bernick's are creative and fascinating, but they also illustrate that "originalism" is not really the sort of monolithic shibboleth it has become for the culture war in the popular culture.

79. See Alexander M. Bickel, "The Original Understanding and the Segregation Decision," *Harvard Law Review* 69 (1955): 1; Richard A. Posner, "Bork and Beethoven,"*Stanford Law Review* 42 (1990): 1365; Cass R. Sunstein, *Radicals in Robes: Why Right-Wing Courts Are Wrong for America* (New York: Basic Books, 2006).

80. See Michael W. McConnell, "Originalism and the Desegregation Decisions," *Virginia Law Review* 81 (1995): 947; Ryan C. Williams, "Originalism and the Other Desegregation Decision," *Virginia Law Review* 99 (2013): 493.

These claims were echoed by leading figures on the religious right. Consider this typical passage from a letter sent to Focus on the Family supporters by its president, James Dobson, concerning President Bill Clinton:

> As it turns out, character DOES matter. You can't run a family, let alone a country, without it. How foolish to believe that a person who lacks honesty and moral integrity is qualified to lead a nation and the world! Nevertheless, our people continue to say that the President is doing a good job even if they don't respect him personally. Those two positions are fundamentally incompatible. In the book of James the question is posed, "Can both fresh water and salt water flow from the same spring?" (Jas 3:11 NIV). The answer is no.[81]

This kind of material was a staple of religious right rhetoric at the time. The notion that Christians should enthusiastically support an ill-tempered, foul-mouthed braggard of a reality television star who had been divorced several times; who boasted of grabbing women by the "pussy" at whim; who had affairs with porn stars and covered them up with hush money in violation of campaign finance laws; who lies whenever it is convenient; who coddles and promotes Russian tyrants; who tweets childish and racist comments at adversaries; and whose religious views seem to run toward a vague kind of prosperity gospel, would have been unimaginable. But the "prophecy" preachers changed their tune, and James Dobson became part of candidate Donald Trump's evangelical advisory board in 2016. Even if Dobson and the "Bible conference" preachers were wrong to conflate biblical Israel with America—and they were—they were right that a leader's character matters.

Of course, pro-life Christians would still rightly be concerned about how the constitutional right to abortion requires federal tax dollars to be spent on abortion services for Medicare and Medicaid patients. Pro-life Christians also rightly would be concerned that the law as a moral teacher should embody greater respect for the unborn. Pro-life Christians also might continue to lobby their state lawmakers to regulate abortion services in ways that are consistent with Supreme Court precedents. But maybe a different focus, based in a more nuanced theology of positive law, would make room for a slower, more patient kind of change.

Finally, the leader these conservatives have anointed, ironically has done more than any American political leader in recent history to *undermine* civil society and the rule of law. President Trump's disrespect for

---

81. James Dobson, online letter, December 1998, https://tinyurl.com/y36p3aek. Quoted in Fea, *Believe Me*, 63–64.

the judiciary; his undermining of his own intelligence officials; his disre-
gard for international diplomatic norms and historic alliances; his unconstitutional executive orders on immigration; his hateful public rhetoric
about Muslims, Mexicans, and other minorities; his refusal to condemn
white supremacist rallies; his campaign finance violations; his penchant
for conspiracy theories; his childish name-calling; his branding of the
press as an "enemy of the people"; his obstruction of justice—all of this
and more is doing grave, lasting damage to the republic. The price of
winning appointment for some originalist justices cannot be this high.

CONSENT, CIVIL RIGHTS, GAY MARRIAGE, AND RELIGIOUS LIBERTY

As we saw in our discussion of Colorado's Proposition 2, although traditional Christian views about marriage are not only motivated by homophobia, the public rhetoric about legal change was driven by fear.[82] That
fear has now shifted toward the belief that Christians in America are
becoming a persecuted minority and that LGBTQ activists are out to
destroy the church and its related institutions. The rear-guard action is
now in the domain of religious liberty.

A threshold question in this battle is whether such institutions must
employ LGBTQ people under laws that prohibit employment discrimination. The Supreme Court addressed this question in 2012 in *Hosanna-
Tabor Evangelical Lutheran Church and School v. EEOC*.[83] The procedural
background of *Hosanna-Tabor* is somewhat convoluted, because the
statute at issue related to retaliation for disability claims, not directly to
employment discrimination against LGBTQ people. In any event, the
court in *Hosanna-Tabor* announced a "ministerial exception" to the civil
rights and employment laws.

Although the conservative Justice Roberts wrote the majority opinion,
the decision was unanimous. This means that *Hosanna-Tabor* did not
depend on a uniquely originalist constitutional interpretation. Writing
for the majority, Justice Roberts stated,

> The members of a religious group put their faith in the hands of their min-
> isters. Requiring a church to accept or retain an unwanted minister, or
> punishing a church for failing to do so, intrudes upon more than a mere
> employment decision. Such action interferes with the internal governance

---

82. Unfortunately, this kind of fear-mongering is nothing new. See Fea, *Believe Me*, chap. 3
("A Short History of Evangelical Fear").
83. 565 U.S. 171 (2012).

of the church, depriving the church of control over the selection of those who will personify its beliefs. By imposing an unwanted minister, the state infringes the Free Exercise Clause, which protects a religious group's right to shape its own faith and mission through its appointments. According the state the power to determine which individuals will minister to the faithful also violates the Establishment Clause, which prohibits government involvement in such ecclesiastical decisions.[84]

Hosanna-Tabor seems to strike at least some kind of workable balance between the rights of religious organizations and the broader society's beliefs about LGBTQ rights. It will not always be easy to determine, of course, whether a particular employee is in the "ministerial" category or not, but a sound theology of positive law would agree, as I argued in chapters 1 and 2, that under a good legal regime the church will enjoy some insulation and autonomy from the state. This must at least mean that churches and church organization possess freedom to express moral views that the broader society might consider wrong.

LGBTQ RIGHTS, CONSERVATIVE CHRISTIANS, AND HIGHER EDUCATION

Although a ministerial exception makes sense, as the *Bob Jones* case illustrates, the freedom of religious groups to dissent from the rule of law as reflected in the consent of the broader public must at some points be limited. Some examples of such limitations should be obvious. Imagine, for example, a group trying to revive Mayan practices of human sacrifice. No one would argue that the Mayan group's religious liberty interests outweigh the state's interest in preventing murders and other ritual killings. More interesting cases involve issues that are more subtle. But even subtle, interesting cases can arise from bad or compromised missional practices. I think this has been the case in the recently hotly contested area of how LGBTQ civil rights intersect with Christian groups or Christian schools in higher education.

My first example of these cases is one in which I think a Christian organization's appeal to the law clearly was wrong. This was *Christian Legal Society v. Martinez*, decided by the US Supreme Court in 2010.[85] Christian Legal Society (CLS) is a theologically conservative organization of Christians in the legal profession that caters largely to an evangelical audience (ChristianLegalSociety.org). In addition to provid-

---

84. 565 U.S. 171 (2012).
85. 561 U.S. 661 (2010).

ing resources for practicing lawyers, including devotional and practical materials, CLS engages in advocacy relating to religious freedom and pro-life causes. The religious freedom and pro-life portfolio suggests that CLS has a culture war orientation, but CLS also supports the work of Christian Legal Aid clinics across the country (ChristianLegalAid.org).

CLS also supports student chapters at many law schools. Student chapters were required to adopt bylaws that incorporated a "statement of faith" and a code of conduct that excluded as members and officers anyone who held religious beliefs contrary to the statement of faith or who engaged in "unrepentant homosexual conduct."[86] A student CLS group applied for "Registered Student Organization" (RSO) status at UC Hastings Law School. Hastings had a nondiscrimination policy that stated as follows:

[Hastings] is committed to a policy against legally impermissible, arbitrary or unreasonable discriminatory practices. All groups, including administration, faculty, student governments, [Hastings]-owned student residence facilities and programs sponsored by [Hastings], are governed by this policy of nondiscrimination. [Hasting's] policy on nondiscrimination is to comply fully with applicable law.

[Hastings] shall not discriminate unlawfully on the basis of race, color, religion, national origin, ancestry, disability, age, sex or sexual orientation. This nondiscrimination policy covers admission, access and treatment in Hastings-sponsored programs and activities.[87]

Hastings interpreted its policy to mandate access to "all comers: School-approved groups must 'allow any student to participate, become a member, or seek leadership positions in the organization, regardless of [her] status or beliefs.'"[88] Because of its bylaws mandating certain religious beliefs and prohibiting homosexual conduct, the student CLS group was not granted RSO status at Hastings. The group asked for a religious exception to the all-comers policy, which Hastings denied.

RSO status at Hastings could

- "seek financial assistance from the Law School, which subsidizes their events using funds from a mandatory student-activity fee imposed on all students";

- "use Law–School channels to communicate with students" by placing "announcements in a weekly Office-of-Student-Services newsletter";

86. 561 U.S. 673.
87. 561 U.S. 670.
88. 561 U.S. 671.

- "advertise events on designated bulletin boards";
- "send e-mails using a Hastings-organization address";
- "participate in an annual Student Organizations Fair designed to advance recruitment efforts";
- "apply for permission to use the Law School's facilities for meetings and office space"; and
- "use [Hastings'] name and logo."[89]

The denial of RSO status did not mean the CLS group was banned from campus. Hastings administration stated that it "would be pleased to provide [CLS] the use of Hastings facilities for its meetings and activities" as well as access to chalkboards and bulletin boards through which to announce events.[90] During the the 2004–2005 academic year, the group operated independently, including "weekly Bible-study meetings . . . [and] a beach barbeque, Thanksgiving dinner, campus lecture on the Christian faith and the legal practice, several fellowship dinners, an end-of-year banquet, and other informal social activities."[91]

In 2004, CLS sued Hastings for civil rights violations, alleging that the denial of RSO status violated CLS's rights to freedom of speech, expressive association, and free exercise of religion under the First Amendment.[92] The case was litigated all the way to the Supreme Court. In a 5–4 decision, which broke along ideological lines, with Justice Kennedy providing a swing vote to the liberal bloc, the court rejected CLS's claims.

As illustrated by the close decision, CLS made some powerful First Amendment arguments. It is easy to see the problem in a policy that requires a religious student organization to open its membership and leadership roles to people who do not share, or perhaps are even hostile to, the organization's religious commitments. As a majority of the court found, perhaps the problem is sufficiently mitigated if the policy is otherwise neutral and generally applicable. Perhaps most potential problems will sort themselves out over time as students choose to affiliate with groups with which they have an actual affinity. Or, as the dissenters argued, perhaps the First Amendment carves out space for diverse groups

89. 561 U.S. 669–70.
90. 561 U.S. 673.
91. 561 U.S. 673.
92. The claim was filed under a statute that was originally part of the Civil Rights Act of 1871, codified at 42 U.S.C. § 1983, commonly called a "1983" claim. The statute was a response to actions by the Ku Klux Klan against black citizens during the Reconstruction era. It allows civil claims for deprivations of civil rights against private parties acting "under color of state law." Claims for violations of civil rights guaranteed under the Bill of Rights, the Fourteenth Amendment, or elsewhere in the Constitution otherwise can be asserted only against the government.

to maintain their own particular standards, and the Hastings "all comers" policy was overly broad. In any event, from the perspective of First Amendment doctrine, it is a legitimate, challenging, and interesting case.

From a theological and praxis perspective, however, I think CLS's decision to litigate was wrong. CLS and the many, many other Christian organizations that filed amicus briefs on its behalf would argue (and did argue) that the case was about precedent in light of a wave of "all comers" policies in universities throughout the country.[93] There is a significant irony in this position, since the religious right usually criticizes efforts to make policy through the Supreme Court rather than through legislation—except in religious liberty cases. But the real issue, I believe, was that UC Hastings's policy, and others like it, included LGBTQ people among the groups that could not be discriminated against.

What was really at stake for the Hastings CLS chapter? The possibility of a very small amount of university funding, some newsletter space, and an email address? The state had not taken any action to shut CLS or its student chapter down. They were still free to meet, and did so, even on university grounds. Why would CLS take the initiative to *start* a lawsuit? What about St. Paul's instruction to the church in Rome, facing much more difficult circumstances than losing access to a bulletin board, discussed in chapter 1: "If it is possible, as far as it depends on you, live at peace with everyone" (Rom 12:18 NIV)? Does the New Testament anywhere even hint at the notion that the church should initiate a lawsuit against Caesar if Caesar refused to give it money and free access to government buildings?

PRIVATE RELIGIOUS COLLEGES AND THE PROBLEM OF CAESAR'S MONEY AND APPROVAL

Christian Legal Society v. Martinez represents the problem of Christian groups with discriminatory policies against LGBTQ people who want access to public university facilities. An even thornier problem relates to the ability of private Christian colleges and universities to obtain access to federal financial aid money or governmental accreditation.

Title IX of the Education Amendments of 1972 states that "no person in the United States shall, on the basis of sex, be excluded from participation in, be denied the benefits of, or be subjected to discrimination under any education program or activity receiving Federal financial

93. For a list of amici, see Christian Legal Society v. Martinez, June 28, 2010, https://tinyurl.com/y5e4b357.

assistance."[94] During the Obama administration, Christian colleges and universities lobbied against a proposed statute, the Employment Non-Discrimination Act (ENDA), which would have amended the civil rights laws to include sexual orientation as a specific category in addition to "sex." When the proposed statute stalled in Congress, President Obama announced plans to issue an executive order prohibiting federal contractors from discriminating based on sexual orientation. Christian colleges and universities lobbied for a religious exemption to the executive order, fearing that without such an exemption, they might lose the benefits of federally guaranteed student loans under Title IX.[95] The president issued the executive order, without any religious exemption, on July 21, 2014.[96] Christian colleges and universities then began to file for religious exemptions through procedures established in Title IX.[97] About half of the schools in the Council for Christian Colleges and Universities (CCCU) sought exemptions.[98]

The schools that filed for Title IX exemptions still want government subsidies. From the perspective on an ecclesial ethic, we could say that these schools want Caesar's money but not Caesar's rules. So the CCCU schools want subsidies from the general public, even if the general public favors broad civil rights protections for LGBTQ people. This raises some very difficult questions about the rule of law and the consent of the governed.

One argument in response to how I have framed the issue is that the "taxpayer's" money is *our* money.[99] In one sense that is true—every taxpayer, religious or not, pays something into the general revenue, and so every taxpayer has a stake in how the general revenue is spent. "No taxation without representation," after all, was a popular slogan against the British crown during the Revolutionary War era and previously in Ireland. The problem is that, concerning Title IX, we *have* representation in Congress and in the executive branch through the president. Taxpayers do not have standing merely as taxpayers to bring claims in federal court to challenge government policies.[100] The issue is that these schools did not like the policy chosen by our elected representatives.

The question, then, is whether these religious schools should receive a conscience-based exemption as a political concession. The Title IX

94. 20 U.S.C. § 1681.

95. See July 1, 2014 letter to President Barack Obama, https://tinyurl.com/yywgnpyf.

96. See Executive Order 13672, July 21, 2014, https://tinyurl.com/y3m2h9za.

97. See Office for Civil Rights, "Exemptions from Title IX," https://tinyurl.com/y5fl2c4m.

98. Sarah Eekof Zilstra, "The Title IX Lives of Christian Colleges," *Christianity Today*, November 23, 2016, https://tinyurl.com/y3d3ajs5.

99. Thanks to Robert Cochran for discussing this argument with me.

100. See Chemerinksy, *Constitutional Law*, 2.5.5.

question provides a difficult contrast to the *Bob Jones* case. Most if not all of the CCCU schools that sought Title IX exemptions would agree that Bob Jones's miscegenation policy was morally wrong. But most of these schools have policies against homosexual conduct. While many of these schools distinguish LGBTQ orientation from homosexual conduct and claim they do not discriminate against LGBTQ people, the same could be said of Bob Jones's policy: black people were free to attend Bob Jones, but they could not have sex with white people, whether married or not.

Further, if we dig deeper into the root of the Title IX problem, the picture becomes even murkier. The root of the problem is that private religious colleges and universities, just like their secular counterparts, for many years have welcomed the cash supplied by cheap government-backed student loans. The average cost of tuition at CCCU schools in 2017–2018 was over $27,000 per year.[101] Many of these schools charge tuition well over $30,000 per year.[102] These schools are worried about Title IX because they cannot sustain these tuition rates without government-backed student loans. There is a deep irony here in that these schools are ignoring the historic Christian prohibition against usury while claiming to represent traditional values about sexuality.

The truth is that if you live by Caesar's largess, you die by it. I don't claim to have an answer to this problem, and as a graduate of a CCCU school (Gordon College, class of 1988), I believe deeply in the value of Christian liberal arts education and intentional Christian community. I would *hate* to see schools like Gordon fold. At the same time, I cannot in good conscience argue that restricting public funds based on generally held public values about LGBTQ people is a threat to the rule of law or to religious liberty. It is the *Bob Jones* issue but with LGBTQ rights as the problem rather than race.

But funding is not the only issue facing private religious schools in relation to LGBTQ rights. Some are also in danger of losing accreditation. Gordon College, for example, faced questions about its accreditation because of its stance on LGBTQ issues.[103] Gordon did not change its lifestyle commitment policy, but it did introduce new initiatives designed to support LGBTQ students.[104] More recently, a Canadian

---

101. CCCU Annual Research, 2017–2018 Tuition Survey, https://tinyurl.com/y48lttou.

102. CCCU Annual Research, 2017–2018 Tuition Survey.

103. See Mary Moore, "Accreditation Board Gives Gordon College a Year to Review Policy on Homosexuality," *Boston Business Journal*, September 25, 2014, https://tinyurl.com /y356hdfm; New England Association of Schools & Colleges, Inc., Commission on Institutions of Higher Education, "Joint Statement by Gordon College and the Commission on Institutes of Higher Education," NEASC, April 25, 2015, https://tinyurl.com/y2bgebrw.

104. New England Association of Schools & Colleges, Inc., Commission on Institutions of

school, Trinity Western University, was notified that its law school would not be accredited because of its code of conduct relating to homosexuality. In response to this decision, the *Wall Street Journal* ran an editorial titled "Canada Attacks Religious Freedom."[105]

Trinity Western is a great example of a Christian liberal arts institution dedicated to the integration of faith and learning. I grieve over the conflict they are facing. At the same time, what they were denied was the temporal government's official seal of approval for their law school. The Canadian government did not close Trinity Western's doors, nor did it forbid Trinity Western from offering courses in law. It's true that a nonaccredited law school cannot compete with accredited schools and cannot produce lawyers who can be admitted to the bar. But should Christians expect a seal of approval from Caesar? Are there other creative ways for a school like Trinity Western to contribute to legal education and training for Christian lawyers without opening an accredited law school? Is this a grave threat to the social order, something worthy of outrage, or is it something to manage with patience and hope? I do not pretend to any expertise in Canadian culture, law, or constitutional jurisprudence. No doubt there are some issues here that differ from the American context. Nevertheless, I wonder if, in missional terms, this fight is worth the further animosity it fosters between some Christians and the LGBTQ community.

Finally, it is crucial to note that these funding and accreditation disputes concern an imposed *code of conduct*, not instructional content. Do private Christian colleges and universities need to organize themselves like monastic communities with a strict rule of life, or can they find other creative ways to encourage their vision of Christian life without a required code of conduct that might conflict with the broader society's moral norms? In the United States, most Catholic universities do not have a required sectarian code of conduct or statement of faith—one reason why I, as a Protestant, can teach at a Catholic law school.[106] Critics, including conservative Catholics, argue that this dilutes the mission of Catholic universities. That may be true, but it depends on the "mission." If the mission is to offer an educational program that interfaces as much as possible with the broader culture, including offering programs that

Higher Education, "Joint Statement by Gordon College and the Commission on Institutes of Higher Education."

105. See Bob Kuhn, "Canada Attacks Religious Freedom," *The Wall Street Journal*, June 21, 2018, https://tinyurl.com/y22vch7a.

106. These schools do, of course, have a code of conduct against cheating, plagiarism, sexual assault, and so on, as required of all accredited universities by law. I mean here a sectarian code of conduct or statement of faith that embeds values and beliefs that are not necessarily accepted by the broader society.

are accredited by professional bodies outside the Christian community while still infusing the campus with a religious perspective and identity, then maybe it is wise to eschew a sectarian code of conduct or statement of faith. If the mission is to create more of an insular, monastic-type community, then a more rigorous code of conduct and statement of faith makes sense. For such communities, from a missional perspective, some legal action to protect property rights and rights of association and speech against the temporal power could be a priority. The expectation of receiving a seal of approval from the temporal government and its professional accrediting bodies, however, might diminish.

GAY WEDDING CAKES

The higher education cases discussed above involve access to government money or government approval. The most recent major legal battle pitting Christians against LGBTQ people involved a conflict between conscience and commerce. This was *Masterpiece Cakeshop*, decided in June 2018.[107]

In that case the Colorado Civil Rights Commission found that the owner of a local bakery in Lakewood, Colorado, Jack Phillips, had discriminated against LGBTQ customers by refusing to supply them with wedding cakes. The case was initiated after a complaint by Charlie Craig and Dave Mullins, a gay couple who had visited Phillips's bakery looking for a wedding cake. The Commission found that Phillips had refused to sell wedding cakes to gay couples on at least six other occasions. Phillips argued that he had a constitutional right under the free exercise clause of the First Amendment to decline to sell wedding cakes to LGBTQ customers. Phillips claimed that his wedding cakes were artistic creations, not merely ordinary commodities, and that as such he should be entitled to a religious exemption to Colorado's generally applicable civil rights laws. A federal appeals court rejected Phillips's argument, but the Supreme Court, in an 8–2 opinion, reversed and held that the Colorado Civil Rights Commission violated Phillips's First Amendment rights.

The *Masterpiece Cakeshop* case is interesting from a jurisprudential and constitutional doctrine perspective. It involves line drawing about when the sale of an otherwise ordinary product—a cake—becomes an expressive act.

If all commercial activity were entitled to strong First Amendment protection, the entire structure of civil rights law would collapse. In

107. Masterpiece Cakeshop, Ltd. v. Colorado Civil Rights Commission, 138 S. Ct. 1719 (2018).

2007, fifteen years after *Romer v. Evans*, the Colorado legislature added sexual orientation to the list of protected classes under its public accommodation civil rights statute.[108] This was the statute Jack Phillips was found to have violated. This history places the *Masterpiece Cakeshop* case into a broader context. Supporters of religious exceptions to generally applicable public accommodation civil rights statutes today argue that they only seek narrow exceptions for a relatively small number of religious people in limited categories of cases. This sounds reasonable, but the history shows that those same Christians first obtained state constitutional restrictions on LGBTQ civil rights through the ballot initiative lost that issue at the Supreme Court, and then lost again when the people of Colorado chose to include LGBTQ people under state civil rights laws.

Not only consistent with the First Amendment, but also consistent with a great tradition of Western legal thought encompassing figures such as Origen, Tertullian, and Lactantius, we should affirm that people such as Jack Phillips ought to enjoy a right of religious freedom. But the limits of religious freedom in the pursuit of a commercial business are not always easy to discern. It obviously cannot be the case that a claim of religious freedom allows a business owner to evade all generally applicable laws concerning health and safety, working conditions, civil rights, and the like. *Masterpiece Cakeshop* exposes difficult questions at the intersection of what we have called Augustinian and ecclesial ethics. When should a Christian assert religious liberty rights in the marketplace?

In cases like *Masterpiece Cakeshop*, state legislatures—that is, the people—have determined that LGBTQ people are entitled to the same equal access to places of public accommodation as any other citizen. Under these civil rights laws, a coffee shop owner cannot hang a "Whites Only" sign in the window, nor can she hang a "Straight People Only" sign. The petitioners in the *Masterpiece Cakeshop* case conceded this point, and in fact Jack Phillips said he was happy to sell LGBTQ people any product other than a wedding cake. The problem, for him, was that a wedding cake was a specially artistic creation that he believed signaled his participation in or approval of the wedding itself. Some florists who have refused to provide floral arrangements for gay weddings have made the same kind of claim.

Anyone has a right to ask a court to enforce his or her rights, but at the same time, no one is *forcing* the respondents in these cases to work as a baker or florist or anything else. Even if the civil rights laws are enforced

---

108. Masterpiece Cakeshop, Ltd. v. Colorado Civil Rights Commission, 138 S. Ct. 1725 (2018).

against them, they could choose to modify their businesses by not selling certain product lines such as wedding cakes, or exit the business entirely for a different trade.

Changing a product line or exiting a trade certainly is a kind of hardship, but in our modern economy, it obviously is nothing like facing execution in the Roman arena. A person who is resourceful and skilled enough to establish a successful bakery or florist shop can find plenty of ways to make a satisfying living that do not involve supplying wedding products. This sounds quite harsh, but largely because in American culture we idolize our careers. Even in our church culture, the notion that our faith might preclude us from some career options seems inconceivable. We demand that society adapt so that we can pursue our faith and our careers without any sacrifices. This is a symptom of how American religious culture blends Christianity and capitalism.

The reality is that those of us who otherwise have the resources and skills to choose one line of work over another routinely voluntarily limit our work possibilities because of our faith convictions. As a personal example, at the start of my legal career I chose not to practice family law because I knew I would not feel comfortable offering no-fault divorce services. Some Christian lawyers offer a full range of family services, including no-fault divorces, and some Christian lawyers offer more limited family law services. Without making any judgments about how those other lawyers decided to practice, for me, I knew I would not be able to discharge my professional ethical obligations to represent my clients zealously in this area of practice because of my religious belief that marriage should be permanent except where there is adultery, abuse, or similar circumstances.

This conviction made it very difficult for me to consider opening my own law practice. A full range of family law services is often part of the bread and butter of solo and small law practices. In a small practice, I could have focused on plaintiff's personal injury law and real estate without family law, but adding family law would have made opening this kind of practice a much easier decision. This was one important reason why I spent my entire practice career at a large, corporate law firm. I did not like the long hours, high pressure, and competitive hierarchy at the big law firm, but at least I was able to engage in a quality law practice and support my family in ways that I felt were not inconsistent with my basic faith convictions.

Even then, there were times when I felt severe tension between my faith and my work. This was not because of my firm's culture, which, I am grateful to say, always adhered to the highest standards of professional ethics. It was because of the inevitable tensions a Christian will feel—I might dare to say *should* feel—when trying to make a living in a fallen world, *especially* in the business world.

At one particularly stressful point in my career I was one of a large team of lawyers defending a big insurance company against class actions brought by consumers alleging fraud in the sale of life insurance policies. One of my key jobs was to oversee the review of many thousands of pages of documents the company was required to produce as part of the litigation for attorney-client privilege. Documents under a claim of privilege were withheld from production and identified on a "privilege log." After receiving the privilege log, it was up to the plaintiff's lawyers to lodge any objections to claims of privilege. Usually this involved a round of negotiation between the parties about what additional documents would be produced, if any, followed by arguments to the court about why certain documents should or should not be produced.

The attorney-client privilege is a particularly important feature of American law practice. A failure to assert the privilege when it should be asserted is a paradigmatic case of attorney malpractice. The stakes are high, which means the incentive is to make very broad, aggressive initial privilege designations and leave any ambiguity to the subsequent process of negotiation and litigation. This can be inefficient and costly, but so long as there is some basis for the privilege claim and the documents are properly designated on the privilege log, it is entirely ethical under the rules of professional responsibility.[109]

I recall finalizing a big privilege log at about three in the morning and thinking to myself, *I'm working through the night with the sole purpose of withholding facts from widows and orphans seeking life insurance proceeds from a huge, wealthy corporation.* I was not doing anything technically unethical. In defending these lawsuits, my client was not doing anything unethical. In fact, the class actions and other cases filed against our client encompassed tens of thousands of individual claims, many of which lacked merit. Litigations like this almost always result in a class settlement in which the individual consumer receives a voucher or some other small benefit, while the plaintiffs' class attorneys receive a substantial fee. I was not really personally fighting against widows and orphans, but I was part of a process that was beginning to make me feel very uncomfortable. I knew that eventually I would have to find a different kind of

109. Even within the literal boundaries of the rules, there are some questionable games lawyers can play. For example, on a fifty-page privilege log listing thousands of withheld documents, a document that would be particularly troubling if disclosed might be moved to the middle of the log, where it might be overlooked by the other side. At some point, games like this can cross the line of professional ethics.

practice if I wanted both to continue working as a lawyer and living out my faith values.

After many other twists and turns, I found a coveted place in legal academia. For me, this was a dream job in terms of my values, but it involved massively lowering my financial expectations. Legal academics make a good living, but the money is nothing close to what a partner in a prestigious corporate law firm can make.

Even as a legal academic, I found that my work presented some ethical dilemmas. Should I accept a nice consulting fee to serve as an expert witness for a party I thought was an abusive organization? How do I feel about the tuition fees that ultimately pay my salary, when my students are taking out significant student loans? As a member of my institution's budget committee, how do I discuss pay cuts or staff reductions in a time of fiscal uncertainty when my own pay and job are at stake as well?

I am not offering these reflections because they are extraordinary but because they are ordinary. Over a span of several decades in the work force, *everyone* will face some difficult decisions and compromises. This will certainly be the case for any Christian who is trying in some way to live out what he or she understands as the teachings of Jesus and of the Scriptures in an economy that is not always congenial to values such as the love command. Jesus said, "No one can serve two masters . . . you cannot serve both God and money" (Matt 6:24), which means that Christians inevitably will experience ethical tension as they try to navigate work in this world.

We should also remember that the *Masterpiece Cakeshop* case seems to reflect a grim history in which conservative Christians in America sided with an oppressive, dominant culture in the name of religious freedom. At every turn in the history of civil rights in America—from slavery, to the black codes of the Reconstruction era, to desegregation and the modern civil rights movement—conservative Christians argued that their religious views about the proper place of black people should be preserved against the encroachment of laws designed to promote racial equality. Conservative Christians today respond that sexual orientation is different than race. Whether or not this is so, or to whatever extent it might be so, this history should sorely chasten us.

Finally, *Masterpiece Cakeshop* is disturbing because it resonates with something so central to the Gospel narratives: eating with "sinners." Luke 5 tells how Jesus attended a "great banquet" held by Levi, a tax collector. The religious leaders criticized Jesus for eating with "tax collectors and sinners" and for not fasting (Luke 5:27–39). In Luke 7, Jesus turns the tables (almost literally!) while having dinner at a religious leader's house, when he allows a sinful woman to anoint his feet—not only eating with sinners but allowing sinners to touch him (Luke 7:36–39). In Luke 19, Jesus is at it again with another sinner and tax collector, Zacchaeus (Luke 19:1–10). These are just a few examples of Jesus's table fellowship with people the religious leaders believed were unclean and undesirable. Sadly, if you Google "Jesus eating with sinners," many of the top links are from blogs or Bible studies explaining that Jesus's table fellowship with sinners was really a disapproval of their lifestyles, suggesting that Christians should be careful to distance themselves from sinful people. The truth is that Jesus had a "right" to avoid contact with the sinners and outcasts of his culture. By exercising this right, he could have won the approval of the religious establishment. He did precisely the opposite, and that is why sinners were attracted to him.

Does this mean people like Jack Phillips should be forced by the temporal law to design fancy wedding cakes for same-sex couples? Does it mean he should have violated his conscience for the sake of the kingdom? No, but perhaps it does suggest a failure of moral and missional imagination. At the very least, it suggests there is not much spiritually edifying or missionally wise about fighting a case like this to the Supreme Court, win, lose, or draw.

Conclusion: Law, Fear, and Eschatology

Why do many Christians get worked up about things like abortion and LGBTQ civil rights but not about pharmaceutical patents? Why do many of these same Christians oppose government-sponsored healthcare plans? The easy answer is that people who care about whether their businesses must serve LGBTQ people tend to be white, middle-class evangelicals who are fabulously well off by global standards and who do not care very much about poor people. There is an element of truth to this response, but the example that led off chapter 4 concerned standards for admitting scientific evidence in US courts. The plaintiffs in these cases usually are American consumers—indeed, mass tort litigation is a uniquely American phenomenon. Both from a local and a global perspective, the relationship between pharmaceutical products and public health is something American Christians *should* care about.

One important and often overlooked reason why LGBTQ civil rights provoke a visceral response for some Christians relates to eschatology. Some prominent voices in the religious right express their eschatological views explicitly, while others operate from default assumptions that they either do not articulate or do not themselves even fully recognize or understand. This eschatology is a form of dispensational chiliasm, which expects a breakdown of social order immediately preceding a time of divine judgment.[1] In its most specific form, the time of divine judgment is called the "Great Tribulation," a seven-year period of massive global plagues and violence predicted in the sequences of seven "bowls" and "seals" in the biblical book of Revelation, resulting in the death of two-

1. For discussion of how this kind of eschatology has influenced the evangelical religious right, see, e.g., Matthew Avery Sutton, *American Apocalypse: A History of Modern Evangelicalism* (Cambridge: Harvard University Press, 2014); Richard T. Hughes, *Christian America and the Kingdom of God* (Urbana: University of Illinois Press, 2009), 183–86; Robert L. Jewett, "Between Armageddon and the World Court: Reflections on the American Prospect," in *The Bible and the American Future*, ed. Robert L. Jewett (Eugene, OR: Wipf & Stock, 2009).

thirds of the human population. As popularized in the Left Behind books and movies, in one popular version of this scenario, believing Christians will be "raptured"—taken directly up to heaven—by Jesus just prior to the start of the Great Tribulation. In some other versions, Christians will be raptured midway through the Great Tribulation, or only at the conclusion of the Great Tribulation. During the Great Tribulation, a powerful world leader, a false prophet portrayed in Revelation as "the beast," will rule the globe.

At the end of the seven years of the Great Tribulation, in this system, Jesus will return to defeat the "beast" and establish a thousand-year political kingdom of peace and prosperity from the throne of David in Jerusalem—the millennium, also referred to in the text of Revelation. Humanity will rebel again at the end of the millennium, however, culminating in the final battle of history, on the plains of Armageddon in Israel. After the Battle of Armageddon, Jesus and the armies of God will defeat evil permanently, the devil and all of the unsaved masses will be thrown into the lake of fire, and the saved will live forever in heaven. (There are a number of variations on the sequence and timing of these events, supporting a vast publishing and media industry, but the basic outline usually includes the elements described here.)

Whether explicitly acknowledged or not, this eschatological framework exerts a powerful influence over the evangelical wing of the religious right in America. This is particularly the case as conservative evangelicals and the religious right have blended with certain Pentecostal and prosperity groups, which also often gravitate strongly toward dispensationalist eschatology. As John Fea suggests, the relationship between Donald Trump and prosperity preacher Paula White connects directly with the conspiracy-theory mindset that Trump so often exhibits.[2]

The dispensational "end times" theology is a key reason why many conservative American evangelicals reflexively support the political state of Israel, since the events leading up to the Great Tribulation involve the reestablishment of political Israel, which will be opposed by the beast, reestablished during Jesus's millennial reign, and permanently established in the heavenly New Jerusalem. Indeed, President Trump recently invited Pastor John Hagee to deliver the benediction at a ceremony marking the relocation of the US embassy in Israel to Jerusalem.[3] Hagee is the editor of the *NKJV Prophecy Study Bible*, subtitled "Understanding

---

2. Fea, *Believe Me*; see also "How Positive Thinking, Prosperity Gospel Define Donald Trump's Faith Outlook," NPR, August 3, 2016, https://tinyurl.com/yyo4m7wn.

3. See Matt Korade, Kevin Bohn, and Daniel Burke, "Controversial US Pastors Take Part in Jerusalem Embassy Opening," CNN Politics, May 14, 2018, http://tinyurl.com/yc4wtldk.

God's Message in the Last Days," and is the best-selling author of books such as *Four Blood Moons: Something Is about to Change* (which suggests that a series of lunar eclipses falling on Jewish holidays signal the end times) and *Earth's Last Empire: The Final Game of Thrones* (which suggests that all is now lined up for World War III and the final Battle of Armageddon).[4] It is also essential to the narrative of crisis and decline that connects the rapid recognition of LGBTQ rights in recent years with the approaching apocalypse.

As noted in our discussion of *Masterpiece Cakeshop*, many religious right groups are convinced there is a "homosexual agenda" mounted by gay activists who wished to dismantle traditional religion through civil rights laws and judicial precedents. Typical of this fear was a statement on Focus on the Family's website:

> For the record, let it be said that Focus on the Family is deeply concerned about elements of the radical homosexual agenda which activists seek to impose on our society. Those elements include: (1) early educational programs promoting homosexuality in our public schools, often against the will of parents; (2) laws redefining marriage; (3) legislation requiring churches, religious for-profit organizations and businesses to hire homosexuals; (4) laws which allow adoption of children by homosexuals; and (5) the redefinition of the family. If we care about our families, our children, and the moral state of our society, we should speak out against these proposals.[5]

Focus on the Family officials have regularly suggested that homosexuality and gay marriage would result in the end of civilization. According to one such official, "They [homosexual activists] don't want us to think that the most important institution, more important than the war, more important than sickness—it is marriage folks. If this goes, civilization goes down."[6] Focus on the Family's founder, James Dobson, has gone even further than this. According to Dobson, "Homosexuals are not monogamous. They want to destroy the institution of marriage. It will destroy marriage. It will destroy the Earth."[7]

While this eschatological framing helps explain why some conserva-

4. John Hagee, *Earth's Last Empire: The Final Game of Thrones* (Nashville: Worthy Books, 2018); John Hagee, ed., *NKJV Prophecy Study Bible* (Nashville: Thomas Nelson, 2015); John Hagee, *Four Blood Moons: Something Is about to Change* (Nashville: Worthy Books, 2013). See also the John Hagee author page on Amazon.com: http://tinyurl.com/y4emmmxt.

5. Quoted in "10 Things You Should Know about Focus on the Family," Human Rights Campaign, https://tinyurl.com/y3vdyc3z.

6. "10 Things You Should Know about Focus on the Family."

7. Quoted in Carmel Perez-Snyder, "Marriage, Family Advocate in State to Support Coburn—James Dobson Spoke to People during a Rally and Urged Them to Consider Brad Carson's Record," *The Oklahoman*, October 23, 2004, https://tinyurl.com/y6nlu5fd.

tive evangelicals are so concerned about the threat they perceive from LGBTQ rights, it does not explain why they focus so strongly on a political and legal response to the threat. If the Earth is about to be destroyed and these people are among those to be raptured, after all, there is nothing to fear and much to anticipate—and presumably the actual timing of these final events is already known to God and cannot be altered.

Incongruously, however, there is a thread of American exceptionalism in popular versions of this theology. America is pictured as a nation that has somehow played a key role in holding off the Great Tribulation, both through its inherent righteousness and its support for political Israel. The chiliastic dipsensational theology becomes commingled with a narrative of "Christian America" that pictures the founding era, and elements of the post–World War II era, as a kind of local golden age, an island of faith in a world of apostasy. America's love of God, democracy, and Israel is holding back the tide of judgment for a while longer so that the nations can be evangelized (and, coincidentally, so that American Christians can go on living their privileged lives). But that love has faded, and the tide will soon breach the dam, unless the cracks can be plugged for a while longer. As religion scholar Richard Hughes has noted, many modern fundamentalists have inherited the American exceptionalism of the earlier generations of American evangelicals who often held postmillennial eschatological views and fused that exceptionalism to their premillennial, chiliastic views.[8] They think "God will use the United States to smite the Antichrist and other enemies of righteousness at the end of time, preparing the way for the millennial reign of Christ and His saints. And God will use the United States in this way precisely because of this country's [supposed] history as a Christian nation."[9]

America's role in this drama was perhaps better understood by the average person in the pew during the Cold War era, when this theology first attained a degree of mass popularity through Hal Lindsey's *The Late, Great Planet Earth* and other books and Bible conferences. In the popular American imagination, there was a sense that America was on God's side against the Soviets and other communists. The hippies, pinkos, commies, bra-burning feminists, and gays were all part of the problem. It was Archie Bunker theology. Today much of that Cold War backdrop has faded from memory, but the sense of American exceptionalism tied to the end times remains. And, of course, many people unconsciously take on much of this baggage without any sense of its intellec-

---

8. Hughes, *Christian America and the Kingdom of God*, 183–84.
9. Hughes, *Christian America and the Kingdom of God*, 183.

tual provenance. The underlying psychological issues—fear, confusion, loss of privilege, and loss of control in a rapidly changing world—remain the same. At the same time, Barack Obama and Hillary Clinton replaced the Soviet Union as the icons of the antichrist. It is strangely ironic that these culture warriors adopted Donald Trump as their political savior.

Pastor John Hagee, for example, argues in his book *Earth's Last Empire* that Barack Obama—whom Hagee dubs "The Socialist Agenda President"—implemented his "socialist" agenda significantly through supporting gay marriage and the Affordable Care Act (Obamacare).[10] According to Hagee, President Trump can reverse this slide and "make America great again" with the coming apocalypse literally at stake:

> If President Trump fails, we will more than likely enter a new progressive era—a prospect that does not bode well for liberty, limited government, and self-evident truths. It will produce a liberal dictatorship that will attack religious freedom and traditional marriage and will advance the slaughter of the unborn and embrace social revolution where tyranny and anarchy in the streets of America overwhelm the police forces.
>
> "Equal justice under the law" will be a mere slogan chiseled over the doors of the Supreme Court building, not a fact of life any longer in these United States. Make way for the New World Order![11]

It is helpful to surface this eschatological frame precisely because it is often assumed but unexamined. Upon the slightest examination, this frame falls apart. A more thoughtful study of the Bible's apocalyptic literature shows that it mostly discusses events familiar to the original readers, and it is not meant to provide a detailed roadmap of future events.[12] Its overarching purpose to encourage the faith community in the face of opposition and persecution and to unmask the hypocrisy and violence of the ruling authorities, whether they were Babylonian or Roman, using highly evocative, figurative language. There is no sense at all in the Bible's apocalyptic literature that a nation state outside of Israel could enact laws that might postpone God's judgment. It is true that the Old Testament's apocalyptic literature warns against moral decline and suggests a renewal of Israel through observance of the Torah and involving a messianic figure, but for Christians that figure is the crucified and risen Christ, not America or any other modern nation state.[13] The New

---

10. Hagee, *Earth's Last Empire*, 208.

11. Hagee, *Earth's Last Empire*, 215.

12. See, e.g., Michael J. Gorman, *Reading Revelation Responsibly* (Eugene, OR: Wipf and Stock, 2017).

13. Sophisticated Dispensationalists note that Jesus did not literally fulfill the Old Testament prophecies of a renewed political Israel and suggest that those prophecies remain to be fulfilled

Testament's apocalyptic literature likewise focuses on Jesus. Any attempt to see a role for America in the New Testament's apocalyptic literature is a transparent fiction.[14]

I am not suggesting that all the people involved in the cases I have discussed in part 2 of this book are crazy, end-times prophets. Indeed, I know some of the people involved in some of those cases, and many of them are thoughtful Christians and fine lawyers and scholars. There is no doubt, however, that at the popular level, this chiliastic eschatology is what stirs up the masses. Responsible Christian lawyers and scholars should recognize this and seek to correct it. It is difficult to argue for a modest, limited engagement with the temporal law when grassroots leaders claim your political opponent is about to "destroy the Earth." A theology and praxis of patient presence and engagement, though, is what we so desperately need today.[15]

In the light of our current political climate, it's easy to see why Charles Colson's 1996 *First Things* "The End of Democracy" essay was not only irresponsible but completely unhinged. Instead of armed rebellion by righteous soldiers for Christ, ideas like Colson's birthed the alliance between the religious right and Donald Trump. In a tragic irony, the idolization of a particular vision of Christian America produced a regime of deceit that undermines civility and the rule of law with every tweet. The rebellion is not armed, but it is well underway. And it is doing grave

at Christ's second coming, in particular during the millennium. This is at least a plausible reading of the biblical narrative and enjoys significant support in the broader Christian tradition, even if the mainstream of Christian theology today takes the Augustinian approach and understands the millennium as a figurative reference to the present age of the church prior to Christ's return. See Craig A. Blaising and Darrell Bock, *Progressive Dispensationalism* (Grand Rapids: Baker Academic, 2000).

14. Calvinism, of course, has also played an important role in American history. Many early American Calvinists were post-millennialists, meaning that they did not believe in a literal thousand-year millennial reign. Instead, they thought the millennial age was already present and that the steady progress of Christianization would cause social conditions to improve. This was an important part of the reform-minded social consciousness of early American Christianity. In more recent times, many neo-Calvinist evangelicals have been attracted to the Dutch Reformed theologian Abraham Kuyper's notion of "sphere sovereignty." There is much to commend in Kuyper's thought, but in his lectures on Calvinism at Princeton Seminary he suggested the American Declaration of Independence and Constitution reflected a prime example of a limited, Calvinist form of government, and this sense of American exceptionalism has influenced some libertarian-leaning neo-Calvinists on the religious right, such as Charles Colson. Abraham Kuyper, "Calvinism and Politics," in *Lectures on Calvinism* (Grand Rapids: Eerdmans, 1931), 79–109. In recent decades, the Roman Catholic Church has also been a major influence in the culture wars through the American Conference of Catholic Bishops and through very conservative Catholic groups that focus on the "church militant." Catholicism also does not adopt a dispensationalist eschatology.

15. Cf. James Davison Hunter, *To Change the World: The Irony, Tragedy, and Possibility of Christianity in the Late Modern World* (Oxford: Oxford University Press, 2010).

damage to the ideals and institutions it claims to support, and even graver damage to Christian witness in America and around the world.

"The arc of the moral universe is long, and it bends towards justice," Dr. King said. The tension between action and patience concerning law and mission, I think, resides in the space between what we do for others and what we do for ourselves. This observation should bring us back to the biblical narrative discussed in part 1 of this book. What do the law and the prophets require? What did Jesus instruct? Prioritize the poor and oppressed. Defend Christians and other people around the world who are subject to real religious violence. Sit at the table with your LGBTQ neighbors and try to hear their stories. If you have an enemy, respond with love and forgiveness. Do not expect too many favors or benefits from Caesar. Respect the routine, regular work of the law, its cultural particularity, its necessary institutions, its seemingly mundane effects on the transactions and interactions that make up most of daily life. Seek reconciliation. Do not be afraid. After all this, if it is still necessary to defend yourself in court, do so with humility and trepidation. These practices are hard, but they seem to me what the *missio Dei* requires of us today.

Acknowledgments

I am grateful to Tony Jones and Silas Morgan for seeing the value in this project and encouraging me to finish it. Thanks also to Robert Cochran for reading an early draft and offering helpful suggestions. I particularly want to acknowledge Angela Carmella, my law and religion teacher as a student and now a dearly valued colleague. My wife, Sue, has been a patient supporter of my halting efforts to learn theology. Finally, special thanks to Patti Atkinson, my high school history teacher, who always knew I could write something like this.

Names and Subjects Index

Aaron, 31, 32
Abihu, 32
Abijah, 40
Abimelek, 39
abortion, 11, 12, 147, 151, 187, 190,
	195–97, 199–205, 207, 208, 223
Abraham, 28, 29, 36, 44, 61, 71, 115,
	163. *See also* Abram
Abram, 28
Acacian schism, 89
Acacius, 89
Achan, 34
Address to the Christian Nobility, 96,
	97
adult baptism, 102
Affordable Care Act (Obamacare),
	184, 227
Africans, 164, 166, 173
Against Celsus, 76
	"Against the Robbing and
	Murdering Hordes of Peasants,"
	98
Ahaz (king), 43
Alexander V (pope), 94
Alexander Severus, 75, 76
Alexandria, 74–75, 87
Alito, Samuel A., 189
Amendment 2, 192, 194

American Revolution, 6, 73, 159,
	213
American School of Ethnology, 166
Amorites, 34
Anabaptists, 100, 101
Anastasius (emperor), 86, 89
Antioch, 68, 87
apocalypse of John, 23. *See also* Rev-
	elation
apocalyptic literature, 64–66, 227,
	228
Apologeticum, 78
"Appeal for Law and Order and
	Common Sense, An," 179
Aquinas, Thomas, 94–96, 117, 120,
	121, 129–33, 180
Aratus, 80
Arian controversy, 87
Aristotle, 94, 131
Arrow, Kenneth, 156
Articles of Confederation, 159–61
Assyria, 43, 45
Assyrian conquest, 49
Athens, 80, 83
Augustine, St., 9, 51, 83–86, 85n98,
	109, 117–21, 127, 128, 134, 180
Augustus Caesar, 130
Avignon, 92, 93
Avignon papacy, 93

Babel, 25, 27, 28, 37, 116
Babylon, 35, 43, 45, 119
Babylonian Captivity of the Church, 96
Babylonian exile, 44, 45
bankruptcy law, 12, 148–51
baptism, 100, 102
Baptists, 73
Barnabas, 68
Barron v. Mayor and City of Baltimore, 169
Barth, Karl, 24, 63, 64, 124
Bathsheba, 40
Battle of Armageddon, 224, 225
Bauckman, Richard, 19, 65, 71
Benedict Option, 11
Benjamites, 39
beriyth (בְּרִית) (rainbow covenant), 26
Berman, Harold, 104
Bevans, Stephen, 72
Bevel, James, 178
Bible, 8, 10, 17–19, 37, 43, 83, 117, 122, 129, 162, 263, 168, 169, 206, 207, 211, 221, 226\
biblical law, 33, 44, 83, 168
Bilhah, 23
Bill of Rights, 147, 160, 161, 169–71, 175–78, 188, 191, 198
black liberation, 124, 125
black theology, 123–25
Black Theology of Liberation, A, 123
Black's Law Dictionary, 2
Blackmun, Justice Harry, 188
Block, Daniel, 18
Blow, Charlotte, 171, 172, 174
Blow, Peter, 170, 172
Blow, Taylor, 173
Bob Jones, 183, 209, 213, 214
Bob Jones University, 182, 183
Boff, Clodovis, 123, 126

Boff, Leonardo, 123, 126
Bonhoeffer, Dietrich, 134, 202
"Bonhoeffer moment," 202, 205
Bonhoeffer: Pastor, Martyr, Prophet, Spy, 202
Boniface VIII (pope), 92, 93
Bowers v Hardwick, 19, 195
Breyer, Justice Stephen, 190
Brimlow, Robert, 134–36
Brown v. Board of Education, 176, 177, 191
Brown II, 177
Brueggemann, Walter, 42
Buchanan, Pres. James, 172, 173
Burridge, Richard, 52, 57
Bush, George H. W., 189

"Call for Unity, A," 178, 179
Callixtus II (pope), 92
Calvin, John, 96, 98, 100, 106, 117, 151, 172, 195
Canaan, 67, 163, 165–67
Canaanites, 34, 37
canon, the, 19, 33, 67, 69
canon law, 97, 98
Carmichael, Calum, 44
Catherine of Siena, 93
causation, 152
Celestine (pope), 87
ceremonial law, 60
Chaffee, Calvin, 172, 173
Chalcedon, 88
Chalcedonian definition, 88
Chalcedonian formula, 89
Christian Cicero. *See* Lactantius
Christian Legal Society (CLS), 209–12
Christian Legal Society v. Martinez, 209, 212
Christian pacifism, 134
Christokos, 87

Christological disputes, 87
church/churchly order, 62
Cicero, 118
circumcision, 53, 69, 70
City of God, 83, 118, 119
civil authority, 97
civil order, 56, 100
civil rights, 6, 7, 12, 133, 134,
    174–79, 181, 182, 184, 187,
    188, 190–92, 201, 205, 206,
    208, 209, 211, 213, 216, 217,
    222, 223, 225
Civil Rights Act (1964), 181–84,
    191, 206; Title II, 191,
    192; Title VII, 191
Civil War (American), 6, 7, 12, 169,
    173–76, 182, 190, 199
Civil War (English, 73
Clement of Alexandria, 74, 75, 79,
    83
Clement V (pope), 92
Clement VII (pope), 93
Clinton, Bill, 196, 207
Clinton, Hillary, 227
Collins, Richard, 193
Colorado, 192, 193, 217
Colorado Civil Rights Commission,
    196
Colorado for Family Values (CFV),
    193
Colorado Springs, 192, 193
Colorado Springs Gazette Telegraph,
    194
Colson, Charles, 195
common good, 6, 8, 95
common law, 1, 31–34, 138, 140,
    146, 171, 177
compositiones, 97
conciliarism, 93
Cone, James, 123–25
Concordat of Worms, 91, 92

Confessing Church, 202
Confessions, 83, 209, 110
Connor, Eugene "Bull," 178, 180
Conquest, 34, 38, 43, 45, 67
conquest narratives, 37, 38
conscience, 7, 55, 67, 100, 127, 129,
    130, 167, 182, 213, 214, 216,
    221
consent, 7, 102, 105, 118, 129–34,
    141, 145, 161, 176, 181, 184,
    208, 209, 213
Constantine, 10, 74, 76, 79, 80, 87,
    129
Constantinian conservatism,   126
Constantinian shift, 10, 13, 90
Constantinianism, 78, 80, 86, 129
Constantinople, 11, 86–89, 93
Constitution, the, 65, 67,1 22, 149,
    159–61, 172, 177, 183, 193,
    197–99
contingency, 108n22, 113, 113n31,
    114, 151
Cornelius, 69
Correction of the Donatists, The, 127
Council for Christian Colleges and
    Universities (CCCU), 213, 214
Council of Constance, 93
Council of Nicea, 87
Council of Pisa, 93
Counter-Reformation, 106
covenant, 18, 25–29, 32, 34, 38, 40,
    47, 50, 58n93, 61, 71, 115, 135,
    140n148
creation, 2, 9, 22, 18, 20–25, 26–28,
    31, 32, 42, 44, 47, 67, 70, 75,
    83, 84, 95, 102, 106–8, 111–13,
    112n31, 114–17, 119, 121, 123,
    136, 138, 140, 145, 171
creation narratives, 20, 20n13, 21,
    22, 25, 25n22
customary law, 2

Cyril of Alexandria, 87
Cyrus (king), 201

Dabney, Robert Louis, 163, 166, 182
Daubert v. Merrill Dow Pharmaceuticals, 153
David, 15, 40–42, 224
Davies, G. I., 45
debtor's prison, 148, 149
Decalogue, 31–34, 70, 116, 163
Decius, 76
Defence of Virginia, A, 163
Defense of Marriage Act (DOMA), 196
Deuteronomic Code, 18
Deuteronomic narrative, 32
Deuteronomy, 32–34, 44, 67, 70, 113
Digest, 122, 130
dikaiosunē (δικαιοσύνη), 28, 113
Diocletian, 79
diophysites, 88
divine command, 15, 51, 106, 113–15
Divine Institutes, 79, 80
divine law, 95, 96
Dobson, James, 192–94, 199, 207, 225
Donation of Constantine, 90n90
Donatists, 86, 127–29
Douglas, William O., 188
Dred Scott v. Sandford, 170, 174
due process, 146, 147, 183, 189, 190, 196–99, 204

Earth's Last Empire, 225, 227
ecclesial ethics, 8, 11, 134–40, 217
Ehud, 38
Eisenhower, Dwight D., 177

Emerson, Eliza Irene (Sandford), 171, 172
Emerson, John, 170–71
Employment Non-Discrimination Act (ENDA), 213
"End of Democracy, The," 228
end of history, 83, 101
Enlightenment, 2, 3, 73
Ephesus, 87, 88
Epistle to the Hebrews, 70
equal protection, 7, 146, 175, 176, 183, 187–90, 193, 195, 197–99, 206
equal protection clause, 126, 187, 188, 190, 197, 198
equality, 11, 81, 178, 220
equity, 80–82, 82n69, 150, 155
Esau, 28, 29
eschatology, 8, 9, 13, 102, 119, 123, 125, 206, 223, 224, 228
eternal laws, 84, 85, 95–96, 120, 180
ethics, 12, 33, 52, 72, 123, 134, 135
Ethics, Discipleship, 202
Eucharist, the, 100
Euthyphro, 107
Euthyphro dilemma, 107
Eutyches, 88
evil, 2, 7, 15, 22–25, 36, 43, 44, 51–53, 56, 59, 62–64, 66, 75, 81, 85, 98, 102, 108n22, 110–13, 128n87, 140, 203, 204, 224
exiles, 35, 40, 43, 45, 50, 88, 201
exodus, 30–31, 36, 116
Exsurge Domine, 96

Farmer, Paul, 156
Faubus, Orval, 177
Fea, John, 224
federalism, 12, 159, 161, 177, 178, 182, 183, 185, 187

Felix III (pope), 89
Field, Roswell, 172
Fifth Amendment, 169
Fifteenth Amendment, 175, 176
First Amendment, 5, 183, 211, 212,
    216, 217
First Council of Ephesus, 87, 88
First Great Awakening, 73
First Things, 195, 228
Flavian (archbishop), 88
flood, the, 25–29, 44
flood narrative, 25n22, 25–26n23,
    27n26
Formula of Concord, 98
Four Horsemen, 184
Fourteenth Amendment, 7, 175,
    176, 183, 187, 188, 190, 191,
    197, 198, 211n92
Free Choice of the Will, The, 120
free will, 24, 59n98
Freedom of a Christian, 96
French Revolution, 73

gay marriage, 151, 187, 188, 190,
    195, 199, 201, 202, 205, 208,
    225, 227. *See also* same-
    sex marriage
Galatians (letter), 57, 57n92, 58, 59,
    59n98, 60, 61, 75
Gelasius (pope), 86, 87, 90
Genesis, 20, 20n3, 21–24, 116, 117,
    166
Geneva, 99, 150
genocide, 26–27n23, 37, 135
gentiles, 48n86, 59n97, 61, 67–70
Ginsburg, Ruth Bader, 189, 190
Gonzales v. Carhart, 189
Girgashites, 34
God, 2, 4, 5, 8, 10, 15, 18, 20–28,
    25–26n23, 30–38, 41–43, 46,
    47, 49, 50, 52, 56–58, 57n92,

    58n96, 59–67, 69–72, 77,
    81–85, 87, 94–100, 104–8,
    108n22, 110–20, 124–27, 129,
    131–33, 135, 136, 140, 141,
    164, 180–82, 206, 220, 224, 226
God's law, 8, 14, 25, 38, 43, 44, 50,
    77, 83, 84, 131
Gorsuch, Neil, 206
Goshen, 30
Gospel (John's), 22
grace, 8, 22, 26, 27, 36, 60, 61,
    94n110, 105, 111, 114, 138,
    201n66
Great Schism, 86, 91, 03
Great Tabernacle, 223–24, 226
Gregory VII (pope), 90, 91
Gregory XI (pope), 93
Griswold, Dan, 194
Griswold v. Connecticut, 188
Grotius, Hugh, 103, 104
Gushee, Dave, 52, 53

hāʾāḏām (הָאָדָ֔ם) (the adam), 20
Haarlem, Divara van, 101
Hagar, 28, 163
Hagee, John, 224, 227
Ham, 166
hamartia (ἁμαρτία) (sin, to miss the
    mark), 31
Hamilton, Alexander, 160
Haran, 28, 29, 29n27
Hauerwas, Stanley, 136–40
Haugen, Gary, 145
Hebrews (people), 30, 31, 36, 116
Hebrews (letter), 17, 70, 115
Henry IV (king), 91
Henry V (Holy Roman Emperor),
    92
herem (holy war), 34
Herdt, Jennifer, 51n62
Herod, 61

Hezekiah (king), 43, 46n57
Hitler, Adolf, 134, 135, 202
Hittite law codes, 33
Hittites, 34
Hobbes, Thomas, 104
Hoffman, Melchior, 101
Holmes, Oliver Wendell, Jr., 4
Holocaust, 203, 204
holy war, 34, 36, 67, 194
homoousion (ὁμοούσιον) (of one substance), 87
homophobia, 199, 200, 208
homosexuality, 11, 56n87, 190, 215, 225
hope, 45, 46n56, 50, 51, 65, 70, 76, 83, 120, 125, 156, 163, 195, 202, 215
Hosanna-Tabor Evangelical Lutheran Church and School v. EEOC, 208, 209
Hughes, Richard, 226
human law, 65, 84, 85, 96, 116, 120, 180
Hunsberger, George, 71
ḥuqqat (חֻקָּה) (statute/ordinance), 30
Huss, John, 94
Hutter, Jakob, 100, 101
Hutterites, 100

identity, 3, 30, 33, 36, 38, 73, 100, 109, 197, 216
infant baptism, 100
intellectual tradition, 4, 8, 9, 117
international law, 1, 37, 67, 73, 103, 136
interpretation, 6, 9, 27, 51, 52, 54, 55, 154, 167, 183, 198, 208
interstate commerce, 160, 183, 184
investiture, 90, 91
IRS, 183, 197
Isaac, 28

ish nabiy' (אִישׁ נָבִיא) (prophet), 38
Ishmael, 28
Israel, 8, 19, 29–40, 42–48, 50, 61, 67, 70–72, 105, 116, 117, 125, 131, 132, 145, 206, 207, 224, 226, 227

Jacob, 28–30, 131
Jael, 38
Jair, 39
James (apostle), 60
James (epistle), 17, 69, 69n2
Japeth, 166
Jay, John, 160
Jebusites, 34
Jefferson, Thomas, 161, 170
Jehoahaz, 43–44
Jehoiachin, 44
Jehoiakim, 44
Jeremiah, 45, 46n58
Jericho, 34, 36
Jeroboam, 43, 43
Jerusalem, 42, 44, 46n58, 50, 68, 224
Jerusalem Council, 68
Jesus, 8, 19, 40, 20, 34, 38, 40, 47, 50–54, 58–60, 62, 67, 69–72, 87, 114, 115, 117, 124–26, 139, 144, 204, 220, 221, 224, 227–28n13, 228, 229
Jesus Christ. *See* Jesus
Jethro, 31
Jewish Christians, 69, 70
Jews, 37, 47, 52, 58n96, 59, 97, 62, 132n106, 200, 203
Jim Crow laws, 174, 176
Joel, 40
John I (bishop), 87
John XXIII (antipope), 93
Johnson, Andrew, 174
Jones, Bob III, 183
Joseph, 29, 30

Joshua (book), 34, 35, 38, 39, 69
Joshua (person), 34, 35, 69
Josiah, 18, 34, 43
Judah (kingdom), 34, 43, 44
Judea, 68, 69
Julia Mammaea, 75, 76
justice, 10, 1, 15, 17, 28, 37, 38, 40,
    45, 47, 48, 50, 51, 67, 70, 72,
    75, 78, 78n45, 79–82, 84, 99,
    108, 110, 111, 113, 117–19,
    121, 122, 136, 137, 139, 146,
    152, 162, 171, 189, 208, 227,
    229
Justice in Love, 121
justification by faith, 69
justification by works, 69
Justinian, 130

Kagan, Elena, 190
Kansas-Nebraska Act, 173
Kavanaugh, Brett, 206
Kaveny, Cathleen, 138–40
Kennedy, Anthony, 184, 189, 190,
    194–97, 211
King, Martin Luther, Jr., 7, 12, 176,
    178–81, 191, 195, 202, 229
Kingdom Ethics, 52
Klawans, Jonathan, 61
Know-Nothings, 172

Laban, 29
Lactantius, 79–82, 82n65, 83, 127,
    217
Late, Great Planet Earth, The, 226
law. *See specific types of law*
law of faith, 58
law of love, 34, 51, 59, 65, 66
Law and Revolution, 105
law of slavery, 168
law of war, 37
Lawrence v. Texas, 196

laws of divine commands, 106
Leah, 29
legitimacy, 2, 3, 7, 104–6, 120, 124,
    130, 132, 141, 184, 195
Leo X (pope), 55, 94, 96
Leonides, 75
Letters and Papers from Prison, 202
Leviticus, 22, 44, 67, 70
lex regia, 130
lex talonis, 51
liberation theology, 122, 123, 126,
    127
"Letter from a Birmingham Jail,"
    178, 179, 195, 202
LGBTQ rights, 147, 183, 191, 198,
    199, 209, 210, 214, 225, 226
liberalism, 130
liberation theology, 122, 123,
    123n58, 126, 127, 127n83
Lincoln, Abraham, 162n4, 174, 175
Lindsey, Hal, 226
literary-symbolic texts, 22n18
Lot, 28
Luke, 220, 221
Luther, Martin, 75, 96–101, 106,
    117, 150, 195

ma'aseh (precedent), 52
Maccabees, 50
Madison, James, 160, 161
Magisterial Reformers. *See* Calvin;
    Luther
Manz, Felix, 100
Mao Zedong, 105, 105n14, 107
Marbury v. Madison, 198–99
Marcian (emperor), 88
Marcion of Sinope, 35
Marcionism, 35
marriage, 36, 88, 182, 184, 196–201,
    205, 208, 218, 225, 227
Marshall, Thurgood, 176

Martin V (pope), 93
Marxism, 125
Mary, 87, 88
Masterpiece Cakeshop v. Colorado Civil Rights Commission, 216–17, 220, 225
Matthijs, Jan, 101
McGuckin, John, 53–55, 62n109
Mennonites, 102, 136n119, 174
Mesopotamian law codes, 33
Metaxas, Eric, 202
Micah, 39, 45, 46n57
miscegenation, 182, 183, 214
mishpat (מִשְׁפָּט) (justice), 49, 113
missio Dei, 9, 10, 67, 71, 72, 105, 115, 116, 122, 157, 181, 229
Missouri Compromise, 170, 173
Missouri Supreme Court, 172
modern liberalism, 130
Mohler, Al, 201
monasteries, 91
Monophysite controversy, 87, 88
moral law, 54, 87, 88, 102, 114, 180
morals, 58, 60, 119, 173
Moravia, 100
Morton, Samuel George, 166
Mosaie law,163
Moses, 18, 30–35, 43, 51, 54, 68, 74, 75, 116, 121, 131, 132
mōwōšia' (מוֹשִׁיעַ) (deliverer), 38
Moyers, Bill, 194
Münster, 101
Müntzer, Thomas, 101
Muslims, 208

NAACP Legal Defense and Education Fund, 176
Nadab, 32
Nanos, Mark, 61
narratives. *See specific narratives*
nation-state, 70, 103, 134

natural ethics, 138
natural law, 2–4, 10, 11, 15, 23, 24, 40, 67, 75, 79, 82, 82n65, 83, 86, 94, 94n110, 85, 96, 102–4, 106–8, 111, 113–18, 121, 138, 140, 141, 145, 150, 152, 154, 165, 168, 178, 180, 204
natural theology, 24, 40, 83, 138, 139
nebia (נְבִיאָה) (prophetess), 31
Nebuchadnezzar (king), 64
Necho (pharaoh), 43
neo-scholasticism, 106
Nestorian Schism, 88
Nestorius, 87, 88
New Deal era, 183, 184
new federalism, 184
New Jerusalem, 22, 65, 71, 101, 224
"New Natural Law" school, 20n20
New Testament, 17, 21, 38, 47, 62, 56, 57, 63–65, 67–71, 83, 113, 114, 163, 212, 228
Nicene Christology, 87
Nicene Creed, 87
nicolaitism, 91
Niebuhr, Reinhold, 51
nihilism, 25, 83
NKJV Prophecy Study Bible, 224
Noah, 26–28, 115, 166
Noahic Covenant, 25–28
Noll, Mark, 162, 187
nonviolence, 135n117, 136, 137

Obama, Barack, 212, 213, 227
Obamacare. *See* Affordable Care Act
Obergefell v. Hodges, 197
O'Connor, Sandra Day, 189
O'Donovan, Joan Lockwood, 104
O'Donovan, Oliver, 104
Osterle, Dale, 193

Old School Presbyterianism, 162, 165
Old Testament, 8, 33, 47, 59n76, 65, 67, 68, 70, 74, 130, 163, 206, 227
On Justice, 79, 80
"On Kingship," 129
Origen of Alexandrea, 36, 63, 64, 74–77, 79, 83, 217
originalism, 199, 201, 205, 206
ousia (essence), 112

pacifists, 100–101, 134, 135
pagans, 118
paidagōgos (παιδαγωγὸς) (pedagogue), 58
Papacy at Rome, The, 96
papal authority, 76, 97
Parks, Rosa, 191
Passover, 30, 31
patriarchs, 50
Paul, 53, 57–64, 67, 69, 70, 80, 83, 114, 115, 163
Pauline epistles, 55, 62n109, 64
peace, 10, 50, 9, 64, 67, 71, 72, 77, 91, 99, 113, 116–120, 127, 129, 131, 177, 212, 224
Peace of Westphalia, 73
Peaceable Kingdom, The, 136
Pentateuch, 45
Perizzites, 34
Persia, 88
Peter, 63, 68, 69
Petrine epistles, 61
Phaenomena, 80
Pharaoh, 28, 30, 43, 44
Pharisees, 50, 53, 68, 117
Philip IV (king), 92, 93
Philip the Arab, 76
Philistines, 28, 40
Phillips, Jack, 216, 217, 221

pharmaceutical product regulations, 151–52
piety, 48, 81, 82, 96, 102, 129
Planned Parenthood of Southeastern Pa. v. Casey, 189
Plato, 74–75, 107
Plessy v. Ferguson, 176, 191
police, 5, 51, 125, 134–37, 139, 141, 178, 227
political ethics, 72
political theology, 8, 12, 51, 62, 63, 82n6, 83, 93, 116, 129, 163, 178
positive law, 1–3, 7, 9–12, 15, 26, 27, 51, 53, 67, 70, 71, 75, 82, 85, 86, 94–95, 98, 102, 104–5n9, 106, 115–18, 121, 122, 129, 130, 135, 138, 140, 141, 143, 145, 164, 168, 181, 184, 193, 201, 203, 205–7, 209
Potiphar, 30
Powell, H. Jefferson, 139
pragmatism, 4, 6, 117
praxis, 1, 9, 12, 68, 143, 201, 212, 228
pregnancy, 188, 189, 200, 207
priestly codes, 69
professional ethics, 218
Prophetic Dialogue, 72
prophetic literature, 8, 45–56
prophets, 41, 45, 45, 51, 53, 60, 65, 80, 228, 229
Proposition 2, 195, 199, 201
prosopon (three persons), 112
p'rū (פְּרוּ), 20
Pulcheria, 88

Quakers, 73
Qumran documents, 50

race, 4, 12, 120, 159–62, 166, 173, 175, 181, 182, 210, 214, 220

Rachel, 29, 30
radical reformers, 99–102
Rahab, 34
Reagan, Ronald, 189
rebaptism, 100, 101
Rebekah, 28, 29
Reconstruction, 174, 176, 220
Reformations, 2, 101
Reformed traditions, 24, 26
Rehnquist, William, 183, 184, 189
Rehoboam, 42, 47
Rendtorff, Rolf, 44
Republic, 118
Republicans, 172, 189
resurrection, 9, 11, 20, 38, 70, 125, 145, 204
Reuben, 29
Revelation, 22, 24, 36, 124, 167, 223, 224
"Rights and Duties of Masters, The," 163
Roberts, John, 184, 189, 198, 208
Roe v. Wade, 288, 201n72, 204
Romans (people) 65, 86, 118
Romans (text), 57, 58, 58n93, 62–64, 67, 69, 71, 73, 87, 176
Rome, 65, 86
Romer v. Evans, 194–96, 216
Römerbrief, 63
Roosevelt, Franklin D., 183
royal power, 89
rule of reason, 95

Samaritans, 69
same-sex marriage, 196–98. *See also* gay marriage
Samson, 37
Samuel, 40, 166
Sandford, John, 172, 174
Sarah, 28
Saul, 40

Scalia, Antonin, 189, 196, 198, 205
Schlabach, Gerald, 135, 136
School of Alexandrea, 74
Schroeder, Roger, 72
Scipio, 118
Scott, Harriet (Robinson), 171
Scott, Lizzie, 171
Scripture, 4, 8–10, 19, 20, 22, 24, 37, 53, 67, 68, 77, 102, 114, 116, 123–25, 129, 138, 150, 157, 162
Second Temple period, 33, 50
secularism, 104
"separate but equal" doctrine, 176, 177, 189, 190
Septimus Severus, 75
Septuagint, 28
Sermon on the Mount, 17, 38, 51, 52, 64, 68, 134
Servetus, Michael, 99
sexual orientation, 190–92, 198, 210, 213, 217, 220
shalom, 62, 71, 113
Shays' Rebellion, 160
Shem, 28, 166
Shema, 33
Shuttlesworth, Fred, 178
Simons, Menno, 102
simony, 91
sin, 11, 15, 21–24, 27, 38, 40, 53, 58, 59, 85, 100, 117, 121, 137, 150, 160, 164, 184
slave codes, 12, 168–70
slavery, 11, 12, 30, 31, 51, 85, 88, 149, 159, 161–76, 184, 187, 201, 202, 220
Solomon, 42, 44
Sotomayor, Sonia, 190
soul, the, 34, 50, 75, 85, 91, 109, 110
South Carolina College, 167, 168
Southern Christian Leadership Conference, 178

Southern Presbyterian Review, 162
spiritual rule, 90
spirituality, 72
Spyer, Thea, 197
Stassen, Glen, 52, 53
Strasbourg, 101
Strawn and Brent, 17
Stromata, 74
Summa theologiae, 94, 120, 130
Supreme Court, 5, 6, 133, 153, 154,
   160, 161, 169, 170, 172, 176,
   180, 183, 184, 187–90, 194–98,
   202, 207, 208, 210–12, 216,
   217, 220–27

Talieferro, Lawrence, 171
Taney, Roger B., 172, 173
technocracy, 27
tehom (תְּהוֹם) (floods), 31
temporal law, 32, 89, 118, 120, 121,
   205, 221m 228
temporal rule, 65, 86, 90, 99
Ten Commandments, 32, 96, 224
teraphim (תְּרָפִים) (household
   goods), 29
Tertullian, 31, 74, 78, 78nn43 and
   45, 79, 83, 83, 127, 213
tsedeqah (צְדָקָה) (righteousness), 28
Theodoret of Cyrus, 88
Theodosius II (emperor), 87, 88
theology of history, 10, 12, 118,
   126, 128, 185
theology of law, 4, 10, 11, 15, 19,
   20, 38, 45, 53, 57, 59, 102, 104,
   121, 125, 133, 134
theotokos, 87
Thirteenth Amendment, 7, 174, 175
Thirty Years' War, 73, 102
Thomas, Clarence, 189
Thoreau, Henry David, 149
Thornwell, James Henley, 162–69

Tillich, Paul, 124
time, 113, 113n31
Title IX, 212–14
Tome, 88
Torah, 17, 18, 27, 37, 41, 42, 44, 45
   47, 49–57, 57n92, 59n97,
   60–62, 68–70, 114, 115, 120,
   129–31, 227
Treatise on Good Works, 96
"Treatise on Law," 94, 120, 130, 131
tree of the knowledge of good and
   evil, 22, 23
tree of life, 22, 26
Trinity, the, 10, 11
Trinity Western University, 215
True Word, The, 76
Trump, Donald, 201, 202, 206, 224,
   227, 228
tsedeq, 113
two powers, 89

UC Hastings Law School, 210, 212
Ulpian, 122, 130
ūmil'ū (וּמִלְאוּ), 20, 21
Unam sanctum, 92
United States v. Lopez, 184
United States v. Windsor, 197
Ur, 27, 28
Urban VI (pope), 93
ūr'ḇū (וּרְבוּ), 20
ūr'dū (וּרְדוּ), 20
Uriah the Hittite, 40
usury, 12, 150, 143, 214

violence, 3, 5, 6,11, 24–27, 29, 30,
   38, 39, 48, 53, 85, 105, 122,
   123, 127, 128, 134–39, 145–47,
   152, 153, 176, 184, 204, 223,
   227, 229
voluntarism, 106

Wall Street Journal, 215
Warfield, B. B., 167
Wars of Religion, 3, 103
Westphalian Settlement, 73, 103, 104
White, Byron, 189
White, Paula, 224
white theology, 124
Whole Woman's Health v Hellerstedt, 190
Williams, Rowan, 120
Windsor, Edith, 197
Winthrop, John, 73
Witte, John, Jr., 1

Wolterstorff, Nicholas, 121
Wright, Christopher J. H., 71, 122
Wright, N. T., 61, 62
Wycliffe, John, 94
Wyeth v. Levine, 154

Yahweh, 18, 28, 29, 38–40, 48, 49
Yhwh, 42. *See also* Yahweh
Yoder, John Howard, 139

Zedekiah, 44, 46
Zeno (emperor), 89
Zilpah, 29
Zwingli, Ulrich, 100

Scripture Index

OLD TESTAMENT

Genesis
1–2 116
1–4 20
1:26–28 20
1:28 20
2 21
2:2 21
4:20–22 . . . . . . 116–17n33
6:1–5 25
7–8 31
7–10 27
9 166
9:4–6 26
9:7 26
9:12–16 26
11 116
11:1–9 . . . . . . 27, 116–17n33
11:6 27
11:7–9 27
11:10–26 28
11:27–32 . . . . . . 28, 116–17n33
12:1–3 28
12:12–20 28
13–14 28
15:5 28
15:6 28
15:18 28

25 29
23–28 29
28–30 29

Exodus
1–2 30
12:14 30
15:5 31
15:20–21 31
18:1–6 32
18:17–26 31
19:16 31
19:23–20:13 32
20:8 114
20:10 114
20–21 32
21–23 . . . . . . 32, 33
24 32
23:10 32
24:11 32
24:12 32
24:19 32
25–31 32
32 32
34 32

Leviticus
1:1 33

Numbers
15:37–41 33
24:5 171

Deuteronomy
1–4 32
5 32
6:4 34
6:4–9 33
6:5 34
7 34
7:1-2 34
11:13–21 33
21 113
21:18–21 18
21:23 . . . . . . 57n92
31 . . . . . . 29, 30

Joshua
6:17 34
6:21 34
8:24 35
8:25 35
8:34–39 35
10:28 35
10:30 35
10:32–33 35
10:34–39 35
40 35
11:1–5 35
11:12–14 35
12 35
13–22 35
34:25–26 38

Judges
1:1–3:5 83
3 38
3:22 38
4 38
4:21 39

6 38
9 38
10:1–2 39
10:3–5 39
10:6–11:7 39
11:1–35 28
11:8–13 39
13–17 39
17–18 39
18:1 39
19 39
19:1 39
19–21 39
21:20–23 39
21:25 . . . . . . 49, 125
21:25–39 39

1 Samuel
3:1 40
4:1–7:11 40
8:3 40
8:5 40
8:7 40
9:17–10:1 40
11:1–12:1 40
13:8–15 40
16:13 40

1 Kings
3:1–28 42
3:3 42
3:13 42
4:29–30 42
4:34 42
5:1–28 42
5:13 42
6–7 42
11:1 42
12:1–5 43
12:14 43

2 Kings
22–23 34
23:28 43
23:29–30 43
24:1–2 44
24:13 44
24:15–17 44
25:1–26 44
28:31–37 44

Psalms
19 . . . . . . 40, 83
19:1–6 41
19:7–9 41
19:10–13 42
19:14 42

Proverbs
8:22–22 117

Isaiah
1 47
1:7 48
1:10–11 48
1:12–13 48
1:15–16 48
1:16–17 49
1:18–20 49
2:3–5 50

Jeremiah
4:23–25 47
7:3–11 48

Micah
3:9–12 45–46
2:34 46
2:44 49

NEW TESTAMENT

Matthew
5:17 47
5:17–18 53
5:25 51
5:39–40 52
6:24 220
19:8 117
22:40 47

Mark
13:29–31 50

Luke
5:27–39 220
7 220
7:36–39 221
19 221
19:1–10 221

John
1:1 22

Acts
5 182
5:12–27 63
5:28 63
10:9–23 69
10:24–28 69
10:28 69
11 69
11:1–18 69
15 . . . . . . 53, 68, 69
15:1–2 68
15:25 68
15:29 69

Romans
1 83
3:19 57

248   SCRIPTURE INDEX

3:27 58
3:27–4:25 . . . . . . 58n93
3:31 58
7:13–25 58
7:21–25 69
12 64
12:18 212
12:14–21 64
12:18 212
13 . . . . . . 67, 69, 182
13:1 77
13:1–7 . . . . . . 62, 63
14 69
15:28–29 69

1 Corinthians
8–10 68
15:28 115

Galatians
1–2 69
2:2–3 60
3:2–3 57
3:10 57
3:19 58
3:24 58
3:37 58
4:1 58
4:28 58

5:13–14 59
5:19–21 59
5:22–23 59
5:23 59

Ephesians
4:5–9 168

Colossians
3:22–4:1 . . . . . . 164, 165

1 Timothy
1 . . . . . . 55, 61
1:4 55
1:5 55
1:6–7 55
1:8–11 56
2:1–4 56

James
2:24 65
1–2 69

Revelation
6:15 65
20:4 65
21:22–27 65
22:2 28